MY LIFE IN DOG YEARS

MY LIFE IN DOG YEARS

A Poodle Named Henry & Other Melodramas

CANDIDA PUGH

Delarouse Books

My Life in Dog Years: A Poodle Named Henry and Other Melodramas
Published by Delarouse Books

Paperback ISBN 979-8-218-50290-4
Ebook ISBN 979-8-218-50292-8
Library of Congress Control Number 2024921142

Cover design by Jeenee Lee
Page design by Beth Wright, Wright for Writers, LLC
Ebook conversion by Erica Smith, Ebook Conversions

To Charles
Who holds me up when I wobble, and picks me up when I topple

and

To Henry
Who taught me not to believe everything I think

Author's Note

In these pages, fellow dog lover, you will encounter plenty of joy and laughter, but also loss and even trauma. Losing a beloved dog crushes the strongest individuals, and I don't count myself among them. I've also included a description of an incident of sexual abuse in my childhood that explains how my bond with at least two of my dogs was reinforced by their ability to be my protector.

Only the names of my dogs, my children, my husband and ex-husband, the wonderful trainer who deserves a mention (Jordan), and my friends Terri, Susan, Gil, and Donna have been retained. All other names have been changed out of respect for their privacy.

Preface

This is a love story dedicated to all the dogs who have enriched my life—to those I've lost and to those still with me.

It's said into each life a little rain must fall. For some, the rainfall is a torrent, and this is true for dogs as well as for those of us with only two legs. Many of the dogs I've cared for needed to overcome bad breeding or a difficult, even abusive, past. These pages are filled with their triumphs.

Watching a dog shake off a dark history teaches us to strive for joyous indifference to a past that might otherwise crush us.

Scrappy

Scrappy broke my heart. It wasn't her fault, and it wasn't mine. It wasn't even my mother's fault.

Before there was a Scrappy, my father plucked from the street the dog who would bring her into the world. I must've been seven or eight. Having a dog was bliss. It was like eating a big bowl of butterscotch pudding, only better because I got to keep the dog after the pudding was gone.

Tippy, the stray, was medium-sized, sporting glossy black sealskin over a scrawny body. She looked like a derelict in an expensive fur coat. Whenever she wasn't eating or demanding to be petted, she planted her inky self in the darkest spot in our house, under a wall-mounted heater in an unlit hallway. My dad, a carpenter, hadn't put a light there, I suppose because—at Mom's insistence—he planned to tear down the heater wall to make their bedroom larger, a task he put off until Mom took a sledgehammer to all the bedroom walls, creating an open floor plan Dad seemed to dislike.

While the wall stood, Tippy would lie facing the heater, concealing the chalky splotches on her nose and toes that had suggested her name. Nearly every night, one of us stepped on her. But since she was a dog, she didn't hold it against us. Still, I thought she should've learned something after so many nights of being trampled.

Within days of taking her in, we found out why Tippy was homeless. She was a runner, scaling our backyard gate with acrobatic ease. Luckily, she always came back. Maybe she knew a good thing when she had it, and maybe she hadn't had it at her last address.

My father built a taller gate, one Tippy couldn't clamber over. *No problem*, she said, and dug her way out. Dad, determined she would not best him, dug a deep trench under the gate and poured concrete. After that, Tippy became a homebody.

She loved anyone her whip-cracking tail and prodding muzzle could reach. Grandma, a stony-faced Swedish immigrant, terrified me, but Tippy adored her, demonstrating fealty by executing an air rumba on my grandmother's shin whenever she sat down. I never understood why Grandma didn't seem bothered. For a fastidious woman, she made peculiar allowances where Tippy was concerned, even when Tippy embarrassed us by jamming her nose into Grandma's crotch.

Unlike the hairdresser with a haystack atop her own head, my grandmother—who raised four children on the loose change she earned as housekeeper to wealthy San Franciscans—took her work home. A dust bunny wouldn't have dared tumble under her bed. My mother, who frequently embellished a good story, told me her future mother-in-law had bent over to wipe up Mom's footprints as she entered her fiancé's home for the first time. Given the spic-and-span condition of Grandma's house, it wasn't difficult to believe that, in this case at least, Mom was telling the truth.

Grandma brought her obsessive-compulsive cleaning from the old country along with other—to me, significant—baggage. She made no secret of idolizing my brother while acknowledging me only as a footnote to the magnum opus of his existence. Her lips caressed the word *boy*. Decades later, as the mother of three young children, I sat on her sofa beside my two sons and my daughter while she crooned, "Isn't it wonderful to have boys?" I said it was and it was also wonderful to have girls.

I don't think she heard me.

Making the backyard into an impregnable kennel came too late. Tippy's middle began to swell. I was ecstatic. Mom didn't share my enthusiasm since she bore most of the responsibility for Tippy's care and felt she had enough to do already. But I think Dad was happy to imagine more dogs in the house.

He built what he called a birthing box. When Tippy got very large, he set it next to the stove and invited her to make friends with it. Mom said she hoped Tippy would keep the mess in the box, but Dad said there wouldn't be a mess because Tippy would eat it and she'd eat all the poop until the puppies were weaned. Mom said, "Ugh."

Every day I asked—first my father and then my mother—when the puppies would arrive. Every day my parents told me again that they had no idea when the puppies had been conceived and, therefore, they had no way to figure out when the babies might sever their ties with Tippy. Dad said this nicely, but Mom said it a bit louder every time I asked.

Every time Tippy lay down, I ran to one or the other parent, calling out, "She's laying down!" Mom said more than once, "No, Candi, she's *lying* down." Dad would say, "She's probably tired."

On a drizzly January morning, I woke to five pups in the box. Tippy birthed her babies there just as Dad had meant for her to do. Each of them looked very different from the others. One could've been Tippy's twin. Another was yellow with a freckled face. The third was almost white, and the fourth looked like a small Dalmatian.

That morning, while Mom fixed breakfast and Dad sat at the table, I saw Mom looking down at the puppies as she pushed bacon around in the frying pan. Finally she said quietly, almost like she was talking to herself, "Imagine that." Dad looked up from the *San Francisco Daily News*. "Yeah," he said. "Really something, eh?"

The fifth pup was Scrappy. She had a shaggy calico coat, and she looked beautiful to me. Best of all, she followed me around while the other puppies didn't seem to know I existed. I gave her a name, hoping that could get Mom to accept her. At first Mom refused to call her by name and ordered me to stop. Dad paid no attention, so eventually Mom started calling her Scrappy too. The others were just "the puppies." If I'd been in charge, I would've kept them all, but even I could see that wasn't possible. They were lovable in their way, but Scrappy picked me. She'd stare into my eyes as if saying over and over, *Keep* me!

She was the first to scramble out of the birthing box. Each time she escaped, Tippy snatched her up in her teeth and rudely plopped her back in with her littermates. Tippy must've tossed her back in a hundred times. Watching Tippy strive to keep her puppy close, Dad said I shouldn't get attached to Scrappy. "She's bull-headed. She'll be tough to train." Mom said I shouldn't get attached to any of them: "They're not staying."

One by one, they went off to new homes my mother had found. By then, I'd spent hours doing some version of skillful whining. I'd follow Mom through the house, the sound of my voice probably about as relaxing as a dog barking at three in the morning. "Please, Mom," I'd say to her back as she reached for the vacuum cleaner to drown me out. "Please, please, please can't I keep her? Can't I?" At the slightest hint she was weakening, I'd add, "Oh, Mom, please let me! Please don't give her away!"

In the end, looking far less than pleased, Mom snapped, "If I let you keep her, will you please shut up?"

Having been stuck in the backyard along with Tippy while my brother and I were in school, Scrappy threw herself at me when I got home. I'd leash up both dogs and hike to the woods above Mission Street. There I'd sit under a tree to watch their fun. Today, I think of those afternoons as some of the happiest of my childhood.

Happiness, like everything else in life, comes at a price.

Poison oak loves the shade, and so do I, which is why, one sunny afternoon, I plopped myself down into a patch of it.

Mom covered my mattress with a plastic sheet, and I lay on it like a corpse waiting for the mummy wrap. Every so often she warned me not to scratch.

"You'll make scars."

I suppose she imagined the threat of a scarred rear end would scare me into ignoring the nonstop shrieking of my itchy bottom. Whenever she wasn't in the room, I dug in.

Dad sat at my bedside and read Little Golden Books while Scrappy lay on my feet. I thought the stories were for younger kids, but I didn't care. I wasn't about to discourage my father from spending time with me. He was a shy man, so intimidated by a daughter that, whenever my mother greeted him with the need to spank his children, he couldn't bring himself to swat me harder than he might've an infant. Nevertheless, I screamed mightily while my brother maintained stoic manliness, afterward smothering his weeping in his pillow. "Yell," I told him. "Then he won't hit you so hard."

Dad sympathized with me in my poison oak misery at least partly because he, as the saying goes, had been there and done that. Many times. Not Mom.

Scrappy

When she was a kid at summer camp, left out of an excursion as punishment for some childish misdeed, my mother-to-be retaliated by collecting poison oak leaves to put in the beds of her fellow campers. Neither Dad nor I could've pulled that trick without suffering far more than our victims.

When it was time for me to return to school, Mom slathered my fanny with a product called So Help Me Hannah. The color of Pepto-Bismol, So Help Me Hannah dulls the itching about as much as calamine lotion does, which is to say, not at all. Once applied, both calamine lotion and So Help Me Hannah form a chalky crust that cracks open to let poison oak ooze its juice through clothing. But So Help Me Hannah, as an innovative competitor, added a lovely pink stain to their concoction.

When I stood up to go to lunch, my classmates were delighted by the salmon-colored blotch on the back of my skirt.

When I was nine, Mom said we had to get rid of the dogs. I followed her around, bawling, but she refused to be moved. Our dogs made a lot of work for her. Their fur stuck to the furniture and covered the floors. They tracked mud in from the yard. Tippy slobbered a lot, leaving grayish shadows on the flooring, and she, more than Scrappy, would jump on us, soiling clothes when her paws were dirty.

"When they both went into heat," Mom complained, "I had to clean the floor every night. What if your grandmother showed up when there was blood on the floor?"

I took my first step into a lifelong career of giving unsolicited advice. "Jody got her dog fixed so there's no more blood. We could get Tippy and Scrappy fixed."

"Don't be silly, Candi. We don't have the money for that."

I kept telling Mom I could help her more. "I'll clean the house. And I'll get the dog food so you don't have to carry it on the bus."

She gave me a wry smile. "You can't lug a sack of kibble home."

"I could buy small bags and just go to the store every day. I don't mind."

"Small bags cost more."

I knew that couldn't be true, but I said nothing because I didn't want to get slapped. But I had a plan. The next day, Mom came home to scrubbed floors, dusted shelves, the table set, and the dogs fed. She peered into the poop-less yard and thanked me. What surprised her was that I cleaned house nearly as thoroughly as she did. At nine, I had officially joined the wackadoodle clean freaks in my family.

I hoped my hard work would keep Mom from getting rid of Scrappy. And for a while it worked. But a few months later she began again to complain about the dogs. Their food cost too much. And no matter how much I cleaned, their fur stuck to the furniture and then to her clothes. I grew desperate.

The *San Francisco Daily News* featured a lovelorn columnist who called herself Miss Cynthia. I wrote to her about my own breaking heart.

> Dear Miss Cynthia,
> My Mom wants to give our dogs away. But Scrappy is my dog. I trained her and I love her. She's a very good dog. Mom says it costs too much money to fix the dogs so they have to go. Please help. I am crying every night.
> Love,
> Candi

My mother helped me with the letter, giving me a stamp and an envelope and showing me how to address it. She wanted to be kind, but I'm sure she believed nothing would come of it. I heard her telling Dad that it might help me accept losing the dogs, if I knew she'd done all she could.

Miss Cynthia published my letter. Mom was surprised. I was excited, convinced that somebody would help me keep Scrappy.

Less than a week later, Miss Cynthia sent me a letter. When I took it from the mailbox, I felt shaky. In the kitchen, I kept moving the envelope from place to place, first to the counter, where I poured myself milk and took two Oreos from the cookie jar. After that, to the table, where I ate the cookies and drank the milk.

In the backyard, I apologized to the dogs. "I can't take you for a walk today."

I brought the dogs and the envelope out front. Propping myself against the house on the wide ledge of the wall dividing the porch from the weedy flower bed, I slipped the letter between the pages of the fairy-tale book I was reading. I longed for the words inside the envelope to tell me how I could keep Scrappy. But I thought it might say that somebody was sorry I was going to lose my dog. Until I read it, I figured I still had hope. But I knew hope wasn't going to help if help stayed in that envelope.

I closed the book and took the letter out.

A kind lady (as Miss Cynthia called her) had offered to get our dogs spayed at her own expense. This was it! Scrappy wasn't going anywhere!

As soon as Mom came through the door, I met her with the good news. "They'll be fixed and you won't have to pay for it, Mom. So we can keep them!"

I knew that it was more than the expense of spaying that made Mom want to get rid of the dogs. But she grew up in an era when what everybody else thought of you was what you were.

The dogs were spirited away and returned a day later. I couldn't meet Mom's eyes, especially because I didn't want her to see all the happiness in mine.

Scrappy and I were climbing the hill when a man staggered around the corner and nearly collided with us. He reeked of alcohol among other odors, but he seemed harmless to me. My girl, however, held a different opinion. She sank her teeth into his leg.

"I'm sorry, I'm sorry," I cried, yanking her back to me. "Please, mister. Don't be mad. She's not a bad dog. Honest."

He scowled at me but said nothing. At a safe distance, he bent to check his wound. When I saw blood, I stammered more apologies. He growled something I couldn't make out, but then turned and limped away. I was relieved Scrappy wouldn't be taken from me and killed, but I felt awful about what she'd done.

My mother held a different view of what happened. "That man was after you," she insisted. "Scrappy knew you were in danger."

I didn't tell her the man didn't even know I was there until Scrappy bit him.

"You can't fool a dog," she said. "They always know what people are up to."

Now that couldn't be true. I'd often pretended to throw a ball so I could watch Scrappy take off after empty air.

When I was twelve, Mom and Dad separated. Grandma took Tippy. Remembering all the trouble Mom said the dogs made for her, I wondered at Grandma's willingness to take on Tippy. With a dog in it, her house surely wouldn't be as clean as she liked it. Still, if that bothered Grandma, she never showed it. And it looked to me that everything in her house stayed as clean and tidy as always. Tippy stayed too, right up until the end of her life.

Mom moved me and Scrappy with her into a storefront apartment on Old Russian Hill. The apartment didn't come with a backyard, just a creepy alley where I had to stash our garbage, which I did while looking steadily over my shoulder, checking for monsters.

Scrappy spent more than eight hours every day alone in that boring apartment. She took to entertaining herself by chewing on things she shouldn't have chewed on. Mom decided Scrappy would have to spend the day locked in a tiny bathroom, crammed with a tub, a toilet, and a sink. It was cruel, but Mom said we had no choice. As it turned out, we didn't even have that choice.

Leaping against the bathroom door in a frenzy to escape, Scrappy shredded the veneer. The door was ruined. Mom said that was it.

"I'll pay for it out of my allowance!"

"She has to go, Candi. Don't be selfish. She's miserable, locked up by herself all day."

Sadly, I knew she was right. I was selfish. If I loved Scrappy, I'd want her to have a better life than being kept in a space hardly big enough to turn around in. But my love wasn't that large. I needed her, and I believed she needed me.

A few days after that, I came home to find a stranger in our living room, on her knees, cuddling my dog. I watched as she scooped up Scrappy and said thank you to Mom.

After they left, I went to my bedroom, which didn't have a door to slam. There I lay on my narrow bed and wailed.

An hour later, Mom came in and said, "Dinner's ready."

I said nothing.

"Candi." One word. Flat. Not a question, just a reminder that when my mother spoke to me, I had to answer. Politely.

"I'm not hungry," I said, and turned over to face the wall. In a small husky voice, I added, "Thank you."

The next day I came home from school to find Scrappy waiting on the doorstep. My heart swelled. I took her inside, gave her water, and sat her in my lap, all but sure Mom couldn't give her back to those people when she saw how much Scrappy wanted to be with me.

Scrappy finding her way back to us amazed Mom. The friend who adopted my dog lived on the other side of San Francisco. But, astounded or not, Mom was more determined than my dog.

When I heard her on the phone telling someone, "We have *your* dog," I wished Mom and her friend would disappear forever and leave me alone with my dog.

Scrappy never came back again.

Try, Try Again

I was in my twenties when I purchased my first hamster. Divorced and living with my four-year-old daughter, I felt our home needed some fur. Our rental house was cold, heated solely by a single space heater isolated in the cramped living room, turning the other rooms into Siberia. The gas stove provided extra heat from the oven and all the burners. But while the living room became a kiln, the kitchen—the only large room—sent the bulk of its heat straight up to the ceiling. These fluctuating climate conditions were probably not ideal for hamsters.

But I didn't realize that. I wanted Becky to have a pet, as I did myself. Sadly, a dog was a nonstarter. My babysitter lived an hour away, and that tacked two more hours of commuting onto my workday—far too long for a pup to stay alone. Friends suggested a hamster. They're easy, they said. Well, picking one out seemed easy enough. They all looked the same. Awkwardly, I juggled a hamster in a box, a cage, bedding material, a water bottle, and a food dish on the rush-hour bus. No way could I have taken a detour to pick up Becky. The babysitter's husband, clued in on my plan, had kindly offered to bring her home after he got off work.

Gerard had a cute face despite his resemblance to a rat. He held his food pellets between miniature paws and nibbled politely. I liked his table manners but was less enchanted by his nightly regimen. His exercise wheel squeaked. While I considered oiling it to get some sleep, I feared the oil would somehow contaminate the cage and do in Gerard. I needn't have worried.

On the morning of the fourth day, his corpse lay on the bottom of his cage. I hustled Becky out the door before she saw the body. Child development professionals may urge frankness in handling young children when

11

there's a death in the family, but I opted for circumspection. Maybe I felt guilty. I did feel guilty. That poor hamster depended on me. Even if I had no idea why he died, it was my fault. I felt sure of that much.

On my way home that evening, I stopped at the same pet store and bought another Gerard. That one lasted a week. The next one lived almost ten days. The longevity trajectory headed upward, but I was unwilling to kill off more Gerards.

I stashed the rodent paraphernalia in the basement and took in a cat that had been sleeping on our porch.

Becky christened her Ezekiel, waving away my protests that she was a female. Zeke was her best friend at the babysitter's, and he'd revealed the source of his nickname to her, although he got mad if she called him Ezekiel.

"I like Ezekiel," she told me, pursing her lips in disapproval. "Better than Zeke. Zeke's a stupid name."

Becky wanted the cat to sleep with her, but Ezekiel was having none of it. That cooled my daughter's interest. Every night the cat came into my bedroom, although not necessarily to snooze.

That small room, jam-packed with furniture, provided an ideal setting for Ezekiel's nightly aerobic exercise. She'd start making the rounds, leaping from table to chair to television set to bed to dresser, beginning slow and picking up speed with each revolution. Eventually I could see only a blur skidding across tabletops. This performance always ended the same way. She'd slam into the glass on the television, fall to the floor, and casually lift one paw to clean it, signaling, I assume, that she'd meant to smash her nose into the television set all along.

The set had other uses for our cat. When it was turned on, its heat proved irresistible. Ezekiel would splay across the top, falling deeper and deeper into sleep until her body began to ooze down the screen. Waking, she'd notice the flickering images and halt her downward travel. At that point, she'd hang down the front, nose to nose with Eliot Ness or one of his *Untouchables*.

Ezekiel resisted my own slide into unconsciousness. She'd arrange herself across the top of my head and start blowing into my ear, like an inexperienced lover. I'd disentangle myself from these amorous sorties, and drift off again, only to wake to the stinging sensation of claws knifing into my scalp, and the hum of purring, again right in my ear. My efforts to discourage this behavior bombed. After a slew of sleepless nights, I banned her.

Whether because of her exile from a favored performing arts stage, or because Becky and I were gone the better part of twenty-four hours, Ezekiel tired of us and found new digs. Becky asked about her but without much interest.

I missed the cat, although never when I turned out the lights.

My Inner Rocking Horse

After a couple of months of canoodling—a word more evocative of developing romance than "dating"—Bob moved in with us. I never had a key made for him, although in hindsight I can't say why. For that reason, unless I was home to let him in, he routinely climbed through the living room window to get inside. It never occurred to me that an unlocked window next to a locked door might seem silly to some people.

Part of what made me fall in love with Bob was the relationship he fostered with my little girl. After we'd been involved for two months, he invited me to go camping. Best of all, he asked if I could get Becky's father to relinquish one weekend with her so she could come with us. "I want to meet her," he said.

Only because of such sweetness did I agree to go. It was early March!

Bob's idea of camping didn't live up to the bountiful food and equipment-rich Yosemite holidays I'd loved as a kid. In Bob's battered truck, a gunny sack hung from the unused cigarette lighter. That sack contained all he needed for impromptu expeditions: a single wobbly burner, a dented pot, some flatware, a tin plate and cup, water purification tabs, and packets of dried soup and one of gorp. He deferred to my need for comfort by bringing along some fresh food and sleeping bags. For two days, I shivered in mine while he and Becky built dams across a shallow creek in the middle of nowhere.

Nevertheless, Bob made putting up with his minimalist approach to life totally worth its minor annoyances. He changed the air quality in our house. Mornings had been a hectic mess of me shouting, "Hurry up, Becky! Put on your shoes!" Now he sat her in his lap, held up first one shoe and then the other, telling my giggling child, "Buster Brown wants a foot in the face for breakfast!"

He cooked with her: outrageous dishes such as blue macaroni and cheese without cheese. They made peanut butter and jelly and cheese sandwiches. Bananas mashed into carrots. As a man happy to behave as the child he once was, Bob entered into my daughter's world in a way I never could. I wished I knew how to take unabashed pleasure in clowning around. It gladdened my heart to see Becky burbling with laughter every morning and every evening. She had a live-in playmate.

But not a dog. I'd like to claim I thought long and hard about getting one. That I considered the ins and outs, the upsides and the downsides. Instead, I listened to my inner rocking horse. Someone brought a box of puppies to the San Francisco welfare office where I worked. I stooped, scratched one behind the ear, and scooped her up. As I watched her tumble around my office, I struggled with validating this rash decision. After all, I had killed off three hamsters and lost one cat while avoiding taking on a dog. I'd told myself I didn't have time for a dog. I told myself I was away too many hours. I was still gone too many hours.

But Bob's workday was shorter than mine. And he'd offered many times to pick up Becky from the babysitter. We could alternate doing that errand, and then I'd be able to spend more time with the puppy. When I wasn't there, he'd be there.

I didn't anticipate objections from him. He was easygoing, and, after all, we weren't married. As a single woman, didn't I have the right to make decisions like this on my own? Light seeped into my head at this point. Either I was single and entitled to act on my own, or I was dependent on him. No way could I be both.

But I dismissed the thought, counting on Bob to reassure me I'd done the right thing because a dog was just what we needed.

To my astonishment, he did object, saying peevishly that we should've discussed it. Well, I pointed out, that wouldn't have been possible, this having happened before anyone owned a cell phone. If I'd gone home, had the discussion, and gone back for the dog, there would've been no dog. The argument seemed unassailable. He disagreed, having visualized a more reasoned approach to the adoption of an animal, one that took into account the availability of dogs in shelters across the Bay Area.

Becky was thrilled, and Daisy found her often gooey fingers far more attractive than my well-washed hands.

I counted on Bob's good nature to bring him around, and soon it did. He grew to love Daisy, who was an adorable flop-eared Snoopy dog. Those incredibly long ears could've made the *Guinness Book of World Records.*

Bob had never owned a dog before her. He and Becky threw themselves into her care and entertainment. I became an also-ran. They taught her to play fetch, although I could see she only ran after the ball to oblige them. Every time she brought it back, they fed her a treat and jumped around, squealing "Good dog!" Well, Becky jumped around. Bob didn't quite enter that far into his childhood.

Soon Daisy was rolling over, standing on hind legs, and playing dead. "How about some of that 'come' and 'down' stuff?" I whined. They ignored me. Life was about fun, not rules and conformity.

By the time she had been impregnated—apparently by some determined stud that leapt our fence—Bob was sold on my belief that no home is complete without dog hair wafting around. Daisy sailed through her pregnancy, happily oblivious to the parenting chores ahead of her. The day of reckoning came one Sunday afternoon when Bob was out somewhere and Becky was with her father. Lugging a bag of clean laundry, I stood at the front door of our shotgun house watching Daisy's ears flying up behind the window in our back door. I often thought she resembled a bed sheet flapping on a clothesline. But this looked like hysteria.

As soon as I opened the back door, she plunged down the stairs to the basement, glancing back to make sure I followed. Five puppies lay snuffling in the birthing box. I brought the box upstairs and put it next to the kitchen stove, as my father had done for Tippy some fifteen years before. Daisy climbed in and settled while the pups found their way to her teats.

By the time Bob got home, she'd mastered canine mothering. I thought she looked amazingly competent for a dog that, only a few hours earlier, seemed to hope I would take over for her. He was less impressed and didn't think she should be on her own, at least not the first day or two. He took off work, supposedly to help Daisy. But I knew the puppies were his real target. I figured he'd learn that blind newborns aren't much fun. I was wrong. When

Becky and I got home, he seemed euphoric. Becky was too, reminding me of myself when Scrappy was born.

Like me, as well, she begged to keep one. Like me, in fact, she wanted all of them. Bob put the kibosh on further additions to our family. In a box, the pups went back to the ancestral manse where my coworkers scooped them up. Considerably lightened by their dispersal, I began planning our wedding. Bob and I married in the fall of our second year together.

Like Tippy before her, Daisy was an avid explorer. When we left San Francisco for Oakland, we rented a bigger house that backed down to a creek hosting truckloads of poison oak. She liked it down there and came back to wipe her paws on me. All the time we lived in that house, I battled poison oak rashes, but I didn't buy any So Help Me Hannah.

Now that we had a living room larger than a closet, we invited friends to visit. One visitor was my brother's ex-wife and her boyfriend. He said he was a dog trainer. He must've been a lousy one because he grabbed Daisy from behind. She whirled around and bit him, shocking me. She'd never shown the least aggression to anyone. I'd watched a baby yank on her ears, a toddler pound on her back, and a cat hiss at her from a foot away. None of it bothered her.

The boyfriend wore an expression that told me what he'd like to do to my dog. I called her into the other room and shut the door. When they left, Bob and I wondered aloud at our dog's behavior. "I didn't like him," I said. "Did you?"

"Not particularly."

"I keep thinking about something my mother said, about dogs knowing character."

"You think they do?"

"I never thought so before. But now I don't know."

A year later we heard my former sister-in-law had disappeared. We also heard her boyfriend had been arrested for racketeering. Maybe Daisy was on to something.

Apart from running, she was a well-behaved dog. During dinner, which we ate in the dining room, she was to stay in the kitchen. She arranged herself nightly at the borderline, a metal strip separating the linoleum from the hardwood floor. She'd place her paws on the kitchen side of the strip.

While we ate and chatted, she waited for her moment. At some point, I'd glance over and see emptiness where our dog had been. Then I'd say softly, "All right." Just those two words. Daisy would shoot out from under the dining room table, and hustle back, repositioning her toes on the correct side of the metal strip.

Around the time Daisy turned five, Eric, our first son, had been born, and we needed more space. We bought our starter house, putting the down payment on a credit card. In those days, modest houses in California could be purchased for less than the price of today's SUVs. The downside was a mortgage interest rate of 14 percent.

Bob rented a van from U-Haul, and he and a buddy ferried load after load of our belongings to our new house, which meant the front door had to stay open a lot. Between attending to the baby and packing, I didn't notice Daisy had disappeared. When at last I did, I took the car and drove around, calling her name. After an hour of not finding her, I went home and called animal control. They reported a dog's body on 580, the freeway not far from our rental house.

That first night in our new home, I didn't celebrate. After I got Eric to sleep, I went in the bathroom and wept.

Too soon, in my opinion, after we lost Daisy, Bob brought home a brindle puppy he named Ginger. Occasionally I can be tactful, so I didn't point out that he hadn't consulted me despite his prior assertion that I'd had no right to bring Daisy home without asking him.

The pup's early months were a model of what not to do with a young dog—or, for that matter, with any dog. Every morning, while he drank coffee and read the newspaper, Bob dangled one hand toward the floor. Ginger amused herself by attacking him. I saw it as her attacking Bob. He saw it as Ginger playing with his hand. Since he had a pain threshold somewhere around Mars, her sharp teeth, even as they penetrated, didn't bother him. His pocked hand bore evidence of Ginger's burgeoning aggression.

I tried to explain why letting her bite human flesh wasn't a good idea. Dogs aren't people, I said. They're partly wild animals. I asked him, "What if she bites Eric?"

"She's not going to bite Eric. Or anybody else. She knows it's only playing."

"That's bullshit," I said. "You can't expect a dog to see the difference between playing by chewing on you and biting to get her own way."

When she was a year old, Ginger took a chunk out of my ankle. I'd accidentally bumped into her while carrying Eric to his crib. Bob said the bite was my fault.

"How can it be my fault? I'm trying not to wake up the baby. I'm not thinking about the damned dog. The dog needs to think about me."

"Why can't you think about the dog? Does carrying Eric require every scintilla of your attention?"

"Bob, she's supposed to get out of the way. If she doesn't, when it's dark in the room, one of us could trip over her. Suppose that happened when I was carrying him?"

"You can't kick a dog and not expect her to react."

"I didn't kick her. I bumped into her."

"Same thing."

Bob had taught her "sit," and that was pretty much the extent of the training he did with her. I tried "lie down," and she bit me. By then I was pregnant again, not working, and imagining this dog around an infant. I already had plenty of qualms about her around my toddler.

Eric was seven months old, not yet proficient on two legs but loudly impatient to get going. With the help of a baby walker, he gaily tooled around the house. Baby walkers currently are engineered. In those days, they consisted of a canvas seat and wheels. Eric navigated by shuffling his feet. The sole drawback to the freedom he got from the walker was that it put his face level with Ginger's teeth.

When Bob was at work, I put her outside. Whenever I took Eric outside, she went back in the house. When Bob was home, I watched her obsessively.

Pleading with Bob to find another home for her turned into nagging. He refused to discuss it. Why he didn't feel that our son needed to be protected from a biting dog, I couldn't fathom, and I bitterly resented it. Bickering over Ginger became more rancorous, but the result was the same—nothing changed.

Bickering is probably the wrong word. Bob didn't bicker, and, for the most part, he didn't argue. My words flew at him while he grew quieter and quieter. He offered no rationale for holding onto a churlish dog. Maybe he knew why no more than I did. Maybe way back then, twenty years before he left me, the seeds of feeling trapped were already taking root in him.

No resolution to the impasse suggested itself. I wanted Ginger gone, and he had no intention of getting rid of her. Between the presence of a dog and the absence of a dog, no compromise exists.

Then she bit Bob. Hard. The next day she was gone. I clamped my mouth around a torrent of recriminations. Ginger would be "put down" (as the euphemism has it), and I had no reservations about where the blame for her demise lay. But I stuffed my resentment under the marital rug, and never again mentioned her.

Which didn't mean I never thought of her.

Chessa

After Ginger, neither of us wanted to take on a new dog. Our sons would be ten and eleven, my daughter a senior in high school, when I began to consider getting one. Bob, perhaps still stinging from his botched relationship with Ginger, didn't object but seemed to lack enthusiasm. The boys clamored for a puppy.

"Not a puppy," I said. By then I had a part-time job. With a job and two young children, I didn't have time to train a pup. "We'll look for one that's already trained."

We picked up Homer in San Francisco. He was about a year old, shaggy black, handsome. He seemed smart and well-behaved. The owners put him through his paces—sit, stand, stay, and lie down, that last, of course, came out as "lay down." I quashed a fleeting inclination to mimic my mother and issue a grammar correction. When she heard that "lay down," my best friend and smartest grammar cop, Terri, corrected me. I told her "lay down" was the command form. For half a second, she swallowed it. Then I told her it was my way of rebelling against my mother, but that wasn't true either. Like my use of the phrase "not hardly," "lay down" came out of a well-carved channel in the speech center of my brain. When I most wanted to appear erudite, that's what flew out my mouth.

When we took Homer, his previous owners made us promise we'd never take him to a shelter. If for any reason we couldn't keep him, we were to bring him back to them. They kept hammering the point: no shelter for Homer. Privately, I hoped Ginger would be my last dog to wind up in a shelter.

In less than an hour, Homer nipped Eric.

After Homer went back to his previous home, I decided we should look for a breed known to be good-natured. "A Lab," I said. "They're pussycats. A yellow Labrador."

"What's a Labrador?" asked Seth.

"A retriever," said Eric. "They go get things."

We found our Lab tied up in a backyard, without access to water or even a soft place to lie down.

"She's wild," said the owner, apparently convinced her faults justified his mistreatment. "Can't do nothing with her."

I wondered how long she'd been tethered, but I didn't ask. The answer might've caused me too much grief.

"She'll calm down when we get her home," I assured Bob as Chessa "attacked" our giggling boys. "A little exercise, and some attention, for Christ's sakes. You can't tie a dog up and ignore her, expecting her to behave."

Little did I know. I had enrolled myself in the first of numerous canine tutorials in the art of "think again."

Chessa was all Labrador, with enough energy to fuel six active dogs. Her rump had never experienced tranquility. In our living room, her muscular tail dominated. As we learned, it ceased moving only when she slept, and sometimes not even then. Having her around turned out to be the equivalent of housing a brigade of monkeys. Years later, when I owned as many as three dogs at once, it seemed to me together they didn't take up as much room as Chessa managed to fill all by herself.

Nicknamed for Duchessa, her registered title, our Lab never achieved the nobility her papers implied. Her only posh assets were her ears. Eric loved to stroke them. They felt like satin. But, with Chessa, elegance ended there.

While she never met anyone she didn't adore—nor anyone she didn't assume adored her—Chessa had a less-than-classy greeting style, with her nose to any visiting crotch, front or back, whichever was handiest. Mary, my stepmother, served as our dog's favorite target, and that was lucky. Mary grew up on a farm in Tennessee. The vagaries of animals didn't faze her. She called Chessa "Dog Bones," and roughed her up, to the dog's delight. With Mary running interference at our door, Dad was spared a Lab inspection. On the other hand, I'm not sure he would've disliked being a victim of her attention. He often said he liked animals far more than he liked people.

Sampling crotch odors wasn't the only way Chessa demonstrated the low regard in which she held the dignity her title implied. True to her breed, she was a food hound, routinely swiping unmonitored vittles from counter or table. In late summer, while I tended my garden, she denuded my bountiful strawberry patch. I tried lacing a meatball with hot sauce, but that was a doomed endeavor. Chessa kept nothing in her mouth long enough to taste. She would've happily ingested a pot filled with hot sauce meatballs. Our dog's gobbling of everything from hot sauce to strawberries led to our discovery of incense. As she lay on her bed and we in ours, we lit up. The scent of vanilla, however, does not purge the stench of flatulence. Pachouli stands a better chance.

To our girl, it was all good. If her plebeian disregard for decorum was hard to take now and then, she nevertheless filled our home with happiness. Chessa erupted from her bed every morning as if she knew the day held something special for a receptive Labrador retriever.

One morning, we headed off to do errands, something Chessa, unlike my children, never found boring. I opened the door for her, and she dashed out, leaping into the air, twirling, and leaping again. I imagined her squealing meant "I'm gonna go! I'm gonna go! I'm gonna go!" She kept celebrating like a delirious hurdler, all the way across the deck to the top of the brick stairs. There, she landed awkwardly, skidding down the steps on her nose. When she got up, blood poured from her mouth. I felt sorry for her, but Chessa, having discarded a tooth, jumped up, caroling more ecstatic verses of "I'm gonna go! I'm gonna go! I'm gonna go!"

Whenever we hiked uphill, Chessa would do ten or fifteen full-scale U-turns before we crested the top, with me huffing like the little engine that couldn't. To our dismay, she somehow made time, even while zipping back and forth, for snuffling, a practice to which she brought all the verve she injected into everything. That meant our hikes sometimes ended with one of her nostrils oozing blood. Off to the vet we'd go, our credit card inching toward max.

Foxtails carpet much of California. These grassy weeds look like miniature arrows, and their nastiness stems from the way in which they lodge in flesh, with spiny flanges flat against the stem until someone tries to pull them out. Traveling backward, the flanges open to stall the effort, like toddlers digging their feet into the carpet to resist going to bed.

Nowadays there's a netting, like mosquito netting, that can be placed over a dog's head. The sight of it is a bit unnerving. Still, it allows plenty of sniffing without peril. Unfortunately, it wouldn't have protected Chessa's vagina against one of those petite spikes. That hike ended in surgery.

One of her favorite excursions was up to Lake Tulloch, where Dad and Mary had a holiday mobile home on a few acres. Every summer, we spent a week there. Every year Chessa got to swim as much as she wanted. Well, anyway, a lot. We'd throw sticks in the water so she could swim out to get them. As she swam, she squeaked like a hinge in need of oil. But she wouldn't stop diving after whatever we threw until we said, *No more.* When she grabbed hold of a water snake, mistaking it for a stick I'd thrown, it curled around her muzzle like a handlebar mustache. The snake wiggled in vain to get free and finally bit her. That worked. He swam away, oddly reshaped into an S.

That was the only time in her life Chessa gave me a dirty look. Probably the only time in her life she gave anyone a dirty look.

At the lake's edge, a weed that must've been five or more feet tall sprouted straight up. From a single stalk, dozens of thin fronds grew upward. My father yanked it out of the ground and threw it like a spear into the lake. Chessa dove in and brought it back to shore. After she dropped the stalk at Dad's feet, she pivoted, plunged back in, and, mouth open, swam in a circle, collecting the floating fronds. Now that's a retriever.

Swimming, a pleasure for her, posed problems for us. The long flaps of her ears created a perfect environment for bacteria. I didn't know then that I could've bought a powder that would dry out her ears. Water in her ears often meant another trip to the vet. How she and I hated the ensuing morning and night ritual of cleaning out her ears and then squirting in the medication. These days, every time my little dog has an ear infection, I light a candle to the gods of research. The vet inserts medication at the clinic, and it works all on its own for two weeks. Hallelujah! No more wrestling matches with a dog.

When we adopted her, the family that gave her to us claimed she was two. I suspect she was closer to five. Whether she'd been two or five, she lived to a ripe old age. Partially blind, totally deaf, and riddled with arthritis, she persuaded us to end her misery by lying on her bed throughout the day. The sight of her immobilized after years of energetic romping tore at my heart. It seemed unfair that she couldn't have gotten from gleeful to dead, and done it without bumping down months of painful decline.

How I Got Henry

As my marriage began to fail, I entered the PhD program in English at Berkeley. Although, in retrospect, I'm not sure that's the way to think about the collapse of matrimonial bliss in my case. It's possible that my enrolling in a doctoral program spurred the fracture of what had seemed a solid union. After all, throughout our years together I'd been my husband's scholarly inferior. He had a master's degree in history. I had nada until I turned forty. Then I began acquiring a BA. Getting accepted into UC Berkeley's PhD program unbalanced what might've been (unbeknownst to me) a precarious equation. I remember a fateful comment Bob made when I tried to get his opinion on my thesis proposal. "You've gone beyond me," he said, and that was all.

I needed a distraction from the sound of bedrock crumbling beneath me. Henry might've been that distraction, but he was also my own mid-life crisis. He came to me as a serendipitous find but also, I have to say, as an affliction. The part of him that qualified as a burden had not been hidden from me. I knew before adopting him what I'd taken on. Well, I knew some of it.

In the beginning, Henry reminded me of Marlon Brando in *On the Waterfront*. In one scene, Brando tells his mobster brother—the man who'd scuttled Brando's shot at becoming a champion boxer by forcing him to throw a vital match—"I could'a been a contenda."

Henry, too, could'a been a contenda.

I used to say Henry thought I was the girlfriend of the leader of the pack. If he'd had a credit card, he would've ordered me a box of chocolates and a bouquet of roses. There were countless times Henry promised me he'd never bite me again.

My road to acquiring this difficult genius dog began with a trip to Oregon to visit Sue and Gil, old friends I'd met through Bob, who had worked with Sue before they moved north. We had never visited them up there, so this was my introduction to their new life, which, by then, wasn't new except to me. Tactfully, they didn't ask where Bob was, but I offered that information anyway. "In the desert," I said. "Where he spends more time than he does with me." I winced at how bitter I sounded. "I love your house," I said, wandering into the kitchen.

Sue and Gil's children had grown and flown. The couple lived outside Portland on several acres backed by woods. Years before, I had been treated to proof of how easygoing they were when Donna, a mutual friend, showed me photographs of a camping trip she and her husband had taken with Sue and Gil. Their two tents squatted maybe twenty feet from a mountain precipice. *Nice view*, I said. *The kids must've had a great time*, I said. *You really captured their carefree joy*, I said, admiring shots of their three gamboling toddlers. Yikes!

Sitting in Sue and Gil's house, I recalled a long-ago dinner under the stars at their charming rental home in Alamo. They'd been my ideal, a romantic couple, drinking wine and eating late because, for hours, they'd been engrossed in talking. Bob and I, each evening promptly at 5:30 p.m., presided over one sulking teenager and two little boys saying yuck about everything on their plates. Our conversations were about as rich as a Western Union telegram.

Sue and Gil owned a coal-black, giant poodle, a canine reprobate. Without sincerity, they bemoaned Maxi's rejection of all that "sit," "stay," "down," and "come" nonsense. Before going off on a month-long holiday, they'd left her in a board-and-train kennel, happily anticipating coming home to a well-behaved dog. It was not to be. Maxi, the trainer informed them while taking their check, was much too smart and therefore unteachable. I thought this one of the oddest rationales for failure I'd ever come across.

I was sure I could've made Maxi into a canine good citizen. However, I buried hubris under good manners, and—as if I knew then I'd wind up with a Henry ready to take my vanity down several notches—that choice of silence served me well. Maybe I remembered that the average life is now and then gouged by errant certainties.

Take my beautiful daughter as a two-year-old. Becky was a delightful child, one who could accompany me anywhere, any time. I never worried she'd throw a tantrum or begin nagging me to go home or demanding to know where her favorite toy was or whining she was hungry but didn't want to eat anything on her plate. A child liberally stocked with sunny smiles. At a party, when she tired, I plopped her down on the host's bed. Parents who'd left their children home for good reasons smothered me in compliments. They asked for tips, which I generously bestowed on them. And then reality intruded. Eric, the first of my sons, joined the family. Soon no one sought my advice. After the second boy, Seth, showed up, I was down to begging anyone who'd listen for their suggestions.

My appreciation of and admiration for well-behaved dogs, however, folded in the blaze of Maxi's charm. After a few hours with my Oregon buddies, I'd fallen in love with their disobedient dog. She'd taken quite a liking to me as well, placing her chin on my knee and gazing adoringly up at me. I felt special until Sue informed me that Maxi took loving possession of everyone who visited.

Like a '60s hippie, their poodle spent hours roaming the woods. All she needed was a backpack, a prairie dress, and a roach clip. Calling her would have given Sue and Gil nothing but laryngitis, so they didn't bother. Maxi came home when she was good and ready. Her anarchism provided them with plenty of laughter—far more pleasure, they finally admitted, than they would've gotten from an obedient dog.

At bedtime, Maxi would refuse to lie down until her beloved stuffed bear rested between her paws. Most nights she found it herself, gripped it in her teeth, and trotted off to the bedroom. But occasionally the three of them had to turn the house upside down to find that bear. If she appreciated their efforts, she never mentioned it.

Sue confessed, however, that Maxi had previously indulged in a habit thoroughly disagreeable to her otherwise permissive, domestic help. Sue and Gil worked full time during the day while Maxi was confined to the house. This would've been fine as, in general, she wasn't a destructive dog. However, she had invented a game to entertain herself during those long tedious hours alone. She developed a fixation on the front door mail slot. Whatever came through, it belonged to her.

Every workday, Sue said, they came home to a carpet of shredded paper. Bills had to be taped back together, but among all that masticated mail, how were they to know which scraps mattered and which didn't? Some nights they sorted and taped only to discover they'd received not a single piece of mail worth saving.

By chance, Sue was enlightened on the source of Maxi's hobby. Home with the flu and lying on the living room sofa, she heard the mailman climb the front steps. *At last*, she thought. *Now I can make her stop chewing up the mail.*

Sure enough, at the sound of footsteps, Maxi charged the door, barking frantically. After a moment, an envelope poked in through the slot, but it didn't drop to the floor. Instead, it began to jerk rapidly back and forth until Maxi seized it. Mild mannered Sue had seen enough. She opened the door. The mailman bobbed up from his stooped position, another envelope already partially inserted. He offered Sue a tentative grin, presumably hoping to engage her in mutual appreciation of his joke. She swallowed her irritation.

"Please," she said gently, "don't do that anymore."

As I drove back to the San Francisco Bay Area from Oregon, my interest in having my own poodle spiraled out of wistfulness into necessity. I wanted a Maxi. I *needed* a Maxi. My very own. Somewhat better behaved, of course. Living in the city without acreage, I needed a dog to come when called.

I wasn't going to buy one from a breeder, given our rickety financial infrastructure. Anyway, what would I do with a poodle bred for dog shows? An unknighted poodle from a long line of un-Sir-Somebodys would suit me just fine.

Fleetingly, I wondered if Bob would object. Recalling his annoyance when I had brought Daisy home without considering him, I was then ready to gamble that he wouldn't care. As it turned out, I was right. When I told him of my intention to bring home a dog, he shrugged and muttered something that might've been "That's nice." He was spending most of his limited at-home time by then in the bedroom he'd converted to a study. Having taken on the job of newsletter editor for a group called Desert Survivors—people dedicated to the proposition that arid, unoccupied land should remain unoccupied, apart from their own excursions—he had little time for me, and less for my whimsical pursuit of a dog after years without one.

But the newspaper want ads, still published in that pre-Craigslist era, offered nothing under AVAILABLE DOGS. My enthusiasm began to wilt. I told myself I could get a perfectly good non-poodle from a shelter. The individual dog mattered, not the breed. But I didn't believe myself.

I knew a trained poodle wouldn't be as entertaining as Maxi. Such a rascal, however, would bedevil me. I lacked my Oregonian friends' tolerance. For me, the charm of a Maxi would wither under the heat lamp of ownership.

But Maxi's joie de vivre kept peppering my fantasy dog. It wasn't just her zesty personality. She was intelligent, a Phi Beta Kappa among dogs. Intelligence in a dog means a lot to me.

I called Terri, my friend and a human Yellow Pages.

"Why don't you call Poodle Rescue?"

"Because I'm on the phone with you?"

"Hilarious."

I thought of Greyhound rescue groups. "Poodle Rescue? Really? For racing poodles that are retiring?" I could almost picture Maxi giving her track boss the finger.

"No, they rescue extroverts as well. Get a pen. I'll tell you whom to call."

"Whom? God that sounds archaic."

I dialed Poodle Rescue's phone number while the phone was warm in my hand. After what I thought were enough rings to summon a gaggle of poodles, a woman answered, sounding out of breath.

"What luck!"

"Pardon?"

"It's amazing," she said. "When you rang, I was on the phone with Fremont. They've just taken in one of our dogs. From the West Bay. When we can't find a foster, we board our dogs at a shelter."

Was this meant to be or was this meant to be? Obviously, the dog of my dreams waited for me in Fremont. There wasn't a moment to lose.

Except it was six in the evening and the shelter closed at five.

The next morning, I set off for Fremont. Making my way through rush hour traffic—surely, I could've waited an hour or two, but no—I pictured my poodle. Sporting a puppy cut, I hoped. The sight of bare dog flesh brings out the prude in me.

When I entered the shelter, I didn't know the sex, the age, the color, or the size of the dog I'd come to claim. I knew nothing beyond the breed. This poodle might be a toy or a miniature. All I knew was I wasn't going to consider anything but a Maxi look-alike, and I felt positive this poodle was a Maxi look-alike. This poodle was my destiny.

The man behind the Fremont counter, wearing a crisp tan shirt that might've been ironed after he'd put it on, frowned.

"Lady," he told me, "you do not want that dog."

"What do you mean? Why don't I want that dog?"

"He's a biter."

I stepped over his counsel as I would've a pile of dog poo. "Let me see him."

He gave a shrug. "It's your funeral. Take her to see Henry, Jorge."

Jorge led me back to the kennels, which were reeking. The barking could've induced hearing loss. How could anyone—human or canine—endure that stench and that racket?

"There he is," Jorge said as if I might've missed the enormous poodle standing before me.

Snowy white, with soulful brown eyes, Henry sported an impressive mustache. A good-looking dog, apart from the fact that someone had massacred his coat. He had lumpy tufts here and there, punctuated by random bare spots. The card attached to his kennel said Henry was five years old. It held no further information, not even that he was a biter. Maybe Tan Shirt made that up. Maybe he wanted this beautiful boy for himself.

Though I stood in front of him, Henry looked past me, thundering like Judge Judy on an opinionated roll.

With one look, and no deliberation, I was in love.

His deep chest provided concert hall acoustics for the solo he performed in that cement echo chamber. His agitation seemed entirely reasonable to me, a proper reaction to that noisy, smelly prison and what had to be grief over having been abandoned by the people he loved. Hell, I thought, I'd bark too.

"Is there a room where I can be with him? Without all this noise?"

Jorge looked skeptical. "You know he bites?"

He unhooked Henry's kennel, looped a noose leash over him, and led the two of us to a small room away from the discord. I expected Henry would settle when the chaos receded.

But he didn't. I was invisible. Irrelevant. Uninteresting. How many ways could he insult me? Well, he would find me plenty interesting once he became my dog.

At the front desk, I took out my checkbook. "How much?"

At my side, Henry stood, at last quiet, his posture regal. He showed no interest in what Tan Shirt and I were doing. I got it. Royalty never concerns itself with money. They have people for that.

And now so did Henry.

"Five dollars."

Blushing, I closed my checkbook. Pointing to the pricey price list posted on the wall, I asked him, "Why only five dollars?"

"He's not our dog." I heard the subtext and was glad Henry's fate wasn't in this man's hands.

Holding the frayed leash clipped to my new poodle's purple collar, I marched him into the clean air and soothing sunlight. There I stopped to contemplate the enormity of what I'd just done. Well, I thought I was contemplating it. In fact, I had no idea of the enormity of what I'd done. Taking home a dog: a major commitment. Taking home Henry: a commitment way beyond major. Henry had acquired a lifetime home with someone determined to love him. I, on the other hand, had grabbed Pandora's Box with its lid jammed in the open position.

I took a minute to scan Henry's folder. It held three slips of paper. Three intrepid souls had volunteered to foster him. Each had submitted a minuscule account of their brief experience with him. The stories weren't encouraging. One woman complained that he had bitten the vet. Another huffily noted that her son, a young boy who "knows how to treat a dog," suffered a bite for merely taking hold of Henry's leash. The third wanted to keep him, but her landlord objected. However, she reported that Henry had bitten a groomer. Which explained the bad haircut.

We trotted over to my little red Acura. Henry leapt into the backseat as soon as I opened the door. I approved of his confidence. A great quality in a dog. I glanced at him in the rearview mirror. He sat upright, surveying his new kingdom. I smiled. I grinned. I practically chortled. He was perfect. He was lovely. He was obedient. He was mine!

Then I switched on the ignition. Fremont is a forty-five-minute drive from Oakland under the best traffic conditions. Luckily, northbound traffic wasn't bad that morning. The moment the motor roared to life, so did Henry. I made myself empathize. He was venting about his ordeal, about being dumped out of his good life into the lives of those who'd had no idea how to handle him. He'd been shifted from pillar to post. What he was doing, I told myself, amounted to a "purge." He'd settle down. He'd find peace. And so would I.

The problem here was that I'm the kind of person who jumps when a door slams. My level of sensitivity is not complicated. In dogs, it's called reactivity. In people, it's a hyperactive nervous system, or, for those who wish to turn an operational defect into moral superiority, I am a highly sensitive person.

That day, inches from my delicate eardrums, throughout forty-five lo-o-ong minutes, Henry pitched his atonal oratorio up into the cheap seats. By the time we arrived at my carport, my nerves were about as steady as those of an acrophobic on the edge of a rooftop. When the motor shut down, so did Henry. *Whew,* I thought. *Okay. He got that off his chest.*

After slapping my ears to get them functioning, I let him out of the car. He bolted, racing around on those impossibly long legs. I was about to lose him! I'd had him for an hour, and all he had to do to shake me was dash down the hill into traffic. I ran around the car after him. He galloped in the other direction, turning to peer at me every time I paused to catch my breath.

"Henry!" I finally snapped. "Come here!"

He came. Oh dear. He'd been having fun, surely for the first time in however long it had taken for me to claim him. Stupidly, I'd spoiled it. This was not how I wanted to start our life together. I apologized and stroked his silky head.

Then we trotted upstairs where my three cats awaited us. When he caught sight of his new roommates, excitement radiated from his body.

"These cats," I told him, pointing at the three who sat unimpressed by the huge poodle invading their territory. "These cats," I repeated, "are *my* cats." For emphasis, I pointed to myself. Then I pointed at him and said, "You, Henry, will not bother them. At all."

Having taken care of that bit of business, I realized it was time for the tasks that normally precede the acquisition of a dog. I had no dishes large enough to hold a Henry-sized meal, which I also didn't have. There was no bed for him and no toys. That ragged leash had to go, along with the hideous purple collar.

Back in the car, Henry let me know that he had not fully rid himself of complaints over his traumatic ordeal, bellowing all the way to the pet shop, which turned out to be more of a pet shoppe. We marched into Furever Friends, the "n" on the sign uncharacteristically (given their prices) faded, leaving a distinctly anti-vegetarian message. This was the sort of pet shop that shames the customers into ignoring their checking account balance. After all, anyone who truly loves their pet would not put money ahead of that pet's happiness and well-being.

Anxious to prove how much I loved my dog, I loaded up, grabbing everything that seemed remotely useful. My arms filled with the essentials plus toys and treats, I signed an astronomical credit card slip and shrugged off the shop owner's unnecessary offer to help me to my car. What I had to carry fit into a bag. The heavy items would be delivered by her son.

Head held high, I stepped outside like a supermodel on a catwalk. As the belled door shut behind us, Henry spied an irresistible spaniel. I had one second to decide whether to let go of his new leash, perhaps permanently, or go down. I held on and face-planted into a thoughtfully located bowl of dog water. My favorite sunglasses snapped. My elbow and my knee discarded slivers of me on the sidewalk. Henry came back to bestow his presence on lucky me. Seated, he waited, seemingly patiently, but I wasn't fooled. He was thinking only of getting back to his favorite yodeling cave. The Met might've envied my Acura's deft enhancing of sound.

Any adult, not in serious trouble except for being splayed on the sidewalk, will long for passersby to avert their gaze and keep passing by. But the owner of the spaniel didn't grasp this truism. Instead, he came over to help me up.

I tossed my sunglasses into a sidewalk trash bin and shuffled to the car, clinging tight to Henry's leash, praying nothing else would send him vaulting away.

On the way home, he relentlessly serenaded me. I had begun to surmise that these earsplitting complaints had nothing to do with trauma in his past and everything to do with the sound of the engine and the movement of the car. He wasn't mourning; he was having a grand time. Maybe he thought if his barking goaded me sufficiently, he'd finally get to sink his teeth into one of those steel animals running away from us.

I exited the car, rattled, and glad for the diversion of the Furever Friends van pulling up behind me. The afternoon would pass in reorganizing the house to accommodate Henry. I was already drawing mental maps and shuffling furniture and dog equipment into imaginary locations before I discarded one idea and launched the next.

By nightfall, I was exhausted, not least from the strain of bringing Henry home. I said goodnight to the cats and took Henry into my bedroom, where I'd placed his cushion. My cat allergy precluded the feline corps from occupying the bedroom, and they readily adapted to spending the night in their designated beds. I was gratified when Henry did the same. We all slept well.

In the morning, the cats, as usual, sat outside the bedroom door, waiting for breakfast. I started for the kitchen when something caught my eye, and I glanced back at Henry. He'd pressed himself against the wall, sliding ostentatiously along while avoiding the slightest contact with the cats.

At the sliding glass door, Henry plopped himself down, Peewee and Sam sitting on one side of him, Chewy on the other. Every morning they waited for Yoda, a free-roaming feline who belonged to my neighbor. Now Henry waited with them. Maybe the cats had told him about Yoda. He seemed to know something was up. As I fixed everybody's breakfast, Henry rose, barking savagely.

My cats gave him six paws up.

Foolish, Moi?

A lovely pink dusk softened the evening air. I'd had Henry for nearly for-ty-eight hours when I decided to take him up to Merritt College for some exercise. The junior college rests on a plateau with a dazzling view of the West Bay. The customary late-afternoon fog had not yet blanketed the Oakland hills. Merritt would be a great place to frolic. I thought.

We played on the lawn fronting an administration building. His haute mustache quivered. Whatever his shortcomings (at that point I knew of only one), he was the poodle I'd dreamed of having.

I twirled until I felt dizzy. Which happened quickly, although not quickly enough. When I came to a stop, Henry was nowhere in sight. I looked down the lawn toward the street. Thankfully, he wasn't there. I looked at the road leading into the campus but didn't see him. He's somewhat hard to miss, I thought, rapidly concluding that the only direction he could've taken would've been toward one of the parking lots. My heart in my throat, I jogged (sort of) toward the closest one, hoping I'd spot him there quickly.

That evening, the lots teemed with people heading toward their cars. Some event must've just ended. Soon Henry would be in real danger of getting in the way of one of those departing cars. I wove through them, frantically yelling, "Henry! Henry!" Parents hustling young children into their family vehicles assumed I had lost my son. A few patted my arm. Some clicked their tongues over the shameful carelessness that had caused me to misplace my child. One gave me a scathing look, muttering "Idiot." I couldn't disagree.

Finally, a little boy in an Oakland A's hat tugged on my sleeve. "Are you looking for a big white poodle?"

My heart settled into a steadier beat. Henry had to be safe if this child knew where to find him. Maybe someone was holding his collar for me.

I followed the kid to an SUV with an open back door. On the backseat, perched next to the far window, sat Henry, staring fixedly away from me. An angry woman twisted toward me from the driver's seat. "I want him out," she said. "Now." Unfortunately, Henry didn't seem to be picking up on her hostility.

"I'm really, really sorry," I told her, reaching for him. And there it was. Without looking over, he favored me with a guttural threat. Mortified, I assured the driver, "He really is my dog." Because I was wondering how I could prove he was my dog, if, say, the police were summoned. With scarcely less venom than Henry was directing toward my efforts to remove him, the woman retorted, "I don't give a damn whose dog he is. Just get him out of my car."

Henry was not ready to cooperate. Even though the air was turning cool, sweat oozed down my back. What if I couldn't get him out? What would happen? Animal control, seeing Henry's aggression, would put him to sleep. Because he wasn't adoptable, at least not by any reasonable person. I didn't fail to note the irony. Had he only been there, Tan Shirt would've relished the moment.

The boy in the cap stood beside me. I scanned him surreptitiously, searching for bite marks, comforted by not spotting any.

The driver started mumbling what sounded like a countdown, reminding me of my mother setting a timer as she put a disheartening bowl of Cream of Wheat in front of me.

Just as I'd concluded there was no way we were going to get out of this situation without something worse happening, Henry seemed to remember me. He got up, his head brushing the ceiling of the van, and clambered down to stand politely at my side, regal as ever. I re-fastened his leash. The boy, no more enamored of my dog than was his mother, leapt into the backseat and slammed the door.

The SUV whizzed out of the lot.

I looked down at my magnificent, exasperating poodle. He looked up at me.

I said, "Did your people have a van like that one, Henry?"

40

Poodle Follies

In short order, one of Henry's other behavioral excesses came to my attention. He had separation anxiety. Whenever I left the house, he urinated and defecated on the living room rug.

And that wasn't all. Although he tried to keep me home, he went away whenever an opportunity presented itself. My fence wasn't secure, and Henry took full advantage. The phone would ring, and somebody would say they had my poodle. Once I had to hand over twenty bucks as a "reward" that felt more like extortion. A couple had called to say Henry had been about to trot down the on-ramp to the freeway when they caught him and wasn't that worth money to me?

The last time Henry took off, I was printing a LOST DOG flyer when the phone rang.

The woman on the other end chuckled. "Do you own a big white poodle?"

"Have you got him?"

"I was weeding my front garden, and I'd left my door open. Your boy trotted up the walk, big as life, like he owned the joint. I went in and found him in the kitchen enjoying my lunch."

Her name was Alma, and she was one of many kind-hearted dog lovers who rescued me from shame by laughing at Henry's offenses. My friends weren't as tolerant. They refused to ride with me and my poodle. He'd turned me into a pariah. I had to do something. And suddenly I knew what that would be.

We made a second trip to Furever Friends for a barbecued bone. An irresistible treat. Henry sniffed the bones on offer. He seemed pleased with my selection. My strategy was to leave it in the car where Henry would happily chew on it as we tooled along in silence. Oh, it was genius.

Henry remained blissfully quiet . . . for three blocks.

When I'd parked in the carport, Henry took more interest in his bone. "Oh no you don't, buster. Only when the car is moving."

As my hand closed on the bone, Henry's teeth closed on my hand. I knew enough about dogs to know that if I lost this battle, he would take the throne, brandishing his teeth as his scepter. I stomped upstairs, grabbed an oven mitt, and prepared to declare victory. His teeth crushed the oven mitt and my hand under it. Someone must've ground his incisors to a razor tip. Either that, or I needed new oven mitts.

The bone was his until he chose to give it up. I left the two of them in the car.

Teaching him a lesson, I called it. Like sending a teenager to her room where digital amusements await.

Thirty minutes later, I checked on him. He was still enjoying the bone. Lesson not yet grasped by him. I, however, was a quick study. An hour later, he'd lost interest in the bone. When I let him out of the car, he pranced upstairs, his body electric with joy.

Well, that's the spirit I had been seeking in a poodle, wasn't it?

Henry soiling the rug got solved by never leaving him at home by himself. He went everywhere I went—almost. On a hot day, I had to find a covered parking lot, and pay for it. Sometimes I had to walk a half mile or so, just so Henry could be comfy and unperturbed by thoughts of abandonment.

The nasty cherry on top of this sundae was that taking him everywhere I went meant enduring nonstop caterwauling. Nonstop.

I tried slamming on the brakes. Sitting without moving for long periods of time. Waiting him out. Ha. No matter how long I sat there, no matter how many times I did that, nothing changed. Well, how could it? When the car was still, so was Henry. When the car roared to life, so did Henry. Did I think he'd engage in some sort of if-then logic?

Quickly, I tired of his bad habits. He never pottied in the house when I was there, but he was a leaky sewer pipe if I had the gall to make an exit, no matter how briefly. Attempts to clean my living room rug left me in despair. My nose assured me that the boards underneath were saturated with urine. Only tearing up the carpet and replacing the floor would cure that problem. But I wasn't about to do that until I could be sure Henry would not stink it back up if I had to leave him home. The carpet cleaning machine I rented at Safeway every couple of weeks soaked the rug without much mitigation of the disgusting odor. I kept the living room windows ajar if not wide open and entertained only in the dining room with the door shut. True, I could've crated him, and that would've solved that. He'd never soil himself, I felt certain of that much. But I wanted him to love his crate. Making it into a prison was a way to ensure he'd never go in it willingly. I so wanted him to do things *willingly*.

After another disagreeable morning driving from one errand to another, I was royally fed up with my royal-standard poodle. The torture had to end, and I thought I knew how. Another brilliant idea, as gratifying as finding a twenty-dollar bill rain-plastered to my windshield. Which, of course, has never happened, and that should've been a clue.

When we got home, I rummaged through a drawer of things I didn't want but couldn't bring myself to toss, since, after all, they might prove useful. Or they would, right after the garbage truck hauled them away.

What I dragged out was a black sleep mask that had come with a jar of face cream. To give myself a few points, I tossed the three-year-old unemployed face cream. Plotting the termination of Henry's earsplitting hobby, I attached the sleep mask to a mesh muzzle I'd bought at the furever-profitable Furever Friends. I'd also purchased a short metal lead. Henry's zeal at the sight of steel prey would end, I reasoned, if he could no longer see cars rushing away from us. The muzzle would hold the mask over his eyes while keeping him from getting his jaws open enough to bark. This was genius. I told myself it couldn't fail.

Muzzled and masked he followed me to the car. There I tethered him to the emergency brake, giving him enough slack that he could lift his head, but less than enough for him to peer through the windshield.

One thing I hadn't considered was how a masked and tethered Henry would look to other drivers. At a stoplight, one couple stared at us, wild-eyed. I toyed with the notion of telling them it was the latest fetish, poodle bondage.

The ignition roared, but Henry didn't. Score one. Then throw in the towel. After a few blocks, he figured out how to peer under the mask at the traffic.

I found out a muzzle doesn't in the least interfere with barking.

Avery

Terri put her feet on the coffee table, balancing a plate on her lap while munching on a (not homemade) brownie. She wore her customary outfit, bib overalls and a light green sweatshirt that echoed the color of her eyes. The overalls made it impossible to see she had a great figure. When I asked her why she wore overalls, she said, "They make me look taller." Years before, she told me she had worn lifts in her riding boots for more than a year. "Didn't help raise my height nearly as much as the coveralls do."

"You need to take some responsibility for this disaster," I told her as Henry sat on the other side of the coffee table, waiting for crumbs to fall from the brownie. "It's at least partly your fault, you know."

She licked her lips and, without much interest, said, "How's that?"

"You gave me the number for Poodle Rescue when I was feeling reckless. As my best friend, you should've enforced a cooling-off period. You could tell I was in no shape to make a rational decision."

She laughed, wiping off her hands. "That bad, huh?"

I shook my head, looking down at my sweet terrible boy. "Ask me about progress with this brute."

"Any?"

"Zip."

Contrarily, she shot her warmest sympathy smile at Henry. After all, I was the wounded party. "Sorry, Henry," she told him, holding up the dish, "but chocolate's bad for dogs." To me, she said, "Have you ever thought about getting a trainer for him?"

"Nope. Our bank account's now officially listed under D for dumpster trash."

Terri drained her cup and set it back on the coffee table. By the gleam in her eyes, I knew she had an idea. Indeed. She reached into her purse and extracted her little black book.

"Her name's Avery, and she's fabulous. She trained Loki." Loki was Terri's long-departed German shepherd, and he'd been a very well-behaved personal protection dog. But that wasn't the sort of training I wanted for my deranged poodle. "At least talk with her, Candi. It couldn't hurt."

"Oh yes it could," I said, but I took Avery's number anyway.

On the phone, Avery gave me twenty minutes of free advice—focused primarily on my need to pay her or somebody else to fix my Henry. She did give me a tip or two, but I thought they were worth what I paid for them.

"Don't take him with you. Leave him in the yard."

"My fence has a lot of gaps. He gets out."

"I heard fences could be fixed."

"I also heard they could be fixed," I said, trying not to sound peeved. "And I heard fixing my fence would cost me money I don't have."

"Well, then you ain't got a choice. Crate him. That takes care of two problems, right-o? The barking and the pooping."

I explained I didn't want to turn his crate into a jail. She guffawed, but said only, "Suit yourself."

Decades before, a psychiatrist pointed out to me that some people—meaning me—hang onto neurosis, using it as a security blanket. The comfort of the familiar. Maybe I was holding onto Henry's disagreeable behaviors the same way. But what was my payoff? Please. Bring me my payoff!

"Crating him doesn't fix anything," I said, sounding as defensive as I felt.

"And neither do you."

True enough.

"You probably need at least eight privates," she said, changing the subject. The word "privates" obviously didn't mean to her what it signified to me. "Henry the punk," she began, sounding like someone mulling over a possible investment. I imagined her at the other end of the phone line—Sherlock Holmes for canine evildoers, one finger propping up her chin as she contemplated the clues. "Could be more. Sounds like he ain't gonna give up his cushy life easy. A dog too smart for his own good. That's a poodle for you."

She went on to describe the equipment I'd need, all of which, happily, I could purchase from her. On top of fifteen hundred for a month of board and train—her most emphatic recommendation. Whoopee. She gifted this tip to a woman who'd just said she couldn't afford to patch a fence.

"Would the eight private—uh—sessions—would those be included or extra?" If I have to ask, I told myself, I can't afford it. And I definitely cannot afford it. So why am I asking? Well, I can dream, can't I?

"The way it works is this. He's here for three weeks. You come in for privates at the end. You get five with B&T." I didn't have to annoy her by asking what on earth B&T might be, because, bright woman that I am, I figured it out. It stood for the help I could not have because it would cost me fifteen hundred dollars.

She paused, and I sensed Avery was a woman of few words, unhappy to be chatting. "How long you had this bad boy?"

"Five long months."

"Right-o. The crap your dog's pulling? Now you're part of it. I ain't saying it's all your fault. He had to be messed up long time before you ever laid eyes on him. But now you're stuck with the mess somebody else made. And all that stuff you been doing—trying to fix him? Made it worse. Every win he chalks up makes it harder to train him. See what I'm saying?"

"I *don't* see what you're saying, Avery. Because Henry doesn't know I'm alive when he's pulling his shenanigans. He's not chalking up wins against me. He's doing his thing."

"What this boy's doing ain't *shernanigans*, missy." I bristled, being, I figured, at least ten years her senior. But her foghorn voice rolled on. "Don't do anything about it, your boy ends up biting serious. He knows you're alive, all right. Henry's got your number."

Shaking off her nonsense, even so I toyed further with the fantasy of getting her help. "Would you hurt him?"

"It ain't about hurting a dog. It's about drawing a line. Setting him up to cross it. He crosses it, you figure out how to stop him. He makes a mistake, you correct him. Every time. Comprenday?"

What I *comprendayed* was that she wasn't a Spanish speaker. "Give me an example."

"Say you're teaching the dog to wait. Does Henry wait at doors?"

"Not if he can help it."

"Right-o. Here's how you do it. You set him up. Make him sit in front of the door. You open it a crack. He stands up. They all do. You shut the door. Make him sit. You open the door. You keep doing it until he gets the message. *I ain't getting out that door till she says I can.*"

"He'd just push past me."

Avery snorted, and I felt her contempt coming out of the telephone. "Think it over and get back to me. If you want to."

Henry and I staggered on. Well, I staggered. With Henry, it was more of a strut. He was the abusive husband, merrily quaffing beer with his buddies, while at home his wife cooked his dinner, desperate to find a way to change him.

One month after that phone call with Avery, Henry decided to be my dog. I'd passed my six months of probation. He finally started greeting me with more verve than he showed everyone else. I figured he'd worked out his angst over having been dumped. The people who owned him before me were fully formed in my imagination, as was the reason they abandoned Henry. I'm good at figuring these things out.

They must've been a young couple, indulgent with their smart poodle until, newly pregnant, they began to develop serious doubts about keeping him. After all, he'd nipped them both. They couldn't risk their baby getting bitten. What if the infant snatched something from him?

This story isn't my invention. When Mom was pregnant with my older brother, my parents had a mutt about as big as Henry. Mom called him Snuffy Smith and said he looked just like the Snuffy owned by the comic strip character Little Orphan Annie. Snuffy Smith had rough curly hair and a square face. He sounded as if he might've been about as bright as a puff of air, but sweet. Even so, with an infant about to join the family, she and Dad wanted to be sure he would stay sweet. They bought a stuffed toy and, lying on their bed, they each stroked it lovingly, cooing as they would to a baby. Snuffy watched.

Then they went out, leaving the stuffed toy.

Well, anyone who's owned a big dog for more than twenty-four hours could've predicted what happened next. Snuffy tore that toy to shreds.

Off to the pound went Snuffy.

In my version of his history, Henry, like Snuffy, was a blameless victim.

Then he bit Seth, my younger son. Having come up from Santa Cruz for a visit, my son sat down on the sofa where Henry held court. As casually as if he'd been offered a piece of Seth as an hors d'oeuvre, Henry leaned over and chomped. No stitches were required, but I lost my benign view of my poodle. Up to then, Henry hadn't bitten anyone but me. Now he'd branched out, and I had run out of excuses for him.

And it got worse.

On one occasion, Henry's bite exceeded the definition of a nip. We'd just gotten off the freeway after spending forty-five minutes in hell. Well, I spent the time in hell. Henry had a blast. Still rolling, so he was still caterwauling, I pulled over, reached in the back, and snapped the short leash I'd attached to his collar in anticipation of doing just that. His teeth clamped down. Hard. Blood spurted, but he didn't immediately release my hand. I stomped on the brakes, and we locked eyes. He let go. I turned and banged my head on the steering wheel. Blood rained over my clothes, the dashboard, the upholstery. Even the windshield sported pink freckles. CSI would've sworn no one could live after losing this much blood.

Nice joke, but I couldn't make myself laugh. I couldn't even tug my mouth into an imitation smile.

"I can't do this, Henry! I can't!"

It dawned on me that anyone observing me might easily conclude that the car's ranting driver—me—was a lunatic. I pulled a clean rag from the glove box and wrapped my bleeding hand. Then I took out a tissue and blew my nose. While I tidied myself up, Henry sat behind me in regal serenity. As the car was no longer moving, he had nothing more to contribute to our conversation.

More than the pain of my throbbing hand and the insult of having a dog I treasured treat me as a chew toy, Henry's obvious indifference to my weeping and his role in causing my misery struck me as outrageous. For one deranged moment, I grieved over the unfairness of his failure to understand English. I willed him to know what he'd done and what I thought of it. Then I did laugh. Well, I chuckled.

Could I endure more of his antics? I had to. It wasn't his fault I'd ignored the warning from Tan Shirt. If I'd listened, I wouldn't be sitting here wondering how to get blood stains out of upholstery.

My fight for Henry's soul was just beginning.

The next day I went to the library and checked out a stack of books on difficult dogs. Cross-legged on my bed, I skimmed through them for a description of any dog vaguely resembling my mammoth pain in the butt. As I feared, Henry seemed to be one of a kind. The authors discussed aggressive dogs. He wasn't aggressive. They wrote about fearful dogs, and that wasn't Henry either. They wrote about how to lure obstinate dogs into obedience with treats or games. No need to lure Henry. Except for biting me, pooping and peeing in the house, and fracturing my eardrums, he was perfect.

Nearly all the recommendations involved spending money. Unsurprisingly, trainers urged me to consult a trainer. Many confessed that (heh heh) trainers don't come cheap. My cut-rate poodle was laying asphalt on my road to bankruptcy.

Cheaper or even free alternatives were mentioned in passing. Classes at pet stores or the SPCA were great, but only for the average dog. Henry could not check any box labeled "average." Anyway, free classes taught commands he already knew. I needed to enroll him in classes taught in a moving car.

I did come across a few nuggets that Henry or circumstance made short work of. One author instructed me to restrain Henry in the car because darting from window to window increased his excitement. I had to buy a doggy seat belt. Okay. I bought a doggy seat belt. Before we left the carport, Henry had chewed through the passenger seat belt to which the doggy seat belt was attached. Ka-ching.

Back to the counsel of the experts. What would most certainly work, one sage asserted, was to put him in a crate inside the car. Nice idea and, yeah, crated he might not bark. Only one obstacle nixed this remedy. I couldn't jam a Henry-sized crate into my Acura's backseat.

Teach him down and stay, said another. Henry knew down and stay, and he performed them admirably. But only on terra firma.

More irrelevant advice: I needed to intervene *before* he got excited. I couldn't figure out how I could manage this one in the nonexistent interval between turning the key and his bursting into song. Echoing this advice, another book—one that should've been printed in ALL CAPS—read like shouting. "Stop him before he escalates!" Henry never escalated. He was like a sports car that goes from zero to eighty in an eyeblink.

One ditzy writer said I should give him treats to discourage every bit of doggy "mischief." (I thought of Avery's aversion to my calling Henry's misbehavior "shenanigans." What would she think of "mischief"?) Timing, this counselor said, was everything, but timing didn't seem relevant to my unhappy interactions with Henry. Should I ignore safety and whip around to stuff kibble in his mouth in whisker-thin moments between barks? Should I feed him goodies whenever he didn't bite me?

None of the experts seemed aware of a dilemma like mine. There wasn't anything I *could* do while driving and nothing I could accomplish when the car stopped. Henry's timing was impeccable. In one sense, Avery was right about Henry being a dangerous dog. I was finding it increasingly difficult to focus on traffic while ineffectually struggling to tune out the din he made right next to my ear. Distraction, reputedly, causes more accidents than alcohol.

I was at my wits' end, an expression that doesn't adequately express how awful my life had become. Unfortunately, none of the advice books cited *wits' end* as a tenable location from which to conduct successful dog training. All the experts stressed that I must practice calmness before I got in the car. I tried to practice calmness. I meditated until my body turned to jelly. But Henry wasn't absorbing my chi. The know-it-alls begged to differ: "The dog picks up on everything you feel." Nonsense. In full throttle, Henry couldn't have distinguished between me and the steering wheel. He might have my number, as Avery put it, but he wasn't dialing it in a moving car.

It seemed to me that Avery, obnoxious as I found her, constituted the only available lifeline to sanity. From her, I wanted the nonsexual version of a "quickie." *Just fix my dog.* If only she could do it in a single lesson. I'd pick out the most abhorrent Henry behavior, she'd give me the lowdown, and I'd live with the rest.

Maybe, I thought, just maybe, she could set me on a better road, and I could apply her technique going forward. If she saw Henry in the car, she might pick up on something I was missing. It was possible, wasn't it?

I put it to her in another phone call. "You could give me one lesson. One private. You know, just show me how you'd handle things if you had to drive Henry around. Would that be possible?"

"A waste of time."

"Why?"

"Because this ain't what anybody can change overnight. Not even me."

"I get that. But you might look at Henry and see what I'm missing. Then you could tell me how to work with him. I know you can't do magic tricks, but I need some sort of direction, something to go on."

A week later, I met Avery for the first time. She was nothing like I pictured her. Because she had a husky voice and an abrasive manner, I thought she'd look like a muscled farmhand, with boobs like a shelf and hands the size of pizzas. The attractive woman I saw was short and petite with curly blond hair and eyes the color of the sky after a windstorm blew it clean.

After warning me about the probable ineffectiveness of what she'd agreed to do, she got into my Acura and took the wheel. Henry and I climbed into the backseat. She had fitted him with a prong collar. I had paid her twenty-five for that and one hundred and twenty-five for the lesson. Ka-ching.

"When he barks," she said, "snap it. Not hard, do it clean."

After twelve yanks, with her having the prongs on upside down on her thigh, I got it right. "Just that much pressure," she said. "No more."

She started the car. Henry didn't make a sound. She rolled down my driveway. Henry seemed lost in thought.

She glanced at me in the rearview mirror. "He barks if the car moves?"

"He does, yes."

"But not now."

Looking over at my woolly dog, I echoed, "Not now." One hundred and fifty dollars. Bye bye. Thanks for the good time, Henry.

"Let's go to the beach," she said. "Maybe find some dogs. That'll wake him up."

On that windy, drippy day, the beach was unsurprisingly vacant of visible life forms, human or canine. Henry stared fixedly out the window as Avery piloted the Acura back and forth. I said, "I think we're boring him."

Avery

All the other dogs in Alameda were snoozing in front of warm fireplaces. We'd cruised the beach several times when Avery snapped, "Look at that!" She pointed at the rearview mirror. "The punk's watching me in the mirror. Cripes. He's one smart cookie."

At last, an elderly man exited his car, leashing up a small terrier. Avery drove slowly past him. Henry didn't twitch a muscle. She made a U-turn and passed the old guy again. And again. The man began watching for us. He looked frightened.

Finally, I said, "He's not going to bark with you in the car, Av. It's hopeless."

After the beach dud, Avery came up with a different idea. This time she called me.

"You mean a shock collar? I thought you said training wasn't about hurting a dog."

"Stim collar," she said, her tone suggesting she'd had to explain the difference to ignoramuses like me before. "It don't hurt unless you use it wrong."

"You know what? If you need a way to use anything wrong, I'm your woman. Look up *klutz*. You'll see a picture of me. I don't trust myself."

"Then you better find him another home. Because you know there ain't no way you're keeping this dog, not how it's been going."

"No way. I'd never sleep again. Even if somebody as dumb as me came along to take him, I figure, one car ride, one bite, one pile of doodoo, and Henry'd be out on his ass."

"Wrong," she snapped. "Anybody else is gonna listen to a trainer, that's what anybody else but you is gonna do."

I reached for a toy in Henry's mouth. I did it absent-mindedly, as if my poodle were any other dog. By that time, he'd somewhat softened his corrections of me so his bite wasn't super painful, but it sunk my already sunken spirits even lower. I wailed. And shouted. I screeched. I was out of control.

To shelter him from my tantrum, I ordered Henry into his kennel and locked it. As he peered up at me, his eyes begging my forgiveness, I picked up my tennis shoe and flung it hard against the crate. And I kept hurling it, over and over, until my rage had been exhausted. While I'd done all this, he pushed against the crate, his eyes begging me to let him out.

Spent, I sank to the floor and let him out. He crawled into my lap, all seventy odd pounds of him. I knew he was sorry and right there I should've begun to understand something about his biting. But I didn't.

Henry gave me yet another bite to think about on a visit to Point Isabel—a gorgeous twenty-three-acre, off-leash dog park in Richmond, abutting San Francisco Bay and offering an up-close view of the Golden Gate Bridge.

As Terri and I sat down on the lawn to chat, Henry trotted off in search of a love interest. Like a kid who's never around other kids, he was clueless about how to initiate play. Normally, he'd start humping the object of his desire. Some dogs took it badly, but many didn't care, and some would start playing with him. There were those owners who objected, usually men. I remember a pit bull Henry mounted. That dog just kept gnawing on his ball. His owner flew into a rage, screaming at me to get my dog off his. A poodle humping his pit bull and the pit submitted—how the hell was a man supposed to put up with that? Women in the park called out one or another version of "Grow up. It's a dog."

At Point Isabel on this day, however, the objector was female. Some distance away, I watched Henry mount her dog. The owner got up and strode toward the pair. I leapt over the grassy field, my speed worthy of an Olympic medal, I thought, getting there just in time to stick my hand under hers as she reached for Henry's collar.

He whipped around and sank his teeth into my fingers. The woman, apparently shocked, said, "Are you all right?"

I muttered something because she had exasperated me and because my dog had let me down. If I'd spoken to her, I would've asked if another dog humping hers was really so unbearable. Maybe it was. I wasn't in any position to criticize her. Henry was the culprit. Maybe I should've had his teeth pulled. That day I was tempted.

He followed me back to where Terri waited on the grass. I told him to lie down, which he promptly did. I dropped down, fully expecting to have to correct him for getting up as soon as he tired of being a model dog. That park was his Eden, and several dogs approached him where he lay. To my astonishment, he didn't move a muscle, didn't even look at potential play-mates. He looked steadily at me. I was certain he felt guilty.

Any dog owner can induce in their dog a posture resembling guilt, sim-ply by yelling about nothing. The cringing isn't guilt. It's appeasement. But someone once pointed out to me that much of what I want my dog to feel guilty about means little to him except a need to get me to stop being angry. If Henry ransacked the garbage, he knew I didn't like it, but my objection to his feasting on perfectly good food made no sense to him. Having bitten me, however, Henry tried to show me he now appreciated that he'd done something bad.

As we started for the park exit, my boy, unleashed and without being asked, fell into the most perfect heel he'd ever executed. He voluntarily glued himself to my hip for the ten minutes it took us to get out to the car.

Apology accepted.

I needed to make another phone call to Avery.

Avery wanted to house him for a month to teach him biting had conse-quences. That didn't strike me as a viable plan. He'd never bite her. He wouldn't even bark with her in the car. But possibly she'd work with the two of us. I went back and forth.

Henry's separation anxiety had finally eased. No longer did he treat my living room as a toilet. I feared banishing him for a month might reactivate his fear of abandonment along with his loose bowels. Shuffling bills like a card shark scamming a pigeon, I'd just hired a handyman to tear up the living room floor. I didn't want to fix that floor twice.

By this point, Bob and I had agreed to a trial separation, seeing each other only during weekly visits to a marriage counselor. Sitting across from him during those sessions almost broke me, but I kept hoping we could work out our troubles. We'd been happy together for many years, and I thought maybe we could be happy together again.

He paid me a monthly stipend, but keeping two residences going took a big chunk out of his salary. I had less money to work with than I'd had before, when it wasn't enough. And it sure wasn't enough to fund Henry's incarceration. The dogs Bob and I had owned together had been his responsibility as well as mine, but I couldn't persuade myself to see Henry in that light. He was my poodle, and my poodle alone. When I'd brought him home, Bob had barely looked at him. I'm not sure he even knew Henry's name.

Avery said, "You wanna keep getting bit? Go ahead. But this punk won't stop what he's doing cause it's working fine for him. If you come to your senses, let me know."

There it was. My life revolved around a husband who wanted to abandon me and a dog that bit me. It seemed deeply unfair. I'd rescued Henry. I'd spent a lot of money on him. Didn't he owe me something?

He's a dog, the more sensible me said to that nonsense. Henry didn't choose to be helplessly dependent on me for everything that kept him alive. I owed him. The notion that saving a life means committing to sustaining it makes sense to me. I'd saved Henry's life, and his life was mine to take care of. I had to stop whining about it. I'd made a decision; he hadn't enjoyed that luxury.

Which left me with the original question: What was I going to do? I thought about Avery insisting he didn't respect me and wanted to dominate me. I didn't buy it. He humped dogs all the time, supposedly a form of dominance, but he never cared when dogs humped him.

Did he respect me? Clearly, he didn't give me the respect he'd given Avery in the car that gloomy pointless day. But, when Henry wasn't frustrating or biting me, I thought of him as a "go along to get along" kind of guy.

Weary of getting nowhere, even in my head, I exited these worthless round-and-round thoughts and asked myself a hard question: Why did I keep repeating behaviors that triggered him? Wasn't repeating what didn't work in the hope that it would eventually work the definition of insanity? Because right then it did seem insane. Whatever Avery thought, I believed Henry would never stop biting if my goal was to dominate him.

There had to be a different way to live with this dog. If Henry rolled over easily—and he mostly did—maybe I should too.

In the living room, he sprawled near the door, catching a little cool air through my calcified weather stripping. He gnawed on a Kong. I called to him, and he lifted his head. "Come here," I said. He rose and trotted over to me, the Kong clamped between his teeth.

I said, "Henry, drop it."

He dropped it, and I picked it up. We went into the kitchen where I gave him a piece of cheese.

Could I bear to think about how long it had taken me to figure this out? I decided to focus on my brilliance in solving the problem without board and train.

I solved his biting of Seth by denying Henry access to the sofa he had taken possession of. He could no longer evict interlopers from it. I accomplished his withdrawal from that throne by buying a scat mat and placing a sheet over it on the couch. The unpleasant tingle wasn't painful—more like pins and needles of a limb that's gone to sleep. Nevertheless, Henry gave up his perch for good. Before the mat retired, however, it claimed another victim. My son Eric came in, burbling about a new girlfriend. I was focused on what he was saying, so I didn't think about where he was heading to sit. He leapt up, crying, "What the hell was that?" I tried not to laugh.

As for the dog park, I'd hone my sprinting skills and keep a close watch on Henry whenever we visited. His biting days were over.

Work remained, however, if I was ever to ride in my car without suffering through a series of transitory nervous breakdowns. If Avery would help me, I was ready to get the e-collar and pay for more training in how to use it.

The E-Collar

The e-collar came in at $500. Ka-ching. Terri loaned me the cash, and I began paying her back at $50 a week. It was tough, but not impossible. But Avery never sold an e-collar without having the buyer take lessons in how to use it. More ka-ching. After a bit of negotiation, she too worked out a payment plan. I'd be eating a lot of pasta and beans for a year, but I could swing this.

And if it failed, I figured Furever Friends could order me up some pricey, dog-proof earplugs. I'd put them on my credit card.

I sat in Avery's consulting room, the size of a doctor's examination cubicle and equally chilly. At least I didn't have to remove my clothes. In her gravelly voice, she instructed me at what seemed breakneck speed.

"Every day for ten days, you put it on, you take it off, you put it on again. You're just putting collars on and taking them off. That way he gets used to the feel of it. So he don't connect the collar to the stim."

"What if I accidentally push the button—whatever—the thing that makes the electricity?"

"You ain't nearly ready to turn it on."

I frowned. "What's the point if I never turn it on?"

Avery offered me a bleak smile.

I took the collar and Henry home. For ten days, I put the collar on and took it off. All good, I thought. He'll never know it's the collar.

Back to Avery for the second lesson.

"See the numbers? Start at one. Then turn it up one and another one—just until Henry turns his head and looks at you. Give him a treat when he does."

"In the car?"

She rolled her eyes. "You ain't ready for the car. Just listen. Nine, ten days go by, you're giving him a treat every second time he looks at you. Then every third time. Finally, just one in a bit. The idea is he will see the little buzz he gets as a good thing."

"A shock collar as a good thing."

"It's a shock collar if you use it wrong."

A horse of a different collar. I knew better than to say that out loud. "What then?"

"Henry knows the tingle in his neck means something good is about to happen."

"What? Like getting another chance to bark in the car?"

"Next you teach him to bark."

"He barks fine. No instruction required."

Skipping over my witticism, she continued the lesson. "You gotta agitate him to bark. Work him up. Rev his engines."

I didn't mention that this was a poor choice of words. "All I have to do is pop him in the car and start the engine. That'll rev him up."

"Forget the car. He's gotta bark when you tell him to. That's the goal."

The only positive I could see in all she was telling me was that I wouldn't be "shocking" Henry. At the same time, I heard a raft of negatives, more things that wouldn't work with my mulish poodle. "I don't want him to bark. I want him to stop barking."

Her patience, never in plentiful supply, seemed drained. She said sharply, "You teach him to bark, then you teach him to stop barking."

"Then what's the five-hundred-dollar e-collar for?" The question wasn't wholly facetious. She ignored it anyway.

"You can use 'speak' and 'hush.'"

"I don't know, Av. I don't see this working."

"Just do it and see, okay?"

"Look, why can't I just increase the stim so he gets a little jab? Wouldn't that make him stop?" Great. In fifteen minutes, I'd gone from humanitarian to Josef Mengele.

"Trouble with that is, you forget the collar, he's gonna bark."

"Wait. What about the ten-day thing? You said he wouldn't know it's the collar."

Avery shrugged that off. "I like to give it a shot, but the smart dogs always figure it out."

The funny thing about Henry was that, although he barked in the car and he barked whenever he spotted one of my neighbor's cats, he was a quiet guy. When someone rang the doorbell, he rushed to see who it was, but he gave no warning bark. He was a greeter. Walmart should've hired him.

Advice books suggested I try jumping around and clapping my hands. Henry curled up on his bed. I bounced a ball, but Henry had zilch in the way of interest in any kind of ball. I tied him to the fence and waggled his favorite toy at him, just out of reach. He yawned.

"Speak, damn you!"

He woofed.

I gaped at him. "Somebody taught you that?" Then it dawned on me. No wonder he'd learned every command in record time. He already knew them.

At last, I was ready to try the "stim" button. Avery had advised me to hide the controller from the dog. He mustn't associate the equipment with what was happening. Right. Like not connecting the collar with the sensation. Except smart dogs figure it out, and Henry was a smart dog.

Besides, hiding the controller wasn't easy. It was nearly the size of a Volkswagen Beetle. I tried holding it behind my back, but Henry gave me a look that said he knew.

With the level at one, I pressed the button, sitting on the sofa with the controller under a cushion. No reaction. I turned it up a notch. No reaction. I turned it up and up. No reaction. At notch 7, he turned toward me, and I gave him a piece of cheese and praised him as if he'd brokered peace in the Middle East and ended hunger in India. "Who's my good, good boy? Henry's a good boy!"

He wagged his tail, looking as pleased with himself as I was with him. He liked that good boy jazz. I'd ask him "Who's a good boy?" and he would plop down in front of me. Then I'd say "Show me!" At that, he'd arrange himself in a perfectly aligned sitting posture, poke out his chest, and smile up at me.

He was my miracle dog.

Throughout the afternoon, I periodically hit the button, Henry would look my way, and I'd stuff him with smaller and smaller bits of cheese. I didn't want to give him arteriosclerosis. Within two days, he looked for the treat whenever I pressed the stim button. Gradually, I phased out the treats.

And then we were ready for the final act in our melodrama. My heart was in my throat. Everything depended on what happened next. The pessimist in me didn't believe his behavior would change in the slightest. The optimist told the pessimist to shut up. Neutral me—well, who am I kidding? There was no room in me for neutrality. If our situation had been depicted in a cartoon, the toon me would've been hanging off the side of a cliff, knuckles white as I gripped a fraying rope. Henry would've been at the top, his bared teeth about to chomp into the rope.

I put him in the car. For good measure, before I turned the motor on, I gave him a piece of cheese and raved about what a good boy he was. He licked his chops, but I could see in his eyes, he was prepping for the chase. Indeed, when he heard the roar, he launched into raucous woofing. To which I said, "Speak!" without moving the car forward. Then, while poking the stim button, I said, "Hush!" and slowly rolled out of the carport.

HENRY STAYED QUIET!!

Henry and Doors

A friend invited me to join her for a small party at the house of people I'd never met.

"They own greyhounds," she said. "Henry will be welcome."

Because she didn't have a car, I drove. The trip took a couple of hours, and, for some reason, I forgot about giving Henry a potty break.

The hosts had been waiting for us. They stood in their doorway. One of their two greyhounds bounded down the stairs with a chew toy she promptly dropped at Henry's feet. An offering to the god he thought he was.

"She always does that."

"It's charming," I said.

Henry glanced at the object but had other fish to fry. He dashed into the living room, squatted, and pooped. If there had been a me-sized hole, I would've happily crawled into it. The hosts cracked up, which was more than gracious. I picked up the excrement and scrubbed at a nonexistent stain on their carpet, silently thanking Henry for producing solid turds. The remainder of our visit was uneventful, thank heavens.

Henry never saw a door he didn't want to go through. Alma, the gardening neighbor who lost her lunch to him, could testify to that. His penchant for assuming everyone wanted to have him as a house guest turned him into my accomplice in crime one frantic afternoon.

I was expecting friends for dinner, and I was way behind schedule, impatient to get home to vacuum, set the table, and decant a five-year-old cabernet

I hoped would live up to its price tag. Only then could I start on the meal. The lead-up to a social event at my house always puts me in a dither. When people arrive, I concentrate on being a good host. Before that, I'm unravelling like everything I've ever tried to knit.

Just up the hill from my house, I was tooling down a street that barely accommodated two cars passing one another when I found myself obstructed by a huge box truck. The driver had enough room to pull over into a wide driveway so that my little Acura could bump over the curb to squeeze past. Instead, he chose to stop in the middle of the road. Having a bad day, I guessed.

I watched him walk up to a house and press the doorbell. A woman came out, spoke to him, and peered out at me. I presumed she'd tell the driver he needed to move his truck. But no. She too must've been having a bad day. I sure was. The driver followed her inside. Who knew how much of a tête-à-tête they planned, after which he would presumably load or unload furniture. I had no time for their rudeness. I didn't think I could back up. I'm shaky driving in reverse, often veering toward parked cars. If I had backed up, I'd be backing into blind curves on a narrow road some drove as if they were in a Formula 1 race. As for a U-turn, which I didn't think I could manage, the route would've taken me more than a mile out of my way, and I didn't want to lose any more time. Why should I? Common courtesy would have me on my way in seconds.

I got out of my car and let Henry out. He trotted up the walkway to the open door and bounded inside. When I reached the door, I was treated to a sight that could've come out of a Buster Keaton movie. I stood at the head of a hall stretching from the porch to the back door. A second hall cut the house into squares. As I stood on the threshold, a cat hurtled down the bisecting hallway and disappeared. A second later, here came Henry, loping merrily after the cat. Behind Henry came the woman of the house, shouting "Stop!" Positive my dog couldn't catch the cat, I refrained from intervening. I did feel it was unfair that her cat had to pay for her lack of consideration, but I had no intention of losing time while she transacted whatever business she had with the driver of the box truck.

The cat came flying from the opposite direction, with Henry in pursuit, and the screeching homeowner behind him. This scenario repeated as the driver ordered me to take my dog out of the house. From his proprietary attitude toward the premises and adjacent street, I wondered if he might be moving in.

"When you get your truck out of my way, I'll get my dog."

He spoke like a spoiled four-year-old. "I'll get my truck when I'm good and ready."

I half-expected him to follow up with "Neeny nonny newny!"

"Okay," I said.

He turned into the house where the chase was going strong. The cat and Henry maintained the pace, but milady was getting winded.

To his back, I added, "I'll move it."

When I climbed into his cab, I saw he'd conveniently left keys in the ignition. The motor kicked in, I released the brake, and gaily plowed onto Cat Lady's lawn. Back in my Acura, I called for Henry, who bopped out looking exceptionally pleased with himself. The driver ran out, shouting "Don't you dare ever touch my truck again!"

I smiled, and off we went, my day having turned considerably more pleasant.

Lost

I set off with Henry one late-ish afternoon. Our normal route on the Sequoia Bayview Trail, his favorite, took us on a three-mile roundtrip. Around the mile and a half point, the path starts to lose definition, and we turn around. Cruising those same miles time after time never bored Henry, but, much as I loved that walk, I'd begun craving some adventure, in particular the distraction of the unfamiliar that might drive my iffy future out of the hamster wheel in my mind.

I thought, *Why not wander up into the woods?*

Here's why not: Years ago, driving alone between two unfamiliar towns in North Carolina, I stopped for gas. In that era, an attendant pumped the fuel. When he'd filled my tank and collected Standard Oil's profit, I exited the station, made a left turn and another left turn and then a third left. Back at the pump, I rolled down my window. The gas jockey quirked an eyebrow. "When I drove in here," I said, "did you happen to notice in what direction I was heading?"

Clearly, I should never go anywhere unfamiliar without a tracking dog. Which Henry most assuredly was not.

I've read you can determine your location in a forest by noting the side on which moss encrusts the trees. I've also read this isn't true. One way or the other, it doesn't matter. Where moss grows would give me no help at all. Even if it does signal true north, I wouldn't know what to do with the information. What are north and south? I'm familiar with up and down and left and right, although, admittedly, somewhat weak on the latter. For a clue to left, I relied on my wedding ring, at that moment occupying my jewelry box while I figured out whether to throw it away.

Tossing myself and my directional dyslexia into the winds of fate, I started to climb. I told myself to pay attention. The whorls on a stump hold a fascinating historical record, had I only known how to read them. In California, the rings on a fat sequoia stump in the national park of that name have been tagged with corresponding events going back to Alexander the Great. Peering at the stump before me while Henry baptized several trees, I tried to imagine what scenes those whorls had witnessed. On reflection, the answer was that they'd witnessed nothing. They'd been inside a living tree trunk, oblivious, while nearby Indians, not yet slaughtered by settlers, turned acorns into flour.

Under a blackberry bush, a clump of feathers told me a predator had lunched on a bird, a red one. Sad. Red's my favorite color. But since I know less about birds than I do about tree rings, the feather gave me no hints about the identity of the deceased. The berries were juicy and warm from the sun. I stained my hands, and no doubt my lips, purple, enjoying them. While I cautiously pawed the vines for the ripest ones, somewhere behind me a blue jay cackled. I looked around. No blue jay. Instead, half-shrouded by ferns, a squirrel cawed like a jay. Seeing I offered him nothing edible, he flipped his tail and hurried away.

I looked up to see tangerine scarves unfurling across patches of startling blue. In the soft air that precedes the coming blanket of late-afternoon fog, I began to feel stirrings of anxiety. The dimming light warned me not to lose any more time basking in a tranquility that was also starting to dim. I needed to get back to my car.

I hadn't seen another human being since we'd left the trail, roughly two hours before. No one to point me in the right direction. Even so, everything would be fine, I told myself. I could figure this out. Since I'd gone up to get where I was, I needed to go down to get back. That bit of Mensa-level thinking ran roughshod over the realities I faced. In short, I couldn't find a way down. In the scarce gaps in vegetation where I could spot a slope, downhill looked more like a cliff than the incline I'd ascended. Moreover, wherever I looked, there was no trail.

Darkness was about to descend, and my serenity was dribbling away.

Spread out like an oil slick on water, an expanse of granite heading downward raised my hopes. Beyond it, I thought I glimpsed a patch of dirt that could be the trail. Thorny bushes flanked the rock to either side, so going around it would've meant more exploring, and I couldn't spare any minutes for that.

The granite looked slippery, but I told myself I had no choice, and even less time. Jaw clenched, I stepped cautiously onto the stone.

Unfortunately, the soles of my shoes had witnessed almost more events than the rings on nearby trees. Lacking traction, one foot shot out, and my butt slammed rudely onto the unforgiving rock. My left ankle throbbed. Just wait, I told myself. It'll stop hurting in a minute or two. It always had. I'd never sprained any of my joints before, and therefore I couldn't have sprained one now. It wouldn't make sense because it was the worst of all possible moments for my formerly faithful ankle to do this to me.

I pressed my foot delicately against the stone. And yelped. Lifting the hem of my jeans, I warily rolled my sock down. The ankle was already swelling, the skin cherry-red. Getting up was not going to be possible any time soon.

The difference between me and those who successfully conclude their hikes and drive home was simple. They were competent. Their directions featured knowledgeable references to north and south. My tips on how to get anywhere normally depended on things like a tilting STOP sign or an abominable purple garage door. When I venture into the territories of left and right, I'm likely to mess up. I recall sending out meticulously edited party invitations, giving incorrect directions to my house.

I've read about intrepid explorers who dragged themselves out of danger on broken limbs. Victims of airplane crashes in the mountains, who crawled through dense brush back to civilization. I'm nothing like those people. I've never shrugged off pain. When I pack for a trip, I dedicate one carry-on to remedies for the slightest discomfort. I noted, however, that my current discomfort went well beyond slight, and all my putative remedies were miles away while I was sadly grounded.

If I hadn't needed to conserve my body's hydration (who knew when I'd have access to water again, if I ever did), I would have bawled.

Henry, who'd been sniffing around, took stock of my predicament and rushed over to rescue me. What a sweetie. I reached out for him, and he stepped on my foot. The injured one. I howled. Henry trotted off, offended.

I was going to freeze to death. I was already freezing to death. The good news, I'd read, was that freezing was far from the worst way to die. The bodies of people frozen to death were often found naked. In the end, the victims felt they were suffering in a heat wave. I almost couldn't wait.

Facing death—everybody at some point imagines how it'll be. It would've been comforting to relive the good times I'd had but, no, I focused on everything I hadn't accomplished and everything that had made me unhappy. I hadn't written a book I felt wholly proud of. Or even a perfect short story. Okay, there are no perfect short stories, but I'd hoped to pen one that was perfect-ish.

Trapped on that slab of granite, I knew I was wasting the precious time remaining to me in grieving over what could never be. I couldn't stop myself. The disappointments came flooding in, like mourning the demise of magazines and journals that long ago published even less than perfect-ish short stories from unknown writers. Not one left, except for the uber-picky *New Yorker*. And maybe *The Atlantic*. I wasn't sure. That was another regret. I never read *The Atlantic*.

Bigger regrets. The biggest, the one that made me think my life was over before this debacle—when my life really could be over—was the long-dragged-out end of my marriage. Once my best friend, now an indifferent acquaintance, Bob told me he no longer wanted to be married to me. He was in love with a younger woman and he'd been living with her the whole time we'd been in counseling. My only respite from misery—and it was minuscule—came from realizing his waste of the counselor's hefty fees justified all I'd spent on Henry.

At that point, I was a graduate student instructor. Cal was paying me slightly less than McDonald's would have. Without an adequate salary, and with practically nothing in the bank, I was drowning in visions of my future wandering the streets of Oakland with my starving dog.

Our divorce seemed on track to take only slightly less time than cleaning an oven with a toothpick. Which made no sense because we owned little beyond debt. His girlfriend proved less amenable than Bob to getting the terms settled. When I didn't cave on accepting a reduction in my share of his retirement so she could get some of it when he keeled over, she pushed him to hire what a lawyer friend of mine said was "a real shark." That week I'd received a letter from the shark that read like the words of a drill sergeant dressing down a hapless soldier. A lot of threats that I laughed off to stop feeling hurt that my husband would sic a person like that on someone he had once loved, someone, in fact, he claimed to still love, albeit in a meaningless sort of way.

I called him to say I'd hire my own shark and we could spend every cent we had plus all of those we might make in the future on lawyers. He asked me if I would read the letter out loud. Maybe his girlfriend had hidden his copy. When he heard the tone and the threats, he said he'd fire his lawyer (and he did). Then he told me the house was mine. He'd sign over his half. The house wasn't worth much anyway. Our hefty mortgage carried a second, and we'd refinanced so many times our equity had shrunk to the price of a week in Hawaii, not including airfare. But I said a sincere thank-you because, mortgaged to its roof or not, that house meant everything to me. I'd find a way to keep it.

As I saw it, I was fifty with no future in a youth-worshipping country. The therapist I started seeing, and then decided not to, had insisted that, if he were in my situation, he would tell himself that he (meaning me) was still young, attractive, and could build a new life. He *was* still young and attractive. I didn't feel either one.

By this time, it was nearly dark. I thought, *My end is in sight.* Why had I left the trail? If only I'd had a good sense of direction, or the good sense to behave as if I didn't. For heaven's sakes, I was three miles from my house! If I'd known which way to go, I could've crawled there.

In death, I was going to be a running joke, a comical tale to energize fatigued joggers.

"Are you hurt?"

I could barely make out the figure of a woman, but I saw her halo. I thought maybe the miracle of her appearance was God's stab at curing me of atheism.

She extended her hand. Wiping my eyes and nose with the back of my sleeve, I estimated the weight of my rescuer and concluded she was considerably lighter than I was. I suggested it might be better to call for the cavalry. But she pulled me to my feet, or rather to my foot, and insisted I lean on her. At first, I couldn't make myself do it. I was positive I'd topple her and we'd both wind up spending the night in the woods.

But this wasn't a woman who screamed "EEK!" at the sight of a mouse or the sight of a big woman incapable of walking.

She piloted me out to the road, put the two of us in her car, and drove down to where I'd parked. After blessing her, which seemed appropriate, I climbed into my manual shift car and whimpered as I made my way home.

Paradise Reframed

Gone was Henry's triple threat—biting, barking, and besmirching my living room. For the most part, I waxed euphoric over his numerous charms. But some obstacles to absolute bliss endured. His coat demanded lots of attention. It seemed to double in size every week. I wondered, if it were never cut, how big would it get?

A groomer was out of the question. Even had I been able to afford one, I couldn't overlook the fact that he'd sunk his choppers into the last person who'd wielded scissors in his vicinity.

His fur was unbelievably silky, something the American Kennel Club (AKC) calls a fault, but I call heavenly. I wondered if poodle wool could bring in enough to cover the cost of a groomer as well as the cost of a defense lawyer because surely—with my luck—a groomer would wind up suing me.

Groomer or no groomer, caring for his coat was a trial for us both. If I brushed him on Monday and again on Tuesday, it took me more than an hour each day. If I brushed him on Monday and then again on Wednesday, it took me about the same amount of time. So I cut back to brushing every other day to spare both of us some grief. Finally, neither of us could endure another combing session, given the extreme length of his fur. So I decided to clip him myself. After all, I had experience. When I was married, I cut my husband's hair. I cut my children's hair until they were old enough to say "We wanna go to Supercuts." Even so, they'd never looked too bad. How hard could it be to clip a dog?

Indeed.

My incomprehensible mistake was failing to confine Henry to one room. Something any eight-year-old would've thought of before picking up the scissors. Instead, I chose to trail my poodle, snipping what I could whenever I got close to him. An hour later I surveyed what resembled either the remains of a slaughtered animal or the aftermath of an interior blizzard. Every room reminded me of my folly.

As artists say about their work, I never finished the task; I simply abandoned it. More hacking was not going to repair the damage I'd done to his looks. His coat had been less butchered when I'd taken him from the shelter.

Occasionally, I took Henry to Lake Merritt. When I opened the car door, he would dig his bottom into the upholstery. No concrete strolls for my discriminating boy. He wanted the redwoods. Sometimes I wasn't sure he was a dog. For most dogs, the dump would've been a splendid destination. If Henry was picky about where I could take him and expect cooperation, he never failed to demonstrate gratitude when I took him where he wanted to go. On his beloved Sequoia Bayview Trail, he'd plunge ahead twenty feet, anoint his favorite tree, then dash back to show me a huge smile. He was saying thank you. Having given me my due, he'd trot away, head high, just like the dandy he was.

Not only did he show gratitude, but he was the only dog I've owned who had a sense of humor. Like a five-year-old child telling a joke fifty times because it got a laugh the first time, he would reenact his gag again and again. He'd be standing a short distance away from me when I'd call him. His rigid body, head averted, said he'd heard me plainly. I'd yell "Henry!" He wouldn't move. I'd shout once more, and still he wouldn't move or look in my direction. When we'd gone through this a few more times, he'd suddenly whip around and gallop straight at me. Had I not known how the joke ended, I would've been petrified. He always came unnervingly close to me before skidding to a stop. At that, he'd sit down and grin up at me as if he'd just done the funniest thing in the history of funny things. I always told him he had.

His reckless glee, however, gave me pause a time or two, as when we strolled around Lake Temescal in the Oakland hills, and he sprinted ahead of me. He shouldn't have. Temescal is not off-leash, although many of us treat it as a fine place for a dog to romp. Shame on us, I know, but, in our defense, there aren't enough off-leash, level hikes in the parks of Oakland. Hills abound. Steep hills. For some elderly or disabled people with pups, this poses a hardship. I concede, however, that at that time I did not qualify as elderly or disabled.

Henry and I were enjoying ourselves when a senior couple teetered toward us, leaning heavily on canes. When I spotted them, my boy was hurtling right at them. My breath hooked on my rib cage. On that narrow path, he could barely avoid them, assuming he'd try. In the seconds before he reached them, their lives flashed before my eyes. Broken hips. Hospitalization. Palliative care. Hospice. A lawsuit that took my house. And, finally, a funeral where loving children and grandchildren glared at me, out on bail.

But just as Henry came abreast of them, he put on the brakes, swerved, and gallantly skirted their frail bodies. Phew.

After my lecture and office hours on the Berkeley campus, I usually took Henry to Ohlone Dog Park, even though it disappointed us more often than it met our needs. Because he wouldn't fetch a ball or catch a Frisbee, Henry had to have compatriots to enjoy himself, as well as to get some exercise brisker than a walk. Sometimes there were only one or two dogs in the park, at others none. However many, the dogs present didn't necessarily appeal to him, or he to them. Nevertheless, it was what we had easy access to in the early-dark winter.

Late on a Thursday, Henry plopped down on the Ohlone grass, unimpressed with the dogs on offer. I figured we'd wait to see if any interesting ones showed up. Sometimes the park got busy toward dusk. Zipping my jacket to my chin, I sat down, took out a notebook, and began to organize my next lecture.

Opposite me, three dogs milled around the feet of two chatting women. Happily, they were far enough away that their conversation arrived at my table only as a murmur. To my left, about twenty feet down the length of the park, a short stocky woman with gray cropped hair perched atop a picnic table. At that distance, she resembled the Iron Lady, Margaret Thatcher.

Tall, pink, and softly fat, one of the two women opposite me, someone I thought of as a typical Berkeley matron, wore a tie-dyed blouse and billowing pantaloons, but no coat. She looked to be a refugee from the '60s, as did her similarly attired (except for the tie-dyeing), much slighter friend. That woman wore straw huaraches without socks, yet I'm positive there wasn't a single goosebump on her exposed flesh. Meanwhile, I shivered in my warm jacket.

Although the two women looked as if serenity would never desert them, there did seem to be a problem. With tender ineffectual whispers of "Shoo," the tie-dyed matron kept placing her hand between a Jack Russell and a small fox terrier, presumably her dog. *Shoo*, however, wasn't working. The Jack Russell relentlessly skirted her hand in pursuit of the panicked terrier.

Finally, the woman took her resistance up a notch, saying a bit more firmly, "Go away." Her voice, tinny as Julia Child's, held no menace. She seemed incapable of anger, or even of mild annoyance. But telling her dog to go away was way too much for Iron Lady. She shot off the picnic table, bellowing, "You can't talk to my dog like that, you bitch!"

The fox terrier's protector blinked, no doubt flustered by the violence of the outburst. Despite her diminutive stature, Iron Lady—like a colossus—came striding toward the large, discombobulated pacifist. Berkeley Matron, her smile faltering slightly, although she clung to it, stood up, and took a hopeful step forward. I suspected what she was thinking. Meeting savagery with goodwill would successfully de-escalate conflict. She wished global heads of state would adopt that principle and make world peace a reality.

Rapidly closing the distance between them, Iron Lady drew back her arm and slapped the other woman across the face. I don't know who among us felt the greatest shock. I'd anticipated a clash, but I hadn't expected it to be physical. The assailant seemed to be acting out the old joke about dog parks: Snarling often turns into nasty brawls, and sometimes even the dogs get into it.

After the slap, the two women launched into a comic ballet, Iron Lady very much on the offense while the other tried to fend her off, remaining admirably passive. Her friend and I stared, at a loss for what to do. As an adult, I'd never been in a fight. Undoubtedly, the two pacifists had never engaged in one either. The poor woman with the fox terrier kept up a hopeful monologue, looking for words that might lure her infuriated opponent into reason. "It's on account of he's a Jack Russell. One of them attacked my baby, and now he runs away whenever he sees a Jack Russell. I was only trying to keep—I like your dog. He's a sweet doggy."

Iron Lady, oblivious to all but her own rage, ended the dance by seizing Berkeley Matron's hand and chomping down, drawing blood. At that, the stunned woman gave up on employing strategies for peace. She snatched Iron Lady's glasses from the woman's face, and twisted them, flinging them down into the grass with a look of triumph. The Jack Russell owner dropped to her knees and began blindly pawing through the grass, growling, "You broke my glasses!"

Holding up her bleeding hand, Berkeley Matron said, "But you bit my hand!"

"Your hand will heal," Iron Lady snapped. "My glasses won't!" At that, she at last closed on her mangled specs, leashed up her dog, and marched out of the park. Her exit left in its wake stunned silence.

After a moment, the disheveled victim crossed the grass to me. "Did you see that?" she asked in her threadbare voice.

Only fleetingly was I tempted to say "See what?" It would've been cruel, not funny, given what she'd gone through. Even so, I had difficulty keeping a straight face when she added, "Can you believe it? And she's in the helping professions!"

A Bullet Dodged

When I returned to the trail after a long hiatus spent healing my sprained ankle, I learned a woman jogger had been raped. I found out when I took Henry to his favorite trail after a long hiatus spent healing my sprained ankle. An Oakland cop stood in front of CRIME SCENE KEEP OUT tape.

"When did it happen?"

"Close to three this afternoon."

Precisely when I'd originally intended to be there. Hearing that I might've been there and the rapist might've picked me to attack, I began shaking. Trying to still the tremors, I wrapped my arms around myself.

"We'll get him," the cop assured me with a compassionate smile. "Don't worry."

The following day I made myself go back. It was hard, but I wasn't about to give up my fragrant redwood cathedral or deprive Henry of his delightfully pungent walk. When we got there, the trailhead was crowded.

On the bulletin board, tacked over yellowing found dog and lost fanny pack notices, a new flyer cautioned women to walk or jog only in groups. Below it, the Oakland Police Department had thumbtacked a sign-up sheet so we could connect with each other.

Judging by the number of signatures on the sign-up sheets, nearly all the women present had already added their names and available times. I didn't want to. I liked my solo walks with Henry. Besides, almost every name on that sheet came with a note saying she wanted to go with a fellow jogger.

I wasn't a jogger.

In fact, I jog more slowly than I walk, slower actually than anybody walks, with the possible exception of a ninety-year-old arthritic elder statesman recently out of hip replacement surgery. I'll never forgive my daughter for the time I gasped my way around a track as she ostentatiously moseyed past me, smirking. I went home and tossed my sneakers.

Most of the joggers there looked capable of taking out an attacker, while I probably couldn't defend myself against anything heftier than a Chihuahua. Arming myself was out of the question. While I'm not a pacifist, I can't imagine stabbing or shooting anyone. For one thing, my upper body strength would be calibrated in negative numbers. Furthermore, a chronic tremor that renders my signature illegible would make my aim precarious. I'd probably wind up shooting my dog. Even were I to carry a gun or a knife, where, but in my handbag, could I put it? Fishing anything out of my purse takes up the better part of my day. Not to mention I hate lugging anything heavier than Kleenex when I walk.

Pepper spray might work, and I had some. The container comes with a nifty little wristband. Years before, I'd purchased some after sitting through a two-hour course in how to press the button to release the spray. That cannister spent its youth in my nightstand drawer. In pepper spray years, it was probably eligible for Social Security.

Giving up on the knives and guns, I identified the only remaining, albeit questionable, option. The sight of Henry ought to prove sufficiently intimidating. On the credit side, unlike a gun or a knife, he could never be used against me. At seventy pounds, he looked formidable, even if he was a poodle. With enough fur on him to keep a battalion in knitted socks, he did a convincing impersonation of a force to be reckoned with.

While Henry might not have had the moxie to follow through, I had evidence already that his size made an impact. On the freeway, when I stuffed my Acura into an opening the size of a small envelope so I wouldn't wind up heading into San Francisco, a fellow driving a heavy-duty pickup took offense. He sped up and hit me, not hard, just enough to claim my maneuver had caused the collision. I didn't stop. The pickup pursued me for miles, finally trying to nudge me into the breakdown lane. His buddy, riding shotgun, rolled down his window to let me know that I had to stop.

And then the pickup roared off.

Merry Christmas, I thought to myself, because it was Christmastime and that meant presents filled up the backseat, and that meant Henry wasn't in his customary position back there. Instead, he was riding up front with me. Big as life.

But Henry wasn't a pugilist. Had he been human, he would've spent his life on a bar stool, regaling other drinkers with stories from faraway places he'd never visited. I had serious doubts about him ever morphing from raconteur into Cujo.

After the rape, our walks got harder and harder for me. Women jogged or strolled by me, but their presence didn't make me feel safe.

Nothing, I told myself, would ever make me feel safe again.

Kidnapped

At the age of twelve, I was kidnapped while walking downhill from our apartment on San Francisco's Potrero Hill. I was headed to Sears, Roebuck to buy material for a sewing class project when a paunchy man of about forty stopped me. He asked me to get in his car to pull on a rope he needed while he tried to work it loose from his trunk. Like a good girl, I did what I was told. He slammed the door on me, jumped in the car, and drove. My pulse flailed around like poor Scrappy trying to escape the bathroom. Sweat dripped down my neck, and I was panting as if I'd been running. I couldn't stop thinking about two kids from the newspaper, two kids close to my age who hadn't survived their kidnapping.

In July of that year Stephanie Bryan, who was fourteen, had been taken by a Berkeley graduate student who raped, murdered, and buried her in Hayfork, California. In the Bay Area, what happened to her was big news, and I was an avid reader of the newspaper.

In August, Emmett Till, also fourteen, was kidnapped by Klansmen in Mississippi, tortured for hours, and then shot dead. That too filled pages in the paper, especially after the all-white, all-male jury joked as they voted to acquit his killers: "Would'a been quicker but we was thirsty and had to go out for a pop." After being absolved, the two defendants gave an interview to a writer from *Look* magazine, bragging about everything they'd done to Emmett.

The verdict on Emmett's killers came in ten days before I was taken. I'd read it in horror. Now, trembling in a strange car, I thought about how there were grown-ups in the world who could kill a child and who would kill a child. In fact, there were adults who believed that murdering a child was a fine thing to do.

What had happened to Stephanie and to Emmett, I felt sure, was going to happen to me. To the man in the driver's seat, I meant nothing.

I wondered how this man would kill me. Getting strangled would hurt a lot, I supposed. The rope I was to help him free up lay at my feet, not stuck at all. He'd use that rope to strangle me, or maybe to tie me up. With my toe, I nudged it under the front seat.

"That's the My-T-Fine bakery, over there," I said as we shot up Mission Street. "Daddy used to get snails from them on Sunday. That was when we lived in Daly City. Do you know Daly City?" He said nothing. "Daddy and Momma liked bear claws. I can't remember what my brother liked. I only liked custard snails. Momma would heat them up in the oven, and they were so good. I loved Sunday mornings. But I didn't like Sunday afternoon a lot of the time because of football. We wouldn't go anywhere or do anything when the 49ers played a game. That made me sad."

Still, the man in front of me didn't speak.

Years later I would read about the four reactions to fear: fight, flight, freeze, or fawn. The first two weren't possible, so for me the choice was between freeze and fawn. I chose to fawn without having the least idea that I was desperately trying to ingratiate myself with my murderer, as I thought of him. I wanted him to like me. Maybe if he did, he wouldn't kill me.

"I just started seventh grade. It's a rough school, you know. Even though they don't have a white-shoe gang like at Horace Mann. That's the worst. But there are gangs, and sometimes people throw rocks after school. One girl had to go to the hospital and get stitches."

Still, he said nothing. I looked out the window, numb. I was asthmatic, and it was getting harder for me to breathe.

Was this the last hour of my life? I'd read about a girl who was kept in a man's basement for weeks. That would be worse.

After about twenty minutes, the car came to a stop. I looked out at the San Francisco dump. The man climbed into the backseat next to me. His breath was stinky. Big craters scarred his face. I turned away and shut my eyes. I didn't want to see him, and I didn't want to see what he was going to do to me.

He lifted my dress and tore my panties, sticking his finger inside me. His fingernail scraped. I tried to think about something nice. Like one of my family's trips to Yosemite. Every summer we spent two weeks at a riverfront campsite. Daddy carried my brother and me from our beds in the middle of the night. He'd cover us up in the backseat of the already packed car. When we woke, it was light, and we were entering the park.

We'd set up our camp and put a watermelon in the icy river. I don't think I did much of anything on those vacations except find a tree to sit under while I read a book. My brother and Daddy would go off to catch fish for breakfast. Mom and Grandma would begin setting out the food and the bedding. We slept in an enormous tent on cots. Daddy called it an army tent. Every morning Grandma would sweep it out, and Mom would fry the trout that had just been pulled out of the river. Even though I hated most fish when I was a kid, that trout tasted wonderful.

The man took his finger out of me, smoothed my dress, and went back to the driver's seat. I wondered if now he'd take me somewhere to bury me.

"Are you married?" I asked.

"I am."

"Do you have kids?"

He sighed. "I do."

"That's nice. Does your wife know about—this?"

"No."

"Maybe you should tell her. Maybe she could help you."

He said, "Nothing can help me."

"I bet she would try to help you get better."

He snorted. "She'd leave me."

"How come you think that?"

"I don't think it. I know it."

After that, he was quiet. I wanted to talk. When I didn't talk and he didn't talk, my thoughts were terrible.

"I bet you're wrong about your wife."

He didn't bother to say I didn't know anything about his wife. I knew what I said about her was a lie because I was pretty sure she wouldn't stay with him if she found out about what he'd done to me. When I was little, Mom said I was a liar, that I lied all the time. My Aunt Marie said it too.

Nana, who was married to Mom's father, said I was sneaky, and to me that sounded like another way I lied. With my family, I sometimes felt like someone who smelled bad, a kid who should be given away.

Now I felt guilty for lying to my killer.

Getting in that car was stupid. He said I could pull on the rope and he'd try to free it from the trunk. Now I saw how dumb that was. But he was a grown-up. If I'd used his first name, I would've had to call him "Uncle." Otherwise, I'd have to say "Mister." I got in big trouble for being rude to my elders. Sometimes Mom slapped me; sometimes she just yelled.

The only time I didn't get in trouble for saying something that wasn't nice, I got away with it because I was asleep.

Sometime after Mom gave Scrappy away, Harry moved in with us. He was going to be my stepfather in a few months. He and my mother slept on a hide-a-bed in the living room of our storefront apartment. One night around two or three, I stood at the foot of their bed and asked him, "When are you leaving?"

As I remember it, he was fascinated, eager to hear what I might say when I was semiconscious.

Mom said, "Go to bed, Candi." To Harry, she said curtly, "She's asleep. She does this."

"You know why I picked you?" my kidnapper asked. "You looked like the sort of girl that wears silky panties."

My panties were rayon. Mom bought them. I wondered if it would make any difference to him if I told him I didn't really like rayon panties. One pair melted when I left them on the heater too long. Mom said I was harder on stuff than Scrappy.

He stopped the car. I saw we were at the corner where he caught me.

"I've been following you for months." He didn't turn around. That felt weird, like his voice didn't have a person attached to it. "I know where you live. So you better not tell anyone about this, or I'll kill your whole family. Now go on. Get out."

As he drove away, I remembered thinking that if I got out of that car alive, I'd be happier than I'd ever been in my life. But I wasn't happy. I wasn't anything.

I headed back down toward Sears. In those days, in junior high, girls had to take sewing and cooking classes. Boys made things in shop that they could give as Christmas presents, stuff like napkin holders and ashtrays. Cooking class was a joke. We made something called Welsh rarebit. I doubt even one of us ever made it again.

When I got to Sears, I went to the fabric department and opened a Butterick pattern book, like someone who knew exactly what she wanted. I kept squeezing my eyes, but the pictures stayed watery. My body felt like cement. I didn't want to make the rotten dress. I wanted to go home.

I gave a pattern number to the lady who located the pattern for me. The fabric I chose felt sticky, and it was ugly. I asked the sales lady if she could please cut four yards for me. After that, I read the back of the pattern and looked for the thread and zipper it said I needed.

The climb from what was then Army Street to the top of Old Russian Hill is steep and many blocks long. My feet did what they had to do. I followed them home.

Mom was sitting on the sofa, knitting. As I came in, she looked up and said sharply, "What happened to you?"

A scream pushed its way out of my mouth. I listened to it from far away.

Mom decided against going to the police. Even if the man were caught, which wasn't likely, she thought a police interrogation and a trial would be as traumatic for me as the kidnapping was. She said that lawyers always took apart the woman or the girl for their client. Mom said they made the victim feel she must be telling a lie or misremembering, or even that she deserved what she got. Sometimes the jury agreed.

I've always felt grateful for her wisdom at that very bad time.

For months, every man I saw terrified me. They were all that same balding man, and they were all plotting to get me. Bus rides to school were a nightmare. Even as my brain argued that the man sitting across from me wasn't the same man who took me, and even as I told myself he hadn't glanced at me, my body shook so violently I thought everyone on the bus could see how scared I was.

One evening, while we were doing the dinner dishes, Mom told me a story about a woman she worked with.

"A man was walking behind her. She felt sure he was following her. She sped up and he sped up. She took off running, and he started running. In a panic, she turned around and threw her purse at him. He picked up the purse and handed it to her. Then he ran and got on a bus that was about to pull away."

I burst into tears. "That's me, Mom. That's how I feel. All the time."

She hugged me, the wetness of her hands seeping into my blouse. "Give it a while," she said. "You'll get over it in time."

Which I did. Mostly. But I never wore that dress. It went from the classroom to the garbage can.

Jessie

Roller coasters don't exhilarate me. If I dared climb aboard one, those safety-tested polyurethane wheels gripping the rail would crack apart, spilling my car—and me—over the side, until the concrete earth cracked me open. Such is the way my mind works. If someone I love is delayed, they've been in a fatal accident or abandoned me forever. Pick one.

My ex-husband Bob was physically fearless but shrank back in terror from any emotional confrontation. He was a bear-like man, nearly six and a half feet tall. When he embraced me, I felt cocooned. I knew he would place himself between me and any danger. But when his adoring father raked me over the coals—as he now and then did for reasons that still escape me—Bob's mind drifted.

He gave me half of what I wanted, what I thought I needed, and for two decades, I was reasonably content. But when the grief over losing him finally eased, I began to accept that he'd set free, not just himself, but me as well.

I've always been a nervous passenger, but—after the divorce and before the rape on the Sequoia Bayview Trail—I had the wheel to myself. With Henry my newly adorable traveling companion, we were cruising together through a pleasant, if unexciting, life. At last, I told myself, I had become a fully qualified grown-up. Independent of any man. These bouts of self-congratulation continued for about two years.

And then came the rape on the trail. I couldn't get past it. The walk had been destroyed. For a while, I made myself go back. Swarms of women blithely jogged or walked by me. I watched their faces the way I watch the flight attendant's face when the plane starts rocking. They weren't afraid. But it made no difference because I was terrified.

Whenever I heard pounding feet, my pulse boomed. My skin prickled at every rustle of a bush. Day by day, my walk with Henry shrank, sending me back to my car on legs that threatened to liquify.

Henry and I went to other trails. Skyline Gate. Temescal. The railroad path above Montclair. Both of us longed for the sweetness of Sequoia Bayview. In the house at night, I felt vulnerable. Periodically, I fell into paralysis. I watched a lot of television: *Perry Mason* and *Murder, She Wrote*. Their predictability and the way good reliably triumphed over evil comforted me. At three one morning, I watched *Lady in a Cage*, a ghastly film about psychopaths trapping an elderly woman in her home. Soporific it wasn't.

Television wasn't doing great things for my mental health. Even I knew the tube was a bad idea. Having it in the bedroom made it harder to get to sleep. If I fell asleep without turning it off, the flicker woke me after an hour or two. If it was off and I woke up anyway, I turned it on for insomnia-provoking company.

Drowsiness made me inefficient at the job I'd recently taken with a Silicon Valley marketing company. Even having financial stability in sight didn't ease my forebodings. My sleeplessness alternated with sleepiness. Twice, the boss had caught me dozing in my office. If I didn't pull myself together, I'd be out of work.

Banging on my door startled me awake.

Terri, looking annoyed, demanded, "Why aren't you answering your phone?"

"Is it morning?"

"No, babe. Sunday evening. Didn't you hear the phone?"

We looked at the empty table where my telephone normally resided. I tried to remember where I'd stashed it. "It's in the basement," I said. "The buzzing drove me nuts."

Terri shook her head. "You've got to snap out of this, Candi. Has that dog been out today?"

Henry looked up, intuiting he was under discussion and possibly about to receive some sorely needed attention. I opened the back door for him. His water bowl was empty. With a sheepish glance at Terri, I refilled it. Someone banged on the door again.

"I found a parking spot." Russ, Terri's new boyfriend, gave me a once-over. I gathered from his expression that I wasn't much to behold.

"You have to stop thinking of yourself as helpless," Terri lectured me. This from someone who, in junior high, had come to my rescue when I was being soundly beaten up by a girl half my size. Hell, Terri was half my size.

Russ decided to chime in. A know-it-all makes a good impression when first meeting his girlfriend's girlfriend, or so he seemed to think. "It's all in the attitude," he assured me. "Just tell yourself you can handle the bastard."

His blasé, mind-over-matter advice didn't irk me, by which I gathered I was in truly bad shape. "He came up behind her," I whined. "How's he going to see my confidence from there?"

"I can show you how to break his hold. It's simple if you know what you're doing." He yanked my body roughly into his, gripping me so tightly I could barely breathe. For one paranoid second, I thought he might be about to attack me for real. No way could I free myself.

"Use your—whoa!" Russ stepped back, dropping his arms. "I'm not gonna hurt her. Take it easy."

Henry stood in front of me, his gaze fixed on my face.

Russ said, "Look, all it is, is you jam your foot into the guy's instep. But you gotta go for it, no holding back. If you don't come down real hard, it's no good."

Terri kissed my cheek. "You need to get out of this house." She sniffed. "But take a shower first."

I stared at Henry, who, as the door closed, resumed taking life easy on his pallet. "Would you protect me, Henry?"

He lowered his chin to the mat and closed his eyes.

If only, I thought.

But maybe Henry *could* be trained to take out a bad guy if one ever showed up. A couple of times, I'd hung around after Avery's obedience class to watch her assistant, Frank, pretend to taunt a dog owner as some dog whirled at the end of a leash, eager to bite Frank's thickly padded sleeve.

He had told me he fantasized about tying pink ribbons on a poodle decked out with a continental haircut. He would take the dog out in public and shout "Attack, Fifi! Attack!"

"People'd either die laughing or run for the hills."

"We don't train 'attack dogs,'" Avery told me. "Personal protection's a whole different kettle of fish. Cops, they got attack dogs. Those dogs go after the bad guys. These dogs, protection's their job. For them, it's a game of keep-away."

Henry could do that, couldn't he?

Avery wouldn't hear of it. "You don't train a biter to bite."

"C'mon. It's not fair to call Henry 'a biter.' He doesn't bite anyone but me."

"Now your son's nobody?"

"Okay. He bit Seth. But that was a while ago."

"How 'bout those people before you got him? You don't know his history. He could'a bit dozens of people."

"If he had—"

"And how about that woman who went to pull him off her dog? Is she nobody?"

"I still say he's not a biter *per se*." *Per se?* That was a good one. I wasn't even sure what it meant, but I was sure Avery didn't know either. Anyway, I was wasting my breath. Neither one of us knew what I was talking about. The difference was Avery didn't care.

"Henry's what—seven, eight? Get him trained, he'd be too old to do you any good anyway."

Two or three months before all this, Henry had gotten sick. The veterinarian diagnosed him with hepatitis and sold me expensive pills. But he expressed less interest in Henry's liver than in his spine. "Take a look at his X-ray," he said, pointing to a white space visible along a portion of Henry's back. He told me there was no treatment for the condition, whatever it was. If he named it, I didn't catch what he said, and I didn't ask anything else. Ignorance is the only path to equanimity at times like that.

Still, in those middle of the night hours when sleep refused to descend, I dwelled on that white spot, hoping, despite knowing better, that it didn't mean Henry's mobility had an impending expiration date. Recalling dogs in protection training leaping in the air, I realized I couldn't do that to him. I imagined my boy with a cane, hobbling toward some evildoer, teeth bared.

Avery said, "I've got a four-month-old puppy. German shepherd. The last of the litter. Wouldn't let nobody else take her."

"Did anybody want to?"

"Oh yeah. One backed out. She was the only one I would'a sold Jessie to. Don't know why she got cold feet. Thing is, Jessie's alpha."

"I read there's no such thing as alpha dogs."

I heard her take a long drink. "Wish I had a damned dollar for every idiot come in here telling me his nasty fear biter's an alpha. Jessie's the real deal. Solid as a rock. I'm betting you can handle her."

I could handle her? Where did that come from? "What makes you say that?" The words sounded more confrontational than I liked, but so what. If I thought anything about this woman, I thought she was honest. Now I wasn't so sure.

"I know. I ain't especially impressed with how you go about working your Henry. But what I like is you don't give up till you get what you want. That, I respect. And I don't see you putting up with macaroni from my Jessie neither. You're too hardheaded for that."

"I don't know, Av. She sounds like she might be more than I can handle."

"Come see her if you want. Up to you."

I thought about it. For an hour.

Well, what would anyone who knew me expect?

Like a rubber beach ball on a pogo stick, Jessie bopped down the steps from Avery's apartment. She was not the noble German shepherd I'd fantasized. Okay, I knew she was a puppy, but reality exerts scant influence over my expectations. I had come to meet Rin Tin Tin. How was this clown—delightful though she was—going to protect me from anything? Maybe I could use her help against a predatory Shih Tzu.

"Take her to Alameda Beach. Throw a stick for her."

"What if she runs off?"

"She won't."

Alameda's summer weather closely resembles San Francisco's. As usual that day—like the one when Avery and I tried to excite Henry—was windy, the sky a steel gray blotting out the horizon. I took a sweatshirt from the back and pulled its hood tight around my face. The beach, not surprisingly, was again deserted. Jessie quickly found a stick and dropped it at my feet. I hoped it wouldn't be blown up into the road.

After we'd been playing for about ten minutes, she dropped the stick and ran back to me. In the distance, I could just make out the figure of a man coming toward us. As he came close, Jessie sat quietly by me, watching him. He and I exchanged comments about the crappy weather. He said, "Looks like a fine dog you've got there."

Staying where she was, she watched him move away. When he had gone far enough, she raced forward to reclaim the stick. When she came back, I knelt on the sand and wrapped my arms around her impatiently wiggling body. I needed a moment.

I bent to kiss the top of her head and whispered in one of her splendid ears, "You're my dog now, Jessie."

Years after I made Jessie my own, after YouTube became the go-to source for "how-to," I watched a video that must've been filmed on the grounds of a doggy day care facility, possibly somewhere in Latin America. Two dark-skinned, dark-haired men stand watching the dogs, who, except for one hyperactive husky, are all playing nicely. The husky, however, can't focus or get control of himself. The men watch without intervening as the husky wanders, bumping into dogs, mounting, or otherwise challenging them. The well-socialized dogs he tries to engage ignore him and move away. Finally, the husky zeroes in on a long-haired German shepherd female who seems cowed by him. As soon as he starts to mount her, a huge male German shepherd lopes over, knocks him to the ground, and straddles him. The shepherd stands over the husky for a while, not looking at him, not showing any aggression. In fact, he looks around as if he's captivated by the surrounding scenery. After a few minutes, when the husky has settled, the big shepherd ambles off.

I watched through tears. The beauty of the shepherd's unflappable discipline of the husky thrilled me. He didn't attack. He calmly made that dog understand he could not continue being disruptive.

To me, that shepherd was an alpha.

Some dogs are born submissive, and no amount of training will turn them into leaders. Most dogs are happy to be in the middle, neither a leader nor a follower. But leaders exist in the dog world just as they do in the human sphere. Sadly, most of us never encounter an alpha, human or canine. Firm and compassionate leadership is in short supply in the world, even among dogs.

Jessie plus protection and obedience training came in at $5,000. I didn't blink. What would've been the point? Nothing on earth was going to stop me from buying this amazing puppy.

While Avery and I were discussing the details of the purchase contract, Jessie kept hurling herself at her older brother, Rolph, who must've weighed well over a hundred pounds. He had the typical shepherd coat, dense and impenetrable, especially around the ruff. As Jessie mauled his throat, he lay on his back, whimpering convincingly. She got off him and strutted around like a prize fighter who just won a Golden Glove.

"He's building her confidence, right?"

Avery glanced over. "As if it needs building. But yeah."

When I got her home, Jessie raced up the stairs and barreled over to Henry on his pad. She saw another Rolph. Henry saw a nightmare. He showed his teeth and let out a low growl. She laughed that off. From that moment, he was her poodle. If another dog tried to play with Henry, Jessie planted herself in front of him, her body language shouting "Back off. This boy belongs to me."

I anticipated her whimpering through the first night. This wasn't the home she was accustomed to. Even so, she merely settled herself on the floor next to me on the bed and went to sleep. When I woke, she lay quietly, watching me.

That morning, I drove to the trail for the first time in two months. Inexplicable though it was, as we passed the trailhead, I felt safe. Why would I? What had changed? My puppy might be descended from champion defenders, but a determined boot could make short work of her.

I chewed over the notion of security. Was it a fact or an idea? No matter what, shit happens. Illness, floods, fire. An earthquake could take my house down. Why did I imagine I could be shielded from harm by avoiding this trail? I needed to stop quaking over every boogeyman in my head. Hadn't I learned that much from the aftermath of being kidnapped? I hadn't, but I promised myself I'd work on it. But first I'd enjoy my walk.

Henry appreciated the woods through his nose. He wasn't much for the view. My own pleasure springs from all my senses. I run my hand down the bark of trees and squeeze fresh bay leaves, sniffing up their sharp familiar scent. I chew on wild rosemary and listen for the birdsongs. But Henry's experience wasn't in the least diminished by plying just one sense. That one sense of his served up a carnival compared to what I got from all of mine.

Jessie thought up a few rougher entertainments. Henry ambled in front of me, and she trotted along, slightly behind us. All seemed well until she surged forward and body-slammed him hard enough that he slipped over the edge. As he clawed into the hardpan, I stretched out on my belly to pull him back up. He wasn't in any real danger, as there was another trail a few feet below him, and he could have slid down to it without injury. But he wasn't pleased, and neither was I. Jessie stood apart from us, her expression suggesting she had no idea why we were making fools of ourselves.

After that, she found a fallen branch, and she raced into us, swiping the back of my knees and Henry's butt. I ended her fun by confiscating the branch. Henry ended her fun by walking on the uphill side of the trail.

One evening Jessie plunged after a man in shorts, her prey drive presumably activated by his running. She leapt in the air, and I thought I saw her bite him on his rear. The jogger ran on without a glance back at us, but I wanted to dig a hole and crawl in. The next evening, as I came off the trail, I spotted him, and steeled myself to ask him if he'd been bitten.

He laughed. "She nipped me, yeah. No problem."

"No blood?"

"No blood."

He waved off my apology, but I felt awful. Well trained or not, Jessie was too young to be loping around the woods unfettered. After that, I leashed her up for every walk.

The clamor of barking dogs filled my answering machine tape. Apparently Henry had developed a new barking hobby, thanks, no doubt, to Jessie. My neighbor was fed up. She'd complained, and I'd promised I'd do what I could. But there wasn't much I could do. The dogs weren't outside; they were confined in the house. The trouble was her living room windows faced my glass kitchen door, which was where the dogs stationed themselves to watch the passing parade. Nonstop barking coming from my house couldn't be escaped at hers. The tape irritated me, but she'd made her point. And I knew too well how it felt to be the helpless victim of a barking dog.

By the end of that week, I purchased a used Nissan pickup with a camper shell. I secured a water dish in the bed and tossed in a couple of bones and several chew toys. From then on, the dogs spent the day with me, and my neighbor got her sanity back. The camper had screened side windows that let in enough air if it wasn't too hot. When the weather did heat up, I'd tie them up under a tree, just outside my office window, where they could look in and see me, and I could keep an eye on them.

At break times, I'd go out to the parking lot to throw a ball for Jessie. At noon I'd take both of them for a walk, although this wasn't as simple as it might sound. The city of Fremont hadn't installed sidewalks around the industrial parks, presumably because the planners figured the workers would be too busy for a stroll. If I had time, I'd take the dogs to a nearby park where Jessie could swim and Henry could wade.

Some weeks, Henry stayed at Terri's house to play with Captain, her golden retriever. On the alternate week, Jessie stayed. Captain liked them both, but it wasn't feasible for the dogs to spend the day at my house. Terri's yard was the better bet for dog playing—meaning flat with solid fencing.

At work I'd been bragging about Jessie's smarts, how she wouldn't let herself get trapped on the other side of a pole.

"What does she do?" Meena, another copywriter, asked.

"Mostly avoids them. But if she's trapped, she backtracks."

"And that's a big deal because?" Meena wasn't a dog lover.

"Most dogs don't know what to do."

"I'd like to see that."

We arranged to drive together to Lake Elizabeth for lunch hour. Henry was at Terri's, which made walking with a friend easier. I was telling Meena about protection training when I felt a tug on the leash. Jessie stood on the opposite side of a pole. I waited. She looked at me. I waited some more. She sat down.

I swear she knew I'd bragged about her and couldn't wait to prove me wrong.

During another walk on Henry's play date, a woman asked if her toddler could pet Jessie. I said "Sure."

The boy approached, raised both hands in the air, and started pounding on Jessie's back. Before I could stop him, she turned and barked in his face. He began bawling. His mother gave me a scalding look and hustled him away. When I got back to the office, I put in a call to Avery.

"Bring her after work," she said. "We'll take care of that."

Avery must've collected every child in the neighborhood. They each held a tennis ball. When we came into the office, the children were jumping, screaming, and bouncing balls. They took turns tossing one for Jessie. They put their hands on her, ruffled her fur, and even pulled gently on her ears and her tail. The session was a success. From then on, whenever Jessie saw children, she was ready to play. She'd even offer a spit-infused tennis ball to an infant in a stroller.

For the most part, however, during breaks we stayed near the office, so I got a chance to eat some lunch after Jessie got a session of fetch. While I threw for her, Henry took up his duties as Sniffer in Chief of the foliage, lifting his leg repeatedly to ensure it held just the right aroma.

Quite far from us, a gardener bent over, weeding the landscaping. I figured Jessie wouldn't get close to him, not with me throwing.

I raised the Chuckit! and flung the ball. Here's the thing about the Chuckit!—a brilliant invention that allows an ungifted athlete such as me to throw a ball farther than the length of my shoe. It's shaped something like a lacrosse stick, with the ball nestled in a cup at the tip of a long plastic stick. The cup releases the ball on a throw and picks it up from the ground on retrieval. A secondary advantage of using it is no longer having my hand slimed in dog spittle. The first time I laid eyes on one, I experienced a frisson of joy. Just what I needed. I couldn't wait to try it out.

The acquisition of that first Chuckit! was major. I drove the dogs to a park and prepared to dazzle Jessie with my newfound proficiency in the realm of fetch. After checking that the ball was correctly positioned in the cup, I got ready. Jessie bobbed excitedly. I raised the Chuckit! and flung the ball . . . at my feet. It rebounded and hit me in the face. Apparently, there was a learning curve.

Over time, I got better, eventually able to pitch the ball about as far as a reasonably athletic woman could accomplish barehanded.

Jessie, at two years old, weighed eighty-five pounds. She looked intimidating. A young man, not yet seeing me, swore he thought she was a wolf. He was probably joking about the wolf, but I could see he was not joking about feeling afraid. Moments like that made me pay close attention to everyone around when we walked on city streets. I didn't want my sweet girl intimidating anybody unless they were a threat. That poor gardener was not a threat.

He faced away from me. But when the ball came to ground behind him, he whipped around, and I saw fear as he spotted Jessie barreling toward him.

I yelled, "It's okay. She's friendly!" Either he didn't understand me, or he didn't believe me. All the gardeners were from Latin America or Mexico, so I thought it possible he spoke Spanish, and maybe not much English. But it seemed equally possible he concluded I had no idea what my dog might do.

His expression didn't relax, even as Jessie sailed past him, grabbed her ball, and dashed harmlessly back to me. I sang out, "El perro amable! No te preocupes!"

He bent to his weeding anew.

I picked up the ball and threw it a second time. It hit him on his leg. *Oh, god. How on earth?* "Lo siento!" I yelled. "Really sorry!" He glared at me as Jessie scooped up her ball.

Many's the ball or Frisbee I've sailed over a fence. While practice makes perfect, in my case practice found its lack of skill level and never budged. I couldn't understand how I'd managed to hit that man. If I'd wanted to, and he'd been agreeable, he would've had to stand there for a month before I managed to get a ball to drop anywhere near him. I'm sure at this point he was worried. I felt confident. No way was a third ball going awry with such disconcerting precision.

The ball bounced off his head. I saw no point in trying to apologize for what had to look like malice on my part. I loaded the dogs into the truck, and ducked back into the office, where I doubled over, laughing. All afternoon, the story of my prowess made the rounds. I was approached with spurious offers to join the company softball team with a record of 6 and 0, or a competitive community bowling team, or a champion beach volleyball team.

I toyed with the idea of agreeing just to scare them.

Jessie liked to sleep on the cool floor next to my bed, the best spot to defend me against marauding brigands. On warm nights, I would leave the sliding glass door open. One night, I kept hearing her get up and trot out the door.

She'd lie down again, get up again, come back, and go out again. I turned on the light and saw her pushing her legs against the wall. This time I followed her out to the run where she squatted as if to defecate, but nothing came out.

Berkeley's emergency vet services told me to bring her in immediately. I gave Henry something to chew and headed out. Jessie somehow clambered into the Acura, which I hadn't yet sold. Luckily. At the vet clinic, I looked at her eighty-pound body and despaired. How would I get her in there? No way could I lift her, and I knew she was in agony. But, when I opened the car door, she tumbled out and walked into the clinic. She had yet to make a sound. I wondered if I were overreacting. Maybe she had indigestion.

The technicians rushed her to the back. Half an hour later, a vet came out to talk with me. He looked tired. I felt exhausted and terrified. The awful fluorescent lights made him gray. I assumed they did my own complexion the same favor.

"She's in complete torsion," he said. "I don't know how she walked in here." I began to cry. "We'll keep her comfortable overnight. We've inserted a tube to keep the intestines open, and we've given her a sedative. I suggest you take her to Walnut Creek first thing tomorrow morning. I'll give the address of a clinic that specializes in the surgery."

At six in the morning, with help, I put a groggy Jessie in the backseat of the Acura. The danger she was in tore at me. No longer were her intestines being kept open. If I didn't get her help quickly, her bowels would strangle and die, and so would she. We were facing rush hour traffic on one of the busier freeways in the East Bay. That morning, Highway 24 to Walnut Creek was a parking lot.

My blood pressure must've topped two hundred as the clock moved faster than the traffic. I was petrified. I kept reaching back to stroke my girl, to make sure she was breathing. For two seconds, I thought about using the emergency lane, but the idea of blocking an ambulance that could save a life kept me on the right side of the law. Plus, I knew, if I got stopped by the police—which would've surely happened—Jessie's condition would become fatal. Nothing could make me risk that.

I was in awe of her stoicism. I'm a person who would happily treat a papercut with codeine. Jessie kept looking around as if we were on a trip to the dog park. She was always more alert in the car than any other dog I'd owned, not counting Henry during his epoch of deafening vigilance. While the car moved, Jessie peered through the window in search of a tree. A tree meant a walk or a game of fetch. She wasn't going to miss out through inattention.

By the time we arrived at the clinic parking lot, my clothes were soggy. Jessie made her own way into the waiting room, where we were expected. She ambled after the technician without complaint, something that surprised me because she always made a huge fuss whenever we were separated.

They said they'd call after the surgery. If all went well, I could pick her up in two days. I drove home in a daze, collected Henry, and drove to work. By the first break, the vet called to say Jessie was doing great. He said he had tacked her intestines to the abdominal wall so she'd never go through this again. And neither would I.

He said, "Breeds like German shepherds, bloodhounds, standard poodles—we see a lot of torsion in those dogs."

Standard poodles. Great. I'd netted a twofer.

Henry's motto was "You throw it, you go get it." Sometimes he'd humor me and trot after a toy two or three times, but that would be it. If I insisted on throwing four times, I was out of luck. A dog that won't retrieve is a difficult dog to exercise properly. Walks are okay, but they don't provide the opportunity to get the heart rate going and build muscle mass.

The evening following Jessie's surgery, Henry dropped her stuffed cat at my feet. I picked it up and waggled it at him, expecting him to grab it for tug of war. He ignored my waggling and stared at the stuffed cat, and waited, looking weirdly expectant. I couldn't figure out what he wanted.

Then it came to me. He was laying a trap. I'd throw it, and he'd watch me play fetch. What fun. I shrugged and pitched the cat across the room, knowing it would stay there until I picked it up, if not the first time, soon after that.

Henry jogged over, retrieved the cat, and dumped it at my feet. I flung it across the room again, and he returned it to me. I was befuddled. What was he up to?

Light dawned as I repeatedly threw the toy across the room and Henry repeatedly retrieved it. Jessie loved a game of fetch. I had to throw that cat for her every evening before she'd agree to settle down. Henry had watched and made his decision. For some reason—who knew why—I required a nightly game. Okay, fine. He could do that. It was asinine, but if I needed it, he'd accommodate me.

Just as long as I didn't bring that infernal German shepherd back.

But, of course, I did.

Jessie's near-perfect obedience was tested during a Saturday afternoon class—her obedience and that of eleven other dogs. Avery instructed us to place our dogs in a "down-stay," after which we were to walk about fifteen feet away. All the dogs did as they were told.

We were to see how long each dog could hold their position. For the first ten minutes, all the dogs stayed put. But after that, as the clock ticked off another minute or two, one or two grew visibly restless. Finally, a dog broke, and that was all it took. One by one, each dog got up. At the end of twenty minutes, a single dog waited to be released.

My Jessie. It was my turn to walk like a queen.

Jessie hadn't seen Rolph since I took her away. Because she settled in with me so easily, I never thought about whether she missed him. Unlike Henry, who for six months had brooded over his missing people—or at least that's what I thought was going on during those months when I seemed to blend in with everybody else who enjoyed his favor. But Jessie surprised me.

We showed up for training one warm afternoon. She was about a year and a half old. Across the yard, in the large kennels, I spotted Rolph and another shepherd that could've been mother to both of them. So did Jessie. She sprinted to them. I watched in astonishment as she lay down and began keening, rolling on her back, from side to side. I have no idea how long she did this—not very long, I'm sure. Rolph and the other shepherd stared at her, cartoon bubbles over their heads asking *WTF*.

After a minute or so, she got up, shook herself, and trotted back to me.

The decision to spay Jessie was a no-brainer. Given my job, pending repairs to the house, an aging poodle, and her, I couldn't spare the time or the patience to deal with a litter. And there was another problem, as I saw it. What Avery had accomplished in training Jessie had given me a magnificent dog. Avery had a huge talent, and I knew I couldn't touch it. If just one pup matched Jessie's temperament, I would be terrified to give it to anyone.

The surgery didn't keep Jessie down for more than a few hours, but the vet suggested she take it easy for a bit anyway. I called Avery to tell her we'd skip the next class.

It hadn't occurred to me she would be upset. "I wanted to breed her."

"That would've ruined her girlish figure," I joked. She didn't laugh. I don't think Avery had a sense of humor.

She was already unhappy with me because I was dragging my feet on beginning Jessie's protection training. When we returned for the obedience class, Avery asked me to come into her office.

"I'm confident, Av. She'll protect me. I know it."

"How you gonna stop her from protecting you?"

"I'll call her off. Her recall is perfect."

"You don't know what you're talking about. When an untrained dog starts biting, you can't call them off. They go into a state, and they ain't hearing nothing."

"Well, it's not likely anyway, is it? I mean I don't expect to be attacked."

"Glad to hear it. But how you gonna keep her from going after somebody because they look funny or they walk funny, huh?"

She had a point. Dogs are Republican. For dogs to be comfortable, everything needs to conform to the established pattern. If I go to bed at ten most nights, my dogs get antsy if I stay up until midnight. That's why, when Frank was training for protection, now and then he would move like a drunk, or like someone with MS. I'd seen a friend of Avery's in a wheelchair roll past the line of dogs waiting to bite Frank. Several of those dogs looked unsettled.

Avery's glacial office kept me shifting around as if I could remain seated on her icy metal chair and be comfortable. I suspected she kept the temperature low to discourage chatting. Let's face it. Give a dog owner a chance to talk about her dog, and she'll gush until the target runs shrieking for the exit. Avery, all business, had no interest in encouraging photo sharing. Her dog pictures were tacked up on the wall. Take them or leave them, but don't talk about them.

I sighed. "It scares me, Av. The thought of her injuring someone, maybe even killing them—I know it sounds stupid. That's why I wanted her. But I was afraid of being attacked. I'm not afraid anymore."

"The rapists all went home, did they?"

"If she bites someone, I could lose everything—even her."

"Hear yourself? That's what I'm trying to stop." She stood up, looking disgusted. I'd never seen her this angry. She headed for the door. As she opened it, without turning around she snapped, "She's your dog."

Which sounded like rejection, and I felt hurt. Wasn't Jessie special to Avery? The crown jewel of the breeding she'd done? *A long line of Schutzhund champions*, she'd said when she'd told me about her four-month-old puppy. Born for the job, she'd meant.

But Schutzhund was a sport. Protection was about biting people in earnest.

A week or so later, something woke me around two in the morning. Jessie stood at the door, letting out soft growls. Henry raised his head but didn't get up. I heard glass breaking, and, at that, Jessie went crazy, her bark a high-pitched screech. She sounded like a dog on crack. I opened the door, and she uncharacteristically tried to shove her way past me to get out. Then I spotted two figures running down the neighbor's driveway behind my house.

"Did you see them?" Mrs. Stutzman yelled, coming out on her porch. Her throaty voice quaked.

"Not too well. Two men, I think."

She pulled her bathrobe around herself more tightly. "Your dog must've scared the poop out of them."

The excitement over, Jessie had settled herself back in her doorless crate.

Mr. Stutzman, coming out behind his wife, shouted, "Your dog sounded like she was gonna rip them to pieces. Glad they didn't stop to figure out she couldn't get at them."

"Better call 911," I said.

"As if that's gonna do anything. Think we'd rather go back to bed."

"Speak for yourself," Mrs. Stutzman said. "I'm calling."

I couldn't fall back asleep. Visions of those men swirled through me, like ice water. In my imagination, they climbed the fence into my yard, mounted the steps to my bedroom—and then Jessie. What would Jessie do? I didn't know.

Terri pawed through my refrigerator, looking for something worthy of her picky taste buds. I was telling her about the attempted break-in and how Jessie had scared off the burglars.

"Not burglars," she said, pulling out a package of Gouda and giving me a thumbs up for quality cheese. "Home invaders. More dangerous."

"Why would someone choose to go in when people are home?"

"I dunno. Got mustard?"

"Top right. In the door."

"How about pastrami?"

"You have lofty expectations of my humble larder."

"Not a larder," she said. Terri was a stickler for language. Before I took a real job, I often thought she should be teaching my class at Cal instead of me.

I reached around her and took out a beer, offering it to her. She wrinkled her nose, as I knew she would. Her drug of choice was pot. For lunch, she would have to make do with lowly salami and cheese.

"The cheese, however, is top drawer," I pointed out.

"Ha ha."

We adjourned to the living room. "How's her training going?" she asked me around a mouthful of sandwich.

I sipped the beer. "Okay." Technically, that wasn't a lie. Her training was going fine, just not the training I knew Terri meant.

"I'd like to come watch."

"Oh?"

"It's a long time since I worked with Loki. It was a lot of fun."

"You mean protection?" She lifted an eyebrow. "We might not do it."

She put the sandwich down and stared at me. "Are you nuts? What the hell did you get her for?"

"I know, I know. But I got cold feet. I keep picturing her mauling somebody."

"You gotta be kidding me. You? The queen of the impulse purchase? Suddenly you're prudent?"

"This is big, maybe the biggest decision I ever made except for getting married and having kids."

"I can't believe it. You're like the rich asshole who buys a champion racehorse and trots it through the park on Sundays. A racehorse needs to run, and a dog like Jessie? She needs to protect. Get over yourself." Terri wiped mustard off her lips. "Got any ice cream?"

"I've watched her chomp through a knuckle bone in minutes. For her, an ankle would be a canapé."

"I repeat. And you got her because?"

The thought of her facing someone who meant to harm me scared and thrilled me. I thought, *Yes! Finally she makes me the equal of any man.* That's what I wanted from her. But my anxiety wasn't about what Jessie might do. Not really. I trusted her far more than I trusted myself. If I was going to get past my uncertainty, I had to find a way to believe in myself the way I believed in her.

Two-Dog Night

Around this time, I drove up to Reno, where my father and Mary had moved after they retired. I hadn't been up there since Bob took off.

I'd bathed Henry, and his white coat sparkled. Before we set off on a four-hour-long trek, I wanted the dogs to have a romp. I stopped at Point Isabel so Jessie could swim. Henry liked to lie down in the water and stay right where he landed. I'd neglected to check on the tides. This occurred to me as we approached the estuary.

Henry romped straight down into the mud. Jessie preferred the rocky, relatively un-mucky beach. For Henry's coat, the damage was done. He wore long black stockings. No way could I put him back in the car. After Jessie had her swim, I hiked them over to Mud Puppies where a sweet young woman asked whether I wanted to wash Henry myself or let them do it.

"I've already bathed him today. This time, I'd like someone else to do it."

Stripping the mud from Henry's curly fur wasn't simple. She worked on him for forty-five minutes. When he was once again fluffy and de-mudded, I thanked her, paid, and gave her what I hoped was a generous tip.

I'd booked a room at Motel 6 because my parents had a cat. If we stayed only during the day, my dogs were welcome. The cat hung out in the garage while we were there. Mary and my father liked Jessie. Mary said she reminded her of a dog she'd had when she was a kid.

"Not a German shepherd. Just a Heinz 57, you know. All mixed up but the prettiest thing you ever saw."

We ate at the casino and came back to television, turned up to full volume although my father had the closed-captioning on the screen. They went to bed around eight, I knew, so I said my good night at seven-thirty.

107

The Motel 6 turned out to be one of the seedier franchises. In the dead of winter, the room felt colder than the outdoors. The heater rattled but produced nothing recognizable as warmth. The bed offered a single thin blanket incapable of keeping me comfortable in Reno's late spring. Clearly, I wasn't getting to sleep without help. I called the dogs over. They stood at the edge of the bed, expectant. What did I want? I patted the bed. They gazed at me. Befuddled. Surely I hadn't invited them onto the bed. They'd been trained to keep four on the floor, and they weren't falling for my bad joke. When they discerned I had nothing interesting to offer them, they settled down on the rug.

I gave up and dragged the poor excuse for a blanket from the bed to join them on the floor. It was a three-dog night, but I had to make do with two.

Protection Training

There was no aha moment, no dramatic event. After Terri left, I brooded over my inability to decide, and I thought about my first day with Jessie, on the beach—her instinct to hurry back to me, her need to keep me safe seeming stronger than her urge to play, even as a puppy. Terri's racehorse analogy made sense. The owner of the show horse was being selfish. Jessie too had been born to do one thing. Protecting her person was in her DNA. In denying her, I was being selfish.

If Avery rejoiced over my about-face, she did it inconspicuously.

Since I hadn't watched a dog advance through the various stages of training, I was curious about how we would begin, and I was starting to get excited.

The goal, I knew, was to shape a dog that would bite on command or, if no command could be issued, would attack when necessary. Otherwise, she'd be friendly, even docile, around non-threats. In the event of an assault, after overpowering the bad guy, she wouldn't pursue him, but would stay near me. If an attacker signaled defeat before I called my dog off, she would release, but remain vigilant. Above all, when I called "OUT!" she was to race back to me.

The first step was to buy a special harness. Houdini couldn't have gotten out of that thing. He couldn't have afforded it either. With a spanking new six-foot leather leash clipped to her yoke, Jessie sat beside me, waiting. She wasn't calm, I could tell that much. *Somehow she knows*, I thought. Maybe she'd watched sessions when Avery still owned her. I'd never let her watch with me.

Frank, Avery's assistant, brought out a whip, and I blanched. "You're not going to hit her?" If he tried, that would be the end of it, DNA or no DNA.

On the sidelines, Avery rolled her eyes. "Just keep her with you. And watch."

Frank raised the whip and snapped it on the concrete. Jessie didn't flinch, but I did. He cracked the whip once more. Jessie barked. And barked.

Avery called to me. "Every time she barks, call out 'Tell him!'"

Jessie produced that high-pitched, crazed clamor I'd heard from her the night the Stutzmans' house was almost invaded. It reminded me of the hair-raising screeching in *Psycho*'s famous shower scene.

"Tell her 'Hush,'" Avery ordered. "Then say 'Watch him.'"

When a dog has a particular behavior in her genetic makeup, the steps to mastering the skills shorten. Films about border collies in the Scottish Highlands showed puppies doing maneuvers practically out of their birthing boxes. They had nothing on Jessie. When I cut off her barking, she fixed her gaze on Frank and didn't look away.

Training is about timing, and my timing was lousy. Still is. I'd watched a woman named Joy work on one of Jessie's littermates, Wolf. He showed a bit less drive than Jessie, but he responded to Joy's every command with precision. Joy tolerated nothing less than perfection.

Now Frank shouted insults at me, and Jessie leapt at him, straining on the leash to reach him. From the sideline, Avery called out "Lesson over."

We spent several sessions reinforcing Jessie's response to "tell him" and "watch him." She did great. Me, not so great. After some introspection, I understood what threw my timing off. My thoughts jumped around. Instead of evaluating Jessie's reactions to Frank, correcting her as she made a misstep, I'd be itemizing what I needed from the supermarket, or wondering where I'd left that library book, or worrying about a bill I hadn't paid. I had to discipline my mind. Like Avery and Joy, I needed to keep my focus on my dog.

Jessie lived for training day. Her next challenge, and mine, was to go after Frank on the command "moosh," a nonword, made up to prevent accidentally triggering a bite. She'd have to wait to bite, partly to build up her frustration so her bite would be intense. Frank would stand just beyond her reach while I held her back. At first, she'd lunge at him repeatedly, but she figured out that he wasn't reachable. Unlike the other dogs, who twirled at the end of their leashes in their frenzy to get at the bad guy, Jessie waited. She lay down. If Frank stepped closer, she sprang at him.

If ever I doubted my decision to do this with her, she validated that decision after every session, sashaying from the training yard with her head high and her body language screaming, "I'm magnificent!" I, on the other hand, usually felt deflated. Joy worked next to me, and I noticed how she unfailingly enforced precision in her dog. Wolf's leash snapped the instant he made a mistake. He didn't have to wonder "What was that about?" When Jessie came back to me, Avery would yell "Correct her!" At that, I'd notice my dog. She was supposed to be parallel to my body, facing forward, her withers lined up with the seam of my pants. Instead, she'd be at a forty-five-degree angle, intent not on me but on her next opportunity to bite.

Avery asked me to come to her office for a bit after class. It felt like the teacher keeping me after school. But she surprised me.

"How do you think she's doing?"

"She's doing great. I'm the problem. I should've taken Wolf, and Joy should've taken Jessie. Wolf lives to please, so it would've worked out better for both dogs, don't you think? Although I wouldn't get anywhere near the level of obedience Joy gets out of him."

"You want to switch dogs?"

I snorted. "Joy told me she'd wanted Jessie at first. Said she realized Jessie was too much dog for her. My God. If my dog's too much for *her*, what the hell am I doing?"

Avery said, "Maybe Joy's too much person for her dog."

"What do you mean?"

"Think perfect's a good thing?"

"Isn't it?"

She gave me a wry smile. "I ain't sold either one of you a machine."

Later, it occurred to me that Avery hadn't said anything that called for a special chat with me. Why had she asked me to meet with her? I thought over what she'd said and I wondered. Maybe Avery read people almost as well as she read dogs.

What Rolph had done for Jessie—perhaps Avery was trying to do that for me. The difference was I *did* need my confidence built up.

When Jessie and I showed up for training, I'd often catch the end of a session with Ned, a gentle Black man, and his laid-back pit bull, Delancy. For a solid year, Frank tried to incite that dog to bite. He never touched Delancy, but he would wield all kinds of noisemakers to excite the unexcitable dog.

Ned lived in a dicey neighborhood, so he needed a dog capable of defending him. I knew the area where he lived, not a place I'd walk through at night. Trouble was, I doubted sweet Delancy could ever be his bodyguard. The dog never bared his teeth. Ned kept bringing him to Saturday obedience but gave up on protection.

I was happy to see his love for Delancy hadn't dimmed at all with the dog's failure to become his guardian.

One Saturday Ned didn't show up for the class. I asked if anyone knew where he was, but no one did. He didn't come the following Saturday either. After a month, he did come back, limping, but otherwise he looked okay.

"Where've you been?" I asked.

"Highland hospital. Head injury."

"Oh, jeez. What happened? Is that why you're limping?"

"It's connected, yeah. Three guys sell dope outside my door. They jumped me. Thought I'd reported them, although I never did."

"I'm so sorry, Ned."

"It's okay. Gave me a chance to find out what Delancy's made of. Those SOBs knocked me to the sidewalk, and my boy tore into them like a hurricane. He had those punks screaming for their mamas." Ned chuckled. "I guess word had got around about me taking Delancy for training and how it never worked out. Only problem was, when the ambulance came, Delancy didn't want to let them take me. I found out they were going to shoot him, but my neighbor came down and took him home with her. She kept him till I got out."

The final phase of training started with Jessie on-leash. Frank, cursing loudly, lunged toward me, holding a Styrofoam bat above my head. As Frank began advancing and shouting, Jessie held her position, watching and then barking and then again watching. After a few minutes of this, Avery said, "Send her, but hold on tight."

Giving her a bit of slack on the leash, I said, "Moosh!"

Jessie was about to get her first bite. But smart dog that she was, she knew she couldn't reach him. She lay down and waited. When he stepped within range, she leapt up and sank her teeth into his bite sleeve.

Afterward he showed me the bruise, proof of the intense pressure she'd exerted on the sleeve.

Jessie was honing her skills, and I was trying to hone my own. Avery's talk had helped. I stopped comparing myself to Joy. Whatever assets I lacked, I knew I could control my dog, and that was all that mattered, especially as Jessie started working off-leash. Without restraint, she showed me just how dangerous she could be.

Avery liked to bring in strangers to agitate the dogs, ensuring they understood people other than Frank could be the enemy. Because Terri's Loki always saw the same bad guy, she used to joke, "If I was attacked, Loki would hop on BART and go bite his trainer."

Avery recruited anyone who was willing to play the agitator.

Paul, Avery's cousin, played the villain once, and only once. He didn't know how to stand, and for that I blamed her. She could be reckless. Paul gave the game his all, shouting insults at me, and raising a "stick" as if to hit me. I said "Moosh!" and Paul extended the bite sleeve toward Jessie. She jumped past it, leaping for his throat. For once, thank heavens, I was focused. Seeing Jessie's jaws wide and inches from his trachea, I shrieked, "OUT!" In midair, she spun around and came calmly back to my side.

That calmness was an important aspect of her training. When the session ended, the bad guy could scratch her behind the ears. Avery's cousin understandably passed on the opportunity to do that. For my part, I was still shaking on the drive home.

Avery kept finding new meat. Christopher, a guy in his early twenties, asked if he could work Jessie, and Avery said, "Sure." But after her cousin nearly had his aorta incised, Avery decided unschooled "bad guys" could work her only when she was leashed.

Christopher acted menacing, and, at Avery's prompt, I sent Jessie. Aware that she had only the length of the leash to get at him, she lay down, waiting. Christopher smirked. "Feeling lazy today, huh?" And he stepped toward her.

Avery shrieked "NO!" before Christopher's arterial system came within range of Jessie's teeth. After that, he showed my dog more respect.

My funniest experience with Jessie in protection work happened when Karen, who owned a mastiff, wanted to get in on the fun. A woman had never played the attacker for Jessie.

Short and stocky, Karen came at me, yelling, "What are you doing here, lady? Get off my property!" Jessie didn't move, merely sat, and looked at Karen. Superfluously, I said, "Watch her." She might've snapped at me (bad choice of words), "I AM watching her." When I said, "Tell her!" she offered two lame woofs. I didn't think much of it because, now that she could bite, she had lost interest in "tell him." That was something we were working on.

Holding tight on the leash, I finally said, "Moosh!" At that, Jessie should've gone down on her belly, waiting for the "bad guy" to step into her booby-trapped parlor. But she didn't move.

Again, I yelled, "Moosh!" She looked up at me. I'd never seen her less interested in biting.

Karen kept screaming, coming dangerously close to us, with Avery shouting "Don't!" Still, Jessie acted as if she were in the car, staring out the window.

"What's wrong with you?" I said crossly. She looked at me, and suddenly I knew.

Avery brought out the Styrofoam bat. Karen raised it over my head.

Jessie attacked.

On hot days, the bite suit had to be intolerable, covering practically every inch of the body with thick padding. Plus, it was a great deal of trouble to get into. Frank rarely bothered with it, opting for the sleeve almost every session. Jessie was frustrated by the sleeve. She wanted flesh. That was why she'd ignored the sleeve when Paul had offered it and why she'd gone for his throat.

When she decided she'd had enough of sinking her teeth into impenetrable material, she tried to go around Frank. He pivoted to protect his rear end, but she pivoted with him. The result was a dance, Jessie trying to get behind him while he spun around to keep her in front of the sleeve. She didn't like to go for it, but she never did outmaneuver him. Eventually, she'd settle for the non-fleshy target.

The finishing touch in the training had Frank playing the part of a home invader. I pretended to be wiping the floor under my dining room table as he stalked across the floor. Jessie, sensing an intruder, went to the sliding glass door through which visitors normally entered. Standing there on guard, some twenty feet away from me, she didn't hear Frank, who wielded a Styrofoam bat. When she saw him, she leapt the distance between them in a single bound, sinking her teeth into his shielded arm. He staggered to the door, Jessie hanging from him. When Frank crossed the threshold, she released him. For the next ten minutes, she scouted every entrance to the house.

I thought I'd investigate a group out in Pinole that gathered every Saturday to work their dogs in protection. According to my emailed invitation, Jessie was supposed to stay in the truck while I watched the dogs work. She could join after that first week, which seemed reasonable to me. I needed to know how the sessions worked, and even whether I wanted her to do bite work with this group.

I walked down to a seat above the lawn on which a man was agitating a dog. He wore a full body suit. I liked that because I'd never wanted Jessie to focus on the sleeve.

Phil, the guy who had contacted me, introduced himself. Then he took a small dog from a crate. I noted she heeled perfectly, head up, eyes on Phil's face, the way Jessie used to heel for Avery although never for me. The little dog took her position next to Phil and the "bad guy" began to agitate. Given her diminutive size, the endeavor struck me as ridiculous.

After he put her back in her kennel, Phil told me, "You can bring your dog out, if you want."

"I'd rather stick to the rules."

"How about I take a look at her?"

We climbed up to the truck, and I pulled the top of the camper shell open. Jessie came over to inspect the stranger. Phil grabbed one of her stuffed toys and softly battered her face with it. She ignored him. When she finally took it in her mouth, she immediately let go. Phil looked at me with pity.

"She's got no drive," he said. I laughed. "My dogs would've ripped that thing to pieces."

I changed the subject. "I love that little dog you worked. She's a real honey." Her concentration on Phil was flawless. If she'd been able to write, she would've composed sonnets for him.

"Muley. I'm gonna get rid of her."

"Why on earth? She looks like a great dog, and she's crazy about you."

"She's not a great dog. She doesn't like to bite."

At that, I got in my truck, waved goodbye, and drove back to Oakland. I wouldn't be bringing Jessie to work with Phil.

Avery exploded when I told her about taking Jessie to Pinole.

"You do not work this dog anywhere but here."

"I don't get it. Why isn't it a good thing to expose her to different people, different ways of doing protection?"

"No. You was gonna put her with somebody you don't know nothing about. I heard about that club. Don't go near it, not with Jessie."

I bristled a bit over her dictatorial attitude, and said, "Whatever."

"Right-o," she replied.

Phil's rapid-fire assessment of Jessie's "lack of drive" wasn't worth the hot air it took to deliver it. But her abrupt release of the toy worried me. Frank had mentioned her bite wasn't as intense as usual, and she was releasing too fast. "I dunno," he said. "Maybe she got spooked somehow."

We talked about what trauma might be causing her to shy away from biting. But none of us could think of anything. It didn't make sense.

Out of ideas, I did what I should've done first. I checked her mouth. One front incisor was half gone and jagged.

Immediately, I guessed how that had happened. When she was five months old and, as usual, ravenous, she carried her stoneware food bowl across the house to where I was sitting, hoping, I suppose, that seeing her empty dish would remind me to fill it. The rim was almost a half inch thick, and the bowl had a ten-inch diameter. That dish probably weighed close to a pound. I suspected her tooth had cracked as she carried it. After six months of protection work, that tooth snapped off, likely on the bite sleeve. No wonder she was letting go quickly.

The vet gave me an estimate for surgery. I approved it, and he took her in the back. When she came out of the surgery, I paid, and we drove home, and I took another look in her mouth.

He'd pulled the wrong tooth.

"She must've broken the other one on the drive home," he said.

"Are you kidding me?"

"We aren't responsible for what happened after you took her home."

"You're responsible, all right. Show me the X-ray."

His face collapsed into a deer-in-the-headlights expression. "We didn't take an X-ray," he admitted.

"Really?"

He sagged. "We'll pull the other tooth without charge."

"Oh, you've already been paid for pulling the right tooth. Don't you dare try to bill me for your damned mistake."

He did pull the right tooth that time, but I mourned the perfect tooth the idiot had trashed.

Nevertheless, free of the pain of a fractured fang, Jessie's bite work went back to ferocious. I half-wished Phil could see her at work.

Imagine the scene. I'm driving my little Acura with towering Henry and hefty Jessie in the backseat. My cell phone rests on the seat next to me. I'm coming back from Berkeley on a route where, at one juncture, it's necessary to move rapidly left through four lanes of traffic if you aren't eager to wind up in San Francisco.

The opening I slipped into wasn't small. The car behind me didn't have to brake. I maintained speed and cruised onto 580. A young man, driving a late-model sports car, apparently resented my successful maneuver. I was in front of him! Horrors! He began a game of cat and mouse, jamming on his brakes in front of me, tailgating me at the back, pursuing me wherever I went on the freeway.

There I was with two huge dogs in the back, one trained for this. If I didn't want to unleash my dogs on this jerk, I could've picked up my cell phone and dialed 911. Instead, all I could get my brain around was that I couldn't let this idiot find out where I lived. He followed me off the freeway. We were stopped at a red light, his bumper practically touching mine.

Abruptly, I whipped my car to the right and turned, making a fast left into a gas station. Leaving all my handy defenses in the car, I raced into the station and explained to the three men present that I was being followed. One of them handed me a phone, and I dialed 911. Just then the door burst open and here's my nemesis, wearing what could have been an Armani suit (who am I to know), his hair coiffed so perfectly I figured the cut had cost him a C-note. He looked the perfect overpaid Silicon Valley IT exec.

"You hit my car, you fucking bi—who're you calling?"

"The police."

His eyebrows flew up in astonishment. "You called the police?" Apparently, he believed I was overreacting. If I hadn't been so frightened, I would've laughed at the irony.

It would be weeks before a different scenario occurred to me, and I gnashed my teeth. If I'd parked and rolled down my window, ordering Jessie to "tell him," the sight of the huge German shepherd, teeth bared, barking hysterically, probably would've made him wet his Ralph Lauren underpants.

Losing Henry

For months I'd been aware of Henry slowing down. I saw pain in his eyes and in his slow-moving struggle to get up. On our walks, he lagged, sometimes lying down. When this happened, I'd call him, and Jessie would rush back to bark in his face: *Get up!* Neither of us wanted to see what we were seeing.

Getting him into the truck meant I had to lift him, and that made him yelp. He started slipping on the steps to the carport. I cut up an old rug and glued strips on the treads. For a while, that seemed to help. But, eventually, I had to take him in and out the front door, a route that didn't require him to descend or climb any stairs.

One night I woke to find him gone from the bedroom. I went into the kitchen, where he lay still on the cool tiles. Putting my hands on him, I whispered, "Let's go to bed, honey." He snarled and showed his teeth. As I had that long ago night in the freezing Reno Motel 6, I lay down on the floor next to him, as close as I could get without disturbing him.

I brought him to Terri's vet. After I described his pain, she said, "You'll have to make a long appointment. We'll medicate him and take a series of X-rays. He'll be under for quite a while."

"But isn't it risky to anesthetize a dog this old?"

She said nothing.

I started sobbing. Another vet, hearing this story later, told me, in Henry's case, the value of an X-ray would've been measured only in cash: "The diagnosis was obvious at that point. Nothing could've been done to change it."

"If you did—" I began, my voice sounding like that of a sick frog. "If you put him through that—is there anything you could find that you could fix?"

Still, she said nothing. Was she mute? No, because she'd spoken of a long appointment and his being unconscious for some time. What on earth made this woman take up veterinary medicine? She barely glanced at Henry. Had she been rejected from all the human medical schools she applied to? Or did she simply prefer patients who couldn't talk? Her indifference to Henry and his suffering shocked and wounded me.

On the way home, I wondered about her. Years before I'd read an article discussing medical doctors and how they felt dealing with terminal cases. Many withdrew emotionally, sparing themselves the misery of impotent empathy. I hoped that vet's coldness came out of self-protection instead of callous indifference.

I dropped Henry at home and went out for groceries. When I got back, I couldn't find him. Panicked, I flew through the house, searching, as if his giant poodle body could be hidden under a coffee table or behind an ottoman. A crazy thought popped into my head. Someone had stolen him. If I hadn't been so upset, I would've laughed hysterically, picturing thieves breaking in to steal my broken-down poodle. No one had taken him, but he was gone.

Disappearing isn't death, but death is disappearance. Soon Henry would be gone forever, and I couldn't bear the thought.

I'd left the back door open. I hadn't expected him to take advantage of it, but I thought the air might feel good. When I finally checked out there, I spotted him lying at the bottom of the steps to the run. He'd struggled down but hadn't been able to climb back up. His pride in keeping our home clean, slowly learned, had pushed him to try to do what he couldn't.

Terri gave me the name of a mobile vet who did in-home euthanasia. On the phone, I said words to Dr. Arthursen that he must've heard hundreds of times: "I don't know if it's time."

"Let me ask you a question." His voice was deep and comforting. "Is Henry's quality of life acceptable now?"

Remembering my beautiful boy lying at the foot of the stairs, I choked out, "No."

Then he asked his next and most excruciating question: "Is he likely to get better?"

A pale punctuation mark—one that grows darker over the years—trails every moment of happiness my dogs have given me. I know from the start that I will lose them. When the cat my parents loved died, they suffered. I knew their agony. I'd felt it and knew I would continue enduring it. But they opted not to get another cat. The pain was unbearable for them.

Their decision saddened me. Losing a dog feels as if some essential organ has been ripped out of my body, but—as the cliché puts it—you only grieve the loss of what you've been incredibly lucky to have.

I swallowed hard. "No. I don't think he will."

That, then, was that. My responsibility for Henry required me to end his suffering, no matter what I wanted. He was about eleven, maybe twelve—his age had been estimated. I'd been told poodles, even giant poodles, live longer than dogs such as shepherds and rottweilers. For years I'd clung to that, refusing to dwell on that mysterious white spot on his spinal X-ray.

With Jessie in the bedroom, I sat on the kitchen floor, Henry's head in my lap. He was having a slightly better day, making my decision even more difficult. But I knew that "better" wasn't the same as "good." There were no good days in his future.

Dr. Arthursen spoke to him gently. Sobbing, I stroked Henry's head, and remembered him playing fetch with me because he believed I needed it.

The vet inserted the needle into Henry's flank and I thought of Tan Shirt. If I'd listened to him, I wouldn't have had years with this amazing dog. At the time, my taking Henry seemed foolish and impulsive, even to me, following our nightmare ride home to Oakland. But Henry rescued me at my lowest point. He was my companion when my human companion no longer cared about me. I'd endure all of Henry's faults all over again if I could once more watch him run back to thank me for bringing him to his beloved trail. How I wished he could play his joke on me one more time.

After a few minutes, Dr. Arthursen put a stethoscope on Henry's chest and shook his head, saying, "He's got a strong heart."

The second dose ended Henry's extraordinary life.

I wanted to visit the place Henry and I had loved together. With Jessie, I drove up to the Sequoia Bayview Trail, where I'd gotten us both lost years before. As we approached the trailhead, I began to cry. Jessie ignored me. She wasn't big on sympathy.

The walk was to be Henry's memorial. I thought of all the trouble I'd had with him, and all the laughter, and all the sweetness. I pictured him galloping to his favorite tree, as he did first thing whenever we came to the Sequoia Bayview Trail. At that tree and only that tree, he'd lift his leg, anoint it, and race back to look straight into my eyes. That was his thank you for bringing him to this wonderful place. Having let me know how lucky he felt, he'd set off on his kind of walk. He never failed to thank me like that.

All dogs sniff, but Henry stopped at nearly every plant and tree, not to mention every blade of grass, or rather every weed stalk. I imagined him as Ferdinand the Bull, from the cover of a book I'd had in childhood that featured a hulking Ferdinand, plopped down under a tree in a field of daisies.

I'd wanted a poodle with spirit. I got one.

Jessie had run ahead of me while I wiped my eyes. She halted at Henry's favorite tree, the one he watered religiously. That tree should've held a plaque inscribed with his name: *Henry peed here. A lot.*

As I watched, Jessie did something incredible. For the first and only time in her life, she lifted her leg and peed. Her own memorial for the poodle she'd loved.

Jessie and I could stare into each other's eyes forever.

Even as Jessie aged, her beauty persisted.

Charles playing ball with Jessie near the end of her life

Beautiful Vela, who won my
heart with a photo

Vela in her glory in
Lake Michigan

Beauty and the Beast
with fond Grandpa
looking on

Pilar and Vela,
always together

I called Pilar "The Flying Nun"
(after the TV show), but she
might've been better dubbed
"Airplane."

Pilar's ear came up;
Vela didn't care.

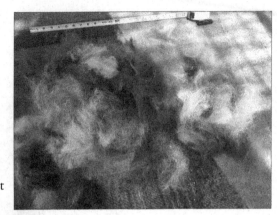

When you have a
German shepherd,
you need an excellent
vacuum cleaner.

Liam's favorite
sleeping posture

So nice to know my
dogs won't bolt through
any open door.

Tildy, the shy dog
I fostered

Sparkle with her best
bud, Zephyr

Who says
Sparkle's not
a lap dog?

The cabin: heaven on earth for dogs

Sparkle and Vela sleeping cheek to cheek—the pack rules!

Vela never found a partner that would tolerate her licking for quite as long as she wanted to lick.

Most dogs like to rest *inside* the donut bed; Liam likes to meditate with his chin on its outer edge.

Liam can be fierce at times.

Sadly, no photos of Henry exist, but this boy's expression is all Henry.

Liam will walk on two legs for me if I offer him sufficiently tasty treats. Who am I kidding? Any treat will do.

Sparkle's favorite game is bubbles; she jumps higher than I am tall.

Controversies in Food

Over the weeks and months following Henry's death, I began to obsess over how to keep Jessie healthy for a long time. She was five then, and—though I didn't yet know it—she had hip dysplasia that her muscular body and her tough mind kept from interfering with her active life.

The first challenge I faced was how to get control of her weight. When I'd been in Mexico with a friend, Terri had kept her. By the time I got back, Jessie weighed one hundred pounds, far too much for her skeletal system, according to everything I'd read.

I bought diet kibble. Three months later, she hadn't lost a pound. Kibble is processed dog food. I knew processed human food wasn't considered part of a healthy diet. Why should dog food be different? Online experts claimed kibble had its nutrients baked out of it, and the source of much of the meat was the floor of the abattoir. In other words, kibble consisted of every part of the animal that couldn't be sold otherwise. The additives used to keep it from spoiling didn't make for ideal dog food.

That's when I debated whether to cook human fare for Jessie. But plenty of veterinarians strongly recommended against cooking food for a pet, insisting only dog food manufacturers know all the nutrients dogs need. Where were all those experts when I began feeding infants?

After scanning the ingredients in Jessie's diet kibble, I decided I couldn't do worse.

For six months, I stewed oatmeal, various ground meats, shredded and steamed carrots, spinach, and string beans. Her weight didn't budge.

Then I came across a site touting the benefits of feeding raw, insisting dogs had no need for vegetables or grain. It occurred to me they might be stepping cavalierly over the reality that dogs, unlike cats, are omnivores. I suspect a vegan diet might undermine a dog's health, but I thought a few grains and vegetables couldn't hurt. Still, I wanted to test one claim on the site: stabilization of a dog's weight occurs naturally with raw feeding.

What I especially liked was the simplicity. Unpack meat, dump in bowl, set on the floor. Jessie went bananas for it. Her coat became glossier, her eyes brighter, and her energy—well, her energy had never flagged. Best of all, within a few months she'd slimmed down to her ideal weight. I was sold.

Falling in Love Again

As I approached sixty, my life seemed okay, if bland. I'd taken a few trips to places Bob never wanted to go, because he'd already been to them long before he met me. My son Eric took me to London; my daughter, Becky, and I went together to Paris; and I toured Mexico City with a friend. But most of the time I was alone and at home. I felt proud of all I'd managed on my own—a remodeled kitchen, a new living room floor, a dry-rotted deck demolished, and a French drain so the basement didn't turn into a quagmire every winter. But I missed being part of a couple. I drove to work, drove home, ate a simple dinner, watched *Law & Order* on broadcast television, and went to bed, where I read myself to sleep.

A coworker suggested I try online dating, the latest fad. She took a picture of me and urged me to post it on a site called Excite.com. I recalled looking for a lover in the newspaper lonely heart ads years before. They weren't promising. And when I scanned Excite, I discovered this fad, like most, pretty much belonged to people in their twenties and thirties.

I thought, *What the hell. Take a chance. What's the worst that can come out of it?* After posting on Excite, I opted to place my profile on several other sites. I wanted to attract men who had some verve left, so I discarded a few years from my age, registering on one site as fifty-four, on another as fifty-two, and on a third, fifty-one, putting down whatever I felt at the moment. Afterward, I had no idea what age I'd entered on which site, and even less of an idea about the birthdate I'd made up. Since I had to enter those to get back in, I was locked out of all but Excite.com, where my first respondent wrote that he'd seen all three ads, and demanded to know which listed my true age. I replied honestly: "None." I didn't bother adding that I was fifty-eight.

The ads from men weren't encouraging. In their sixties many wanted to "start a family" with someone who had "no baggage." *No baggage*? I had luggage that could've housed the population of Rhode Island.

Over twelve months, I exchanged messages with nearly a hundred men. Several clued me in to a nasty disposition by making disparaging comments about "the ex-wife." Some had political leanings at odds with my own. Many had no visible means of support or, worse, felt obliged to report the kind of car they drove. One wrote without capital letters or punctuation. When I told him he was "too lowercase for me," he replied, "what do u mean."

Three months in, my M.O. was fine-tuned. If the first email message intrigued me, I'd invite more, resisting overtures to meet, waiting to learn we had everything short of "chemistry" going for us. A year in, I'd agreed to only a handful of dates. None developed beyond "It's been nice, thanks."

I was ready to yank my ad. What I didn't know was that a man had spotted it and taped my photo to his monitor. When Charles finally made his move, he wrote "You're so beautiful, I thought you were out of my league," a compliment that plunged him straight into the category of "promising," a category I'd all but discarded weeks before.

I relished his educated, slightly sardonic tone. After a couple of email messages, he pressed me for a meeting. I countered, "Let's wait on that."

"A very long correspondence," he replied, "was not what I had in mind. And, by the way, have you read *A Very Long Engagement*?" In the remainder of his very long message, he recounted every salient fact about himself, concluding with "Now can we meet?"

Of all the novels he might have mentioned that I either would not have read or not admired, it hit me that he had picked one so lyrically written, so haunting. I'd loved it. I told myself it had to be kismet. I'm big on kismet.

We arranged to meet at Lake Merritt for a stroll through the dark. I told him I'd be bringing my German shepherd. He replied that I'd know him because he'd be the one without a German shepherd.

He had his back to me as I approached with Jessie. Our conversation began awkwardly. My jokes fell flat. His talk bored me, showing none of the quickness that had attracted me to his writing. A date such as this always ended with a handshake and a firm "goodbye."

Yet when he said he'd had a great time and could he telephone me, I felt inexplicably disappointed that he wasn't inviting me to dinner, as most of the other men I'd agreed to meet had. "Sure," I said, confused by my mixed reactions. Since I knew he didn't have my phone number, I took this as *his* firm "goodbye." But he emailed an hour after I got home, asking to see me again.

He was two years out of his own long marriage. Later I would learn that the coup de grâce had been administered by a puppy. Just before Charles went off to a conference in Brazil, he lowered the boom on his wife's proposal to bring a dog into their household. He didn't want one, and he told her so. A month later, she and a springer spaniel greeted him at the airport. He was furious. They had agreed not to get a dog, hadn't they?

Alarm bells rang. "You don't like dogs?"

"I didn't think one would fit into our lives. Both of us working full time. And I didn't think she'd clean up after it. Which turned out as I expected. Luckily, no one called the health department on us."

"But you're open to living with a dog?" This was brazen. We'd spent—what?—two hours? Three?—in each other's company, and here I was, practically proposing.

"I had dogs when I was a kid. A dachshund. He slept with me."

That was more like it.

He told me about how he and his wife had struggled over replacing their couch. Her father had burned it up, napping with a lighted cigarette, and the firefighters had pitched the smoldering granny-style sofa out an upstairs window. As someone who is fond of old objects, including the sofa (and, eventually, me), Charles set out to find its twin. His wife dissented. She wanted something more modern. They compromised on a very similar Victorian settee in pink instead of yellow.

"I viewed it as an opportunity to work something through to a satisfactory compromise," he said. "Actually, I felt good about it. But she didn't see it that way at all."

"Perhaps," I ventured, "because you won."

When we'd been together for three months, Charles had to attend a month-long conference celebrating his sixtieth birthday, a ritual mathematicians honor, at least for some of their ilk. He planned to drive, and he wanted me to come. While I couldn't take a month off work, I could take a week. I flew to Chicago for the final week of the conference.

At the end of the week, we packed up his Miata and took off. He drove as if he had to get someone mortally wounded to the hospital. We were in the car all day, stopping only for gas and fast food. At night we stayed in some of the worst motels I've ever seen, motels with antennas for the television set and a single lamp for the bed. One place must've been truly vile because he came out and said we had to look for somewhere else.

As we crossed into California, I finally exploded. "You're burning up my vacation!"

"What?"

"We haven't seen anything. We haven't done anything. I've had no fun at all. And you're driving like a maniac. You in a hurry to get rid of me?"

"No," he said, looking shocked. "Of course not. I thought you understood. It's Saturday."

"So it's Saturday. So what?"

"The kennel's closed tomorrow. If we don't get there by five, we'll have to wait until Monday to get Jessie."

"Oh." I looked out the window. "Okay," I said. "I feel moldy."

"What?"

"It's what my kids used to say when I said something stupid. 'You're moldy, Mom!'"

We got there at 4:50. Charles said he'd wait in the car. Which puzzled me. I knew he was eager to see her. "Why not come in?"

"Nah. I don't want to spoil your reunion. I'd be a distraction for her."

I laughed, shaking my head. "I doubt that. What I want to know is how're we going to fit an eighty-pound dog and her ginormous food bucket in this eensy-bitty car when we're already packed to the gills. Have a plan?"

He shot me an enigmatic smile. "Go get her."

When Avery brought Jessie out from a back kennel, she raced at me, shrieking, nearly knocking me down. It took several minutes to get her calm enough to take her out to the car.

Charles had put the top down. I gazed meaningfully up at a sky the color of ashes. My hair whipped across my face and stuck to my lipstick. "I'm cold," I said.

"It's a short ride. You drive. Jessie sits in my lap. Food bucket goes right here." He placed it on the console between us, wrapping his arm around it.

I hadn't thought I'd ever top the sight of my Henry in a sleep mask, tethered to the handbrake, but this looked to be even weirder. On a frigid Bay

Area summer day, we were driving alfresco. Charles could see nothing because Jessie's head blocked his view. I couldn't see well because my hair kept blowing over my eyes. Jessie, in the catbird seat, could see everything. Sitting atop Charles, she was grinning as if she'd just been given a pound of steak.

Around us, drivers gaped, plainly flabbergasted by the sight of two blind people in a sports car guided solely by their seeing eye dog.

We took my pickup truck to Charles's cabin in the woods. He'd invited me to it within days of our meeting, but I'd resisted until I felt confident our relationship had legs. Jessie was dozing behind our seats when we stopped for lunch. It was a hot day, so I parked in deep shade and left the windows all the way down. We were enjoying ourselves on the café patio when Charles said he wanted to grab his sunglasses from the dashboard of the truck.

Jessie, abruptly awakened by a hand reaching in the window, lunged directly at his face, open-mouthed. At the last second, she clamped her teeth, cushioning her sharp incisors with her snout. Even so, Charles's cheek split open below his eye.

With all the blood pouring down his face, I thought he'd lost his eye. I got some ice from the people in the café, and we finally got the bleeding stopped. Neither of us felt much like finishing our lunch. We got back in the truck.

Charles, sporting a soggy Band-Aid and a darkening eye socket, turned around in his seat and affectionately ruffled Jessie's fur. "She's a good dog," he said, inviting her to resume her parrot's-eye view of the road with her chin on his shoulder. "Nobody's stealing anything while Jessie's on the job."

That was the moment I decided to marry him.

Charles loved his cabin, and so did Jessie, but the drive gave her one fretful moment. That was each time we passed the off-ramp to Point Isabel, when she'd whimper loudly, as if shouting, "Go back! You missed the exit!"

Jessie always knew where she was and what lay ahead of her. She'd mapped out the routes to all the dog parks in Oakland, the trails, and, most of all, her beloved Point Isabel. She also knew when we were heading to the cabin, although not until we turned off Highway 101, close to 128 heading into the Anderson Valley. Although at that point we'd still be an hour and a half away from the cabin, Jessie would begin singing, her body electric with joy.

Which gave Charles a heaping dose of pleasure.

The isolation of the cabin, two miles off paved roads, made the woods around it ideal for wildlife. Whenever a deer came into view, she pitched herself forward, practically knocking her nose into the windshield. The only other moving objects to elicit such a response were motorcycles. Her superior hearing tracked them before we could, which resulted in our jumping out of our skin as she erupted in deafening barking inches from our ears.

After we unloaded the pickup, Charles suggested a walk. Uphill, naturally. We wended our way through an ocean of foxtails that turned our socks into prickly porcupines. At the top of the property, we came to a road where we encountered a yapping dog. Charles said, "Don't worry. He won't come off the property."

"He will," I said. "But I'm not worried."

He did come off his property, yapping. For a second or two. Jessie's only reaction was to lower her head slightly. That dog took another look and fled back to safety.

The way dogs read each other intrigues me. At times, it looks like ESP. On walks in the redwoods, Jessie and I sometimes came across a dog flat on its belly, with the owner shouting, "Get up! What's wrong with you?" After we'd pass, that dog would stand up and move on.

The dogs that did that hadn't even seen Jessie yet, but her scent spoke to them of her character. Dogs have no problem prostrating themselves before a superior. And Jessie had no problem accepting their deference.

Wild turkeys abound in the countryside around the cabin. On a walk down the gravel road, Jessie got a shot at them. She raced over to apprehend her prey but looked bewildered. What should she do? After a moment's reflection, she apparently decided a dance was in order. She started hopping up and down. Her antics didn't please the turkeys, but we enjoyed her foxtrot.

She'd had one other experience with loose fowl and had come to the same conclusion then about how to handle it. The people who lived next door to me kept chickens in a coop with a serious flaw in its architecture, a flaw, that is, unless I am mistaken in assuming the purpose of a chicken coop is to *coop* up the chickens. I had let Jessie out of the car without first checking the perimeter as I normally did after those chickens became resident. They were roaming the driveway, and Jessie bolted toward them. She was encircled by flapping wings, to which she responded by bobbing up and down as if she were testing the elasticity of the asphalt.

What food-driven dogs won't ingest hasn't been identified. At the cabin one afternoon, from a distance, Charles and I watched in dismay as Jessie inhaled a cube of butter. Not long before, we'd heard of a dog, only a tad smaller than Jessie, rushed to the emergency vet with pancreatitis brought on by eating far less butter than a cube. After her feast, Jessie enjoyed a pleasant nap in the sun. She had the digestive tract of a Texas pie-eating contest winner, which she proved to me more than once.

Beate—a gourmet cook from New York who was staying with us—asked if she could prepare our dinner and invite three friends. What was I going to say? No? I went to work happy.

When I came home, everything had been done. Table set, food prepared, the guests savoring a fine wine and creamy cheese. Soon after I arrived, we sat down to eat. When we'd stripped the serving dishes of every particle of her cooking, Beate went to get the dessert she'd purchased, seven slices of cheesecake and seven fruit bars. As she started for the steps to our sunken living room, it hit me what she would most certainly find down there.

At the top of the stairs, she hesitated. It took only two or three seconds for her to process what she saw. Then, she said dryly, "So, Jessie, what was wrong with the fruit bars?"

Having never owned a dog, she'd placed dessert on the coffee table. My German shepherd had downed seven slices of cheesecake along with two fruit bars. Pancreatitis? Nah. She sank into a post-prandial nap while the seven of us shared five fruit bars.

Weighing almost fifty pounds more than Jessie, I couldn't imagine ingesting even two pieces of cheesecake without suffering. An imperturbable digestive tract is a boon to a dog with an appetite for anything, including—as it turned out—rodent bait.

Charles had cakes seeded throughout the cabin. I objected, but he insisted Jessie couldn't get to them. That was my primary concern, but I had another.

"How does it work?"

"The cakes attract the mice, they eat one. They bleed internally and die somewhere else."

"What I don't get is this. You don't want rats or mice in the cabin, right?"

"True."

"So why attract them?"

He scratched his head. "Hadn't thought of that." He got up. "Just take me a minute."

When he came back, I asked, "All gone? Where'd you put them?"

"In the metal garbage can. Lid's tight."

"Sure you got them all?"

"Every one."

A few hours later, Jessie's mouth fizzed with green foam.

We were an hour away from help. The vet I reached by phone advised us to pour peroxide down her throat and follow that up with charcoal pellets. With none of that in the cabin, we raced to the Philo grocery store, about half an hour away. I bit my nails until my hand finally closed on a bottle of peroxide. We stood Jessie on the tailgate and poured it in her gullet, after which she vomited a lot of green foam. We kept pouring until nothing more came out of her.

The local market didn't sell charcoal pellets. The clerk said Walmart in Ukiah had them, adding, "You can't miss it." In the years since that expedition, whenever we're having trouble locating an address or a business, we say emphatically, "You can't miss it." Indeed, Walmart would seem to be the sort of place you can't miss.

We drove in circles until we stopped "missing" Walmart. The charcoal pellets, however, were not to Jessie's liking. She spit them out as fast as we stuffed them in, the net effect being we came out with soot on our hands, while she successfully kept them out of her stomach.

Physically and emotionally exhausted by the time we got back to the cabin, we dropped into our chairs, staring into space. Within a couple of minutes, Jessie appeared in front of us with another cake of rat poison between her teeth. She made no attempt to eat it, simply looked at us as if to gauge our reaction. That was a horrible day, true. But my clearest memory isn't of how frightened I was, but of her bringing us that last cake. I couldn't have been more astonished or delighted if she'd offered me a cup of coffee.

The bitterest substance known, the insert proclaimed. *Never appeals to household pets.*

Too bad Jessie couldn't read.

One midnight, I drove out to pick up Charles from Oakland Airport. When I got there, I discovered his flight had been delayed, and it would be some time before it landed. I didn't want to pay to park, so I drove back to a residential block close to the airport. Because there were no streetlights on that block, and no illumination seeped from the windows of the nearby houses, the full moon provided the only light.

It was a warm night, so I lowered my window and waited, checking my phone every so often to see if the plane had finally landed. Jessie sat beside me in the passenger seat. After we'd been waiting for about half an hour, I caught sight in the rearview mirror of a man coming up the street toward us. Without my dog, I would've rolled up the window, made a U-turn, and roared past him. But my breathing stayed calm. I felt as if I were lounging on a beach. Well, not a beach. I hate sunbathing. I felt as if I were reading a book with my back against the trunk of a redwood tree.

Jessie stayed calm as well.

He didn't spot her until he came up even with my window. When he did see her, he billowed sideways. Jessie watched, but didn't react.

"Can I talk to you?" he croaked from several feet away.

"Go ahead."

He lifted one finger, pointing past me. "What about the dog?"

I smiled the smile of the poker player with four aces. "You don't bother me," I said, "she won't bother you."

He cleared his throat and thought about that for a moment. Then he worked up the courage to ask, "Can I have five dollars?"

I might've given him some money, but he didn't look as if he wanted to come close enough to take it from me. And, in fact, immediately after making the request, he waved his hand dismissively. "Never mind."

In the rearview mirror, I watched him make his way back to the main drag.

Security is only a state of mind, but that state of mind is vastly improved by access to an eighty-pound, personal-protection-trained German shepherd.

Jessie and I especially liked to walk on one of the three off-leash trails spiking off the Skyline Gate parking lot. Well shaded by towering pines, the trail was a pleasure, and best of all nearly flat.

We had a routine. I'd say, "Jessie, go find a pinecone." She'd sprint up a slope, nose around, and, after a moment or two, come back with one between her teeth. *Game on.*

On the downhill side of the trail, the grade was steep enough to provoke vertigo. Jessie loved the challenge. I'd toss the pinecone, she'd bolt downhill, and claw her way back up with her prize. When my sister-in-law came for a visit from New York, I took her on that walk, showing off California's redwoods. But mainly showing off my amazing dog.

As Mary watched, I kicked a pinecone down the steep grade. I'd done this more than once in the past, but I'd always done it with athletic shoes firmly bound to my feet. This time I wore sandals, one of which gaily bounced down after the pinecone. I didn't even briefly consider sliding down to get it.

Looking and feeling foolish, I repeatedly called out to Jessie, urging her to find my shoe. Each time I shouted, she looked up at me, awaiting an instruction she could comprehend. One never came, so she resumed hunting her pinecone.

I eyed the trail glumly. Between twigs, rocks, and mixed debris, it didn't promise smooth sailing to a barefoot woman. Maybe I could switch feet into the remaining sandal with each step.

"Don't worry," Mary said. "Any minute a young man eager to help an old lady will come along."

Almost before Mary's mouth closed on the words, two strapping young men ambled toward us. She flagged them down.

One fellow half-scrambled and half-slid toward the sandal. It took him a bit of time to locate it because it had callously hidden under some brush. But when his hand closed on the shoe, he hoisted my treasured footwear as if it were the Olympic torch, his big grin assuring me he hadn't minded helping out.

While it's true that what goes up must come down, it's not true that what goes down will inevitably come up. Repeatedly, the young man tried to get a foothold on the climb. Repeatedly he skidded backward. He kept at it. And at it. His friend began to look worried. I began to be worried. Only Mary and Jessie looked unperturbed.

Then the cartoon lightbulb popped above my head. "Here," I told his buddy, handing him Jessie's sturdy leather leash.

He dangled it over the side, his friend grabbed it, and together they conquered the hill Jessie repeatedly mounted. To be fair, her claws gave her an unbeatable advantage.

Her mastery of that incline astonished more than one hiker. A group of German tourists stopped to watch her. They applauded as she reached the top, and then stayed to watch several more ascents. When they started to move on, Jessie raced to get ahead of them. There, she turned sideways, as if to keep them from moving forward. Well, no, it wasn't "as if." She definitely wanted them to stay and admire her some more. I thought I had never caught such a show of vanity in her, but then I remembered her strutting out of protection training, her body singing its own praises.

The Germans were so charmed by her maneuver, they did stay and watch her a few more times. After that, she permitted them to walk on.

Cajun was Terri's black-and-white collie, his name suggesting a dish of "blackened collie." He and Jessie were good friends, her only friend since Henry died. After he was gone, she showed no interest in other dogs. But she took to Cajun right away, so we included him in many outings, and Terri included Jessie in several of hers. Walking the two of them in the redwoods was a special pleasure. Normally a docile dog, Cajun took on the air of a conquistador when he walked with his bolder girlfriend. They'd trot along, shoulder to shoulder, showing the dogs they passed they were not to be trifled with.

Every Wednesday, on my way to work, I'd take Jessie to spend the day at Terri's house. As soon as I turned right off the driveway, she knew where we were going, and she'd begin yipping excitedly.

By the time I got there, Terri would be at work, so I had a remote opener for her garage door. From there, the dogs had access to the backyard. When Jessie ran inside, her first order of business always was to establish her primacy by putting her chin on Cajun's withers. I could almost hear him whine, *Is it Wednesday already?*

He had reason to find her annoying, as did Terri. Cajun had a treasured basketball. He'd played with it for months. When Jessie spotted it, she pounced. In two seconds, she turned it into a placemat. She similarly victimized the ball I bought to replace it. My indebtedness to Cajun and Terri mounted.

And mounted. Her neighbors had a small terrier that took a dislike to Jessie. He ran along the fence, barking at her hysterically. Through several visits, she ignored him, but I guess she tired of his bad temper. He stuck his nose through the fence one time too many, and she bit it. I paid a hefty vet bill. After that, the little dog ceased offering his nose to Jessie, thank heavens.

Charles, ripe with ideas, suggested we take Cajun with us for a weekend at the cabin. Terri could flit around town guilt-free for two days, knowing her dog wasn't sitting in the yard, thoroughly bored, as he had to do much of her workweek.

On our way north, we detoured into St. Helena for a late lunch on the patio of a charming little restaurant. The detour added a lot of time to our trip, so that when we reached the cabin, Charles and I were ready to go to bed.

The dogs, however, had been cooped up in the truck half the day. To make up for it, we left a door open for them, and they went outside to explore.

Around one in the morning I woke to the sound of dog toenails skittering across the floor, and Cajun panting. Several minutes later, when I had just nodded off again, here comes Jessie, heading straight to Charles's side of the bed, jamming her snout against his. She wanted to tell him all about her breathtaking adventure.

I woke to the sound of his "Ugh!"

"What is it?" My nose answered the question.

Jessie had been skunked in the face. She'd rarely seemed more joyous.

While we were lounging at the cabin one fall evening, a faint pop sounded in the distance. I barely caught it, but Jessie reacted. How could she have known it was gunfire? Even if she did know it was the sound of a gun being shot, how could she know a gun was a potential threat? That's a mystery I never solved.

For the first time in her life, my valiant dog experienced fear. After that, she reacted to any explosive sound. The Fourth of July—never a problem during the first seven years of her life—became a nightmare. Nothing I did calmed her. And while we rarely experience thunder in the Bay Area, we would soon move to a place where thunder was common.

Toronto

Jessie had begun to show early signs of hip dysplasia. To get in the car, she now had to clamber. I made an appointment at Berkeley Dog & Cat. The vet, Dr. Morrison, gave us Metacam for her pain and made an appointment to see her in a week. When we got home, I gave her a dose, and I did that every morning that week. Except I wasn't giving her anything. When I thought the medicine dropper was sucking up medication, it held only air because I didn't turn the vial upside down. Jessie must've wondered why I'd kept opening her mouth to squirt nothing in it. Just before we were due to return to Berkeley Dog & Cat, I realized my mistake. When Dr. Morrison asked me if the Metacam was helping, I said, "Well, you know, it's hard to tell."

When I started actually filling the dropper, the Metacam made a huge difference. She still couldn't leap into the car, but she moved much more easily, especially in getting up from the floor.

In the dead of winter, we packed up to spend a month in Canada, where Charles would be working with a colleague at the University of Toronto. I'd sold the truck, and we bought a Maxima. For the trip across country, Charles glued memory foam to a board that spanned the distance between one passenger door and the other and covered the floor space behind our seats. That became Jessie's perch for the trip. She had room to turn around as much as she needed to, and softness for her tender hips.

At last, we were ready to set off. Our ignorance about our northern neighbor could have filled buckets, much like our ignorance about winter—well, *my* ignorance about winter. Charles had grown up on the East Coast. My rude winter awakening came when we stopped in Nebraska to give Jessie a potty break and a little exercise. The temperature was 8°F, and the wind chill factor probably took that down to -10°F or even -20°F. But I was determined to do right by my dog.

My understanding of Jessie's unflagging need for the great outdoors, regardless of ambient conditions, had been shaped years before, when I'd taken her and Henry to Point Isabel during a violent rainstorm. The wind whipped my drenched coat against my soaked body, and my canvas shoes gushed water with each step. You might ask why I'd wear such pathetic clothing to walk in pelting rain. Canadians say there's no such thing as bad weather, just bad dressing. That day I had dressed as if I swallowed the hype about it never raining in California.

My dogs, however, had a grand time.

With acres of empty park around us, we made our way around the estuary and then back. As we neared the truck, I came across a woman with a small dog, just starting out. She was as inadequately dressed for the weather as I was and looked equally unhappy about it.

"We have to be nuts," she said. I had to agree.

When I opened the tailgate, urging the dogs to get in, they gazed at me with palpable disappointment. I could almost hear them whining, "What the hell was that supposed to be? Don't think you're getting points from us for that outing."

In frigid Nebraska I assumed I'd get the same lip from a dog that had been cooped up in the back of a sedan for three days. I took the Chuckit! out of the trunk, trying to protect my face from freezing by turning away from the wind. Surprise. It didn't help. Jessie hopped out and did her business. I lifted the Chuckit! and pitched, not bothering to watch her go after the ball. Following each of three tosses, I covered my stinging face with my mittens. I couldn't go on.

I apologized to my dog and braced myself for "the look" that said I was a sorry excuse for a dog owner. Instead, she scrambled into the car as if she were escaping a slavering pack of wolves. Then the light dawned. Like Henry, taking up the task of retrieving to please me, she'd been willing to accommodate my incomprehensible need for this diversion, but she was relieved when at last I gave in to common sense.

Driving through sleet and subzero temperatures, we arrived at the Canadian border around midnight, pulling up to a small kiosk. The man inside slid open the window and took our passports. With a glance at Jessie, he said to us in a delightful French-Canadian accent, "I suppose you have papers for that beast in the backseat."

As I began fishing in the glove compartment, Charles said, "Sure. You want them?" The question was perfunctory. Of course a government official wanted the papers. A rabies certificate was a requirement to enter the country.

"No," he snapped. "Welcome to Canada." With that, he slammed the kiosk window. Apparently, he too found the weather unbearable, in his case despite his good dressing.

The ignorance about Canada that I mentioned led us to mistake St. Catharines, a few miles from the border, for Toronto. Our day at that point had consisted of nearly sixteen hours of driving so maybe our brains were as numb as my feet, which were resting on the uninsulated floor of the car. We were so relieved to have reached our destination—until we read the signs. Toronto was still two hours away.

Around three in the morning on a Saturday, we arrived at the house we'd rented for the month. The delay arose from our failure to bring along a map of Toronto. We had to stop at several gas stations before we found one. In front of the house, street signs warned us not to park without a permit. Unfortunately, there was neither garage nor driveway to stash the car, and it was crammed with our belongings. We penned a note to the effect that we would obtain a permit on Monday, left it under the windshield wiper, and took what we needed overnight into the house.

More ignorance about Toronto caused me to stare in bemusement at a swamp cooler hanging from the ceiling. I'd assumed all of Canada froze year-round. While this is true of some parts, it's not at all true of Toronto.

We found Canada surprising in other ways. It slightly exceeds the US in size, but 80 percent of its territory is uninhabited, and 90 percent of residents live within 150 miles of our common border. As a primary school student in California, I learned about the countries to the south. In school in Massachusetts, Charles studied Europe. Canada receives short shrift from American educators.

Over the next several years, we learned Canadians are passionate dog lovers, which makes me a passionate lover of Canada.

I opened the back door for Jessie, and she plunged into a foot of snow, bobbing through it like a snowplow on a trampoline. Charles and I stood, holding hands, and watching her. Her joy inspired ours. At last she tired, and we all went upstairs and fell into bed.

In the morning, when we went out to finish unloading the car, we found a ticket over the untouched note. After we'd put everything away, we leashed up Jessie and went for a walk. There wasn't much to see, but we were all glad not to be cooped up in the car. A block from the house, Jessie went down, splayed helplessly on the snowy sidewalk. We were startled, and frightened that something was seriously wrong with her. With her usual fortitude, she scrambled to her feet, albeit with effort, and soldiered on. At home, I examined her paws and saw salt embedded in the fissured pads. She needed booties.

On Monday, while Charles went downtown to get a parking permit, I took Jessie out, looking for a place to walk her. Within a few blocks, I discovered a small pet shop, where I bought four booties in Jessie's size. The owner squatted to show me how to put them on. When they were cinched up, a very unhappy dog stood still, lifting first one paw, then another, then another. She was marching in place, and her expression wasn't sanguine.

Outside on the icy sidewalk, however, I think she realized those boots were made for walking.

Unfortunately, the neighborhood didn't appeal to me. Tidy but boring homes lined the block where we were staying. The surrounding area had passed its heyday, if it had ever had a heyday. It held several sad little shops, most permanently shut, and unmarked doors, probably leading to cramped apartments. Weeds and trash blotched the gaping holes of vacant lots. More garbage spilled into the gutters.

Across the street from an enormous Loblaw supermarket, we cautiously made our way down steep, icy steps. At the bottom, I found a trail wending through spindly trees. A fair bit of refuse had been disposed of here and there, and the soil gave off a sour odor. At the end of the trail, we came to a slope where shrieking kids were sliding downhill on saucers.

The walk wasn't long enough nor was it pleasant enough, but it was the only piece of nature close to the house. How I missed our redwoods! Jessie was more upbeat about the whole thing. I think she liked the stench of that soil.

New York

One of the pleasures of being Charles's wife has been traveling. Who knew mathematicians went anywhere? I had thought they stayed in rooms and scribbled on paper. He's taken me to cities all over the world, sometimes for a month or more. Twice we stayed in New York City.

The second time we were a block from Riverside Park. I took Jessie to its dog park every day. The first time we went, I stopped at a waist-high wall to look across the river. She put her front paws on the wall to check out what held my interest. Pretty quick, the view bored her, and she left me to it. But, after that, every time we went to the park, I'd get her to join me at the wall. She'd oblige me, even though she clearly found it pointless. Which it was.

Dogs indulge me, even when I'm idiotic like that. Their generosity often exceeds ordinary human kindness. For that reason, among others, I don't think of them as little people in fur coats. While dogs are as helpless as children, the love I feel for them is of their doggishness, that wildness that now and then communicates with me as clearly as the roar of a waterfall. For me, those are the exhilarating moments of entering a dog's world.

For the most part, they are a mystery to me in ways I believe I am not to them. Ironically, I find dogs most readable whenever they pretend not to know what I want. But what joy it is when I get to witness a dog's determination to connect with me beyond tail wagging.

I relish the memory of a day when Jessie cleverly made up for my lack of physical coordination. Predictably, during a game of fetch, I had thrown her ball over a fence. As I went inside for a replacement, our neighbor came out on his porch. When I returned, he was laughing, and Jessie held the errant ball in her mouth. "I couldn't miss it," he told me, shaking his head. "She looked hard at me, and then down the fence. Then, hard at me and down the fence. She kept it up. She couldn't have done better if she'd yelled 'Hey dummy! Look where I'm pointing!'"

Once she'd gotten back her ball, Jessie's connection to the neighbor broke. I would've spent time apologizing, thanking him, offering bits of banal conversation to ease the shift from interacting to ignoring. Dogs would never do that, even if they could. They live in the present, and they keep their eye on the main thing, not obsessing over what to them are trifles. Apart from the rare OCD dog, trivial obsessions are human stumbling blocks. For a ball-driven dog, there is nothing insignificant about that little bouncy object. When it's available, it's the dog's *main thing*. But when Frank tossed a ball toward Jessie as she lunged for him, she barely glanced at it. Attacking him had become the main thing.

At Riverside dog park one afternoon, I encountered a sad example of fixating on what most people would regard as unimportant. The day was exceedingly hot. I was throwing for Jessie, and in between chases, she veered off to the water bucket to cool her burning feet. At home, she routinely stuck her paws in her water dish. During her lifetime, my kitchen floor could've hosted a variety of water sports. When I got another shepherd after she was gone, I had hopes of being able to cross my floor without galoshes. Nope. That floor will never be dry, not as long as there's a dog around to flood it.

As I reached for the ball with the Chuckit!, a woman in an apron came over to complain bitterly that she had emptied and refilled the water bucket eight times, only to watch Jessie return for a ninth foot bath. "It's not sanitary!" she wailed.

"What," I asked, as gently as I could, "would you like me to do?"

We stared at each other through half a minute of silence. Then I told her we were leaving.

For Jessie, dog parks provided the space to play fetch, but they aren't ideal for that game, which is almost as much of a nuisance for other dog owners as if I'd brought a prized toy for all the dogs to fight over. But Jessie couldn't spend two months lounging on the rug. She had to run, and in New York City there just wasn't anywhere else she could.

On one occasion at Riverside, a hound paced her, stride for stride, back and forth, as she retrieved. She tolerated it for a while, but that boy kept moving closer. Finally, she lifted her lip to tell him to shove off. That's all it took. He had no interest in her ball or her ball game. He wanted to fight. So, they did. Dog fights look scary, but luckily they rarely draw blood. It's more like a wrestling match than a fist fight.

The offending dog's owner dawdled before taking control of his animal. As he started to drag the ill-tempered cur away, Jessie turned around and nipped the dog's butt.

I couldn't stop myself from whispering "Good girl."

Toronto Redux

A year after our first Toronto sojourn, Charles got a second offer to teach math there, this time for two months in the summer. The trip across was uneventful except for one nearly devastating incident. We'd stopped somewhere in the Midwest, the only place we'd seen where it was possible to throw a ball—a huge vacant lot back from the road. The lot was severed by a deep pit I assumed held only dirt. Jessie had gone down there after the ball several times before I realized the pit reeked, and so did she, her long, thick fur embedded with gunk all the way up her legs and onto her chest and belly. I panicked. No way could we put her in the car in that condition. Even had we been stoic enough to tolerate the stench, she would plaster the car with whatever was issuing that foul smell.

Just as I began to fear we'd have to pull out clothes and sacrifice them to the task of wiping as much crap off her as we could, I saw a hose. It came out of a building that looked as if it had been deserted for a long while. No way could that hose be operational. It must've been shut off months before. But hope springs eternal and all that, so I walked her over to it, and turned the spigot. To my astonished relief, out flowed clean water.

Shades of the angel that rescued me above the Sequoia Bayview Trail—a last-minute reprieve from an unendurable ending.

We had found a house in The Danforth, an area of Toronto that's also called Greektown because its main street is lined with Greek restaurants. After we unpacked, I took Jessie for a walk and discovered Withrow, an off-leash dog park. The Danforth proved much more likeable than the neighborhood of our previous stay. The area was pleasant, full of large houses, some displaying Victorian architecture. Best of all, nothing stank.

The weather too helped brighten my mood. Toronto in the summer is an entirely different city. As a native of cold and foggy Julys and Augusts in San Francisco, I looked forward to real summer. What I hadn't thought of were summer thunderstorms. The first one drove Jessie into a panic. We were a quarter mile from home when it struck. She pulled me all the way back, flinging herself at our door like a battering ram. After that, I kept an eye on the weather forecast.

Jessie and I spent lots of time at Withrow, where I demonstrated the kind of athletic prowess that had caused me to hit a gardener in the head with Jessie's ball. This time my missile was a Kong, a large thick rubber bell with a rope attached. Dogs love it because it bounces erratically, like prey. Jessie and I were having a great game when the Kong went straight up instead of straight forward. It landed in a tree.

Kongs aren't cheap so I was determined to get it down. First, I tried leaping. Well, leaping doesn't quite describe my attempt to go airborne. Adding an eighth of an inch to my reach didn't give me much hope of putting my hand on the thing. It would be more fruitful, I decided, to find a downed tree limb and use that to make contact. With difficulty, I located a branch long enough and thick enough to do the job.

Perhaps it could have accomplished what I wanted had I been more in control of my swing, which inclined toward the wild side. As a child, I'd always floundered at the bat. I have a vivid memory of dashing home from a baseball game, shouting "Mommy! I hit the ball!"

"Good for you!" she said. "So, what did you do different?"

"I kept my eyes open."

My eyes were wide open as I stood under that Kong, sweating, and getting nowhere. Along came a man. A certain kind of man—and that's the kind I like to marry—wants to save any damsel in distress. He was that type of man. He took the branch from me and began whacking away. But he was having no more success than I'd had. After ten minutes, I grew embarrassed for him and suggested we give up. "It's only a Kong. I can get another."

Kongs have been problematic for me. At Point Isabel, when I had both Henry and Jessie, I always brought one to throw into the water for her to retrieve. When it was time to go home, I'd take it from her, leash up both dogs, and walk to the parking lot. At the truck, I'd lower the tailgate and

Jessie would jump in while I hefted Henry. To pick up Henry, I had to put down the Kong. Why I never put it on the truck bed escapes me, but I didn't. I'd lay it on the ground behind the truck. And drive away.

My parking space became a free Kong warehouse.

My kind stranger wasn't giving up, no matter what I said. For more than half an hour, he swatted ineffectually. The interesting thing was that another Kong hung in a different tree. Nice to know I wasn't the only klutz throwing Kongs into the canopy.

I directed my knight toward that tree. He went over, thwacked it, and we watched the second Kong tumble to the grass. For some reason, I never set that one on the ground and left it. They say the word "free" is the most attractive word in the English language. Maybe I valued my free Kong far more than the ones I paid for, because that one stayed with me for a good twenty years.

Living in Canada

While we were staying in Canada the second time, the math department at the University of Toronto offered Charles a part-time teaching position for two years. He'd retired from UC Berkeley the year before, but he wasn't ready to fully retire. I agreed, although the thought of moving to Canada unsettled me. I told myself change is a good thing. I told myself I'd be fine.

As we prepared for the move, Jessie stopped eating. My own uneasiness might have triggered anxiety in her, but dogs know when changes are in the wind. Not having any say in the matter, and not knowing what those changes will be, has to cause some anxiety.

For me as well. I didn't know what to expect of a long-term stay. I didn't know anyone in Toronto. What I knew about winter didn't lighten my mood. I feared being cooped up in a much smaller house, having no friends, and glimpsing the sun only occasionally.

By the time we climbed in the U-Haul truck to go back to Toronto, Jessie's ribs were prominent. Her eating didn't pick up on the trip. When we walked her around rest stops, people stared. They probably thought we starved her.

Once our furniture had been installed, I called all the utilities to start service. When I contacted Enbridge Gas, the agent put me on hold for what seemed a very long time. When she came back, she said, "Are you sure you have gas there?" Well, no, I wasn't sure. In fact, thinking about it, I realized there weren't any gas appliances. Before that, I hadn't known there were any houses on the continent without gas.

Our little row house had charm, but no heat other than weak electric heaters attached to the baseboards. That winter I spent a great deal of time dipping my hands into hot water. We decided the electric heaters had to go.

Workers came to run gas pipes into the house, after which a crew installed a gas furnace.

A thunderstorm was looming when I had to run some errands. I couldn't take Jessie. She'd freak. I talked to one of the installers.

"She'll go nuts when the storm comes in. It's okay, nothing to worry about. Just ignore her."

He nodded, and I went out. The storm rolled in, bringing booming thunder and brilliant flashes of lightning. I tried to finish up quickly so I could hurry back. The sun was out when I came in, drenched. I asked how Jessie had been.

"Huh?"

"The dog. Did she go crazy?"

He looked over at her. "She pretty much slept through it."

My turn to say "Huh?" The only difference I could think of was my absence. I thought back to a time my son and I were having a very loud argument. Jessie loved both of us, and I saw her confusion. She ran down to the basement. Maybe her reaction to thunderstorms was part of the same thing—she felt the pressure of not being able to protect me.

Jessie's eating picked up, and she put on weight. We did a lot of walking, which she loved. About a mile from our new house, I found another dog park. The walk along Bloor Street to get to it passed several shops. Canadian small business owners are friendly to dogs. The hardware store welcomed dogs. The guy behind the register loved her because when he gave her a treat, she took it from between his fingers without touching him with her teeth. One of the guys who worked there, a heavily tattooed young man, routinely got down on the floor with her.

At the bookstore, too, Jessie was welcome and given a treat. On one occasion, the clerk gave her a biscuit that resembled a fancy cookie. I remarked on it, and he said mournfully, "Yeah, the dogs are going to be disappointed when these run out."

I didn't say the dogs would not be disappointed, not as long as the bookstore continued to stock dog treats of any shape.

The gift shop kept treats too. The bank didn't, but they didn't mind her coming inside. Within a short time, Jessie was a well-known character on Bloor. Passersby sometimes asked if they could give her something. I thought if we stayed in Toronto too long, she might turn into a blimp.

Our front door had a mail slot. If I was out when the mail carrier came, I'd return to scattered envelopes pockmarked like old IBM punch cards. I remember wincing as my husband handed an usher a pair of liberally pierced tickets. Naturally, I thought of Maxi in Oregon, and the wag who waggled the envelopes in the slot.

Normally, when the mail arrived, I'd be upstairs working on my computer, oblivious to whatever was happening below, unless Jessie spotted a squirrel or a cat. I could tell by the intensity of her barking which species had dared to put in an appearance. That the cats insulted her most baffled me. She'd launch into typhoon-strength barking, and they would flee. The squirrels—targets of fierce barking that didn't, however, rise to the level of a cat invasion—stood up on their hind legs, peering complacently through the glass door, looking as if they'd never been more entertained. Sometimes, I swear, they chuckled.

On one occasion, I happened to be downstairs when the mail arrived. Jessie rushed toward the door. Remembering Maxi, I stopped to watch. An envelope nudged the slot open. Before the individual on the other side could push it in all the way, Jessie seized it, tossing it over her shoulder to get back into position for the next piece. After a moment of silence, I heard a soft, tentative knock on the door. The guy probably wasn't sure he wanted that door to open. But we exchanged friendly hellos. It was Canada, where the mail takes forever because postal workers are so amiable. (I relish my memory of a Canada Post employee delivering greeting cards to me while singing a round of "Happy Birthday.")

Visibly flummoxed, this man asked me, "Was that you?"

At that moment, Jessie poked her head around the door. His eyes widened. He muttered, "Oh. Sorry." When he got to the sidewalk, I watched him bend over, hiccupping laughter. He'd probably been wondering for some time what could possibly make a person yank their mail inside before he could let go of it.

One of my sweetest memories of a Jessie greeting came following a trip we'd made to Argentina. Coming back to Toronto in midwinter, we waited for a bus outside the terminal. I wasn't wearing a warm coat, and the temperature was in the low twenties.

We were the first to reach the bus stop, and we waited for a frigid twenty minutes. Many people came, moving in front of us. When a bus finally arrived, they boarded, the driver shut the door, and we were left on the sidewalk. I nearly bawled. Extreme cold gives me stomach cramps, and I began to feel sick.

When at last we reached the house, I went up to bed. Charles drove off to the kennel to collect Jessie. I'd almost fallen asleep when I heard the door open and close, followed by footsteps on the stairs. The bedroom door was open, so I had a clear view of the landing as Charles came up with Jessie. He told me afterward he'd never seen her so dejected. She showed none of her usual enthusiasm when she saw us after we'd been away.

It surprised me that her nose didn't tell her I was there—but I remembered Frank breaking into my house and Jessie not picking up his scent. Maybe she lacked some of the baseline 150 million canine scent glands. Anyway, not until they got to the top of the stairs did she see me. At that, she flung herself at me, sobbing in a way I'd never heard from her or any other dog. With her paws on either side of my head, she nuzzled my face. For a dog that had licked me only once in all our time together—looking, by the way, thoroughly disgusted afterward—this passionate show of her love was overwhelming. I wept. Her welcome home gift was the most intensely moving event of all my years with dogs, and right up near the top in all my years with people.

Our second year in Toronto we took Jessie up north for Christmas, staying in a small cabin that had a hot tub. The snow nearly reached the level of the deck, so plodding around in it was a chore for Jessie. But the owner had a German shepherd puppy that wanted to play with her. The puppy showed up at our door each morning and Jessie bounded out to join him, acting like a puppy herself. Even though I worried about the strain on her, I felt happy to see her exuberance. When we got back to Toronto, she spent a week sleeping.

The following Christmas we rented a house, again up north, but where we saw no other people or pets. I had packed Jessie's red snow boots. I remember coming out of our house in Toronto one November afternoon as a woman exited her car in front of our gate. She glanced over at us, and said, "Nice boots." I looked down. I was wearing sneakers. She said with feigned exasperation, "The dog, not you."

After we had set ourselves up in the vacation rental, Charles suggested a walk. I went upstairs to get Jessie's boots. For several seconds, I stood in the bedroom, puzzled, dog booties in my hand. I'd packed only two.

In Toronto, I came downstairs one morning to find no dog waiting. Jessie had been sleeping downstairs for about a year because it had gotten too difficult for her to mount our steep staircase. I sorely missed having her on her mat at the foot of our bed, but I liked her morning greeting following a night apart.

I called for her, but she didn't come. Then I saw blood. Seemingly everywhere. My heart in my throat, I stumbled down to the cellar where she lay on her side, panting.

"A bleeding ulcer," Dr. Salvador said. "Happens with these anti-inflammatory drugs. She's taking Metacam, right?"

Why hadn't I been warned this could happen?

"She'll be fine. She just needs to rest. You can pick her up tomorrow."

At home I went online to research bleeding ulcers and drugs. As he'd said, site after site discussed the link between the type of drug she took for pain and ulcerated stomachs. I kept reading throughout that day.

"Misoprostol," I told Dr. Salvador when we picked up Jessie. "Can you give me a prescription?"

"What for?"

"They say it guards against bleeding. She's got to have the Metacam, but I sure don't want this to happen again."

He shook his head. "I don't see how misoprostol can help."

I pressed him. Finally, with a shake of his head, he gave me the prescription. From that day to the end of her life, Jessie took misoprostol along with Metacam, and she never had another bleeding ulcer. I realize that when one event follows another, that doesn't prove or even imply a connection. After all, plenty of people drink coffee before getting in their cars to go to work, but coffee doesn't cause driving. Nevertheless, in the absence of evidence to the contrary, I'm convinced Jessie would've had another bleeding ulcer without misoprostol.

A few months after this, Jessie went down and couldn't get up without help. Dr. Salvador diagnosed a slipped disk. He said he could medicate her to keep her comfortable, but it probably wasn't worth doing surgery.

"For old dogs, you get problems with anesthesia."

Charles looked at me, and we spoke at the same time. "We want her to have the surgery."

The first step was to schedule an MRI, which meant she had to be sedated. The anesthesiologist came out after they'd scanned her.

"Are you sure this dog's eleven? Her vitals stayed rock solid throughout."

She was eleven going on twelve, but his words made us feel more positive about the upcoming surgery, which she sailed through as well. What she didn't sail through was being hospitalized. Dr. Salvador had encouraged me to visit her while she was recuperating.

"She'll have to stay with us for two or three days."

I told him I couldn't visit her. It would be too upsetting for both of us. He called the next morning to tell me how she was doing. I heard her loud screeching over the phone.

"You were right about not visiting. If she's like this with me, I can't imagine how she'd be with you. The staff here wants you to get her this afternoon. She didn't shut up all night."

He was chuckling, but the night crew probably saw nothing amusing about her behavior. We drove over to get her. She walked out of the clinic and into the car. Our parking space in the alleyway behind our house was some distance from our gate, but she hobbled all the way. Not until we reached the back door did she let herself collapse.

For a few days, she rested. Apart from having a reverse mohawk—with a bald alley down her back—she looked good. When I took her out for her Bloor Street walk, strangers came up to me to say how much better she was walking. I was startled to think how many people had noticed her difficulty and cared enough to tell me of their relief over her recovery.

As we came up to the door at the hardware store, her favorite treat dispensary, she turned to look at me, clearly wanting to go inside. I smiled and said, "Don't need hardware today, Jessie." Her eyes twinkled, and her mouth widened. I'm sure she laughed.

By the fourth year in Toronto (well beyond the original two), Jessie's physical problems were mounting. Our walks were shorter, and I restricted her ball chasing a bit. One wintry day on Bloor, two lovely Japanese tourists, their long jet-black hair topped by magnificent white fur hats, stopped us. In lilting English, one asked if she could pet Jessie. She crouched in the snow to stroke Jessie's neck. After a moment, she bent down to whisper in that perfectly erect ear, "Have a long and happy life, Jessie!"

Tears sprang into my eyes. It was becoming clear that Jessie's life wasn't going to be a whole lot longer.

The worst day of Jessie's life and one of the worst of mine happened in Toronto on a day I met a friend for coffee. On the sidewalk, I tied Jessie to the iron fence that separated our patio table from where she lay, close enough that I could reach through the fence to stroke her. As she aged, she slept hard and often, and soon she drifted off.

As I chatted with my friend, I didn't at first notice a little boy weaving along the sidewalk on his bicycle. The training wheels must've been just removed because he wobbled badly, barely managing to keep the bike upright.

I watched fear contort his face as he spotted Jessie. Although she lay a good six feet away from him, panic drove him straight into her. His bike slammed down across her back, and he, trapped in the bike and on her body, stamped his feet, screaming. Jessie woke to what had to be unbelievable pain and shock. She bit him on his thigh, twice.

His parents snatched him up and called for EMTs and the police. I was too upset to clearly grasp what was happening. I was concerned for the child, but he didn't appear seriously injured, just rather vociferously hurt. What terrified me was the possibility that he might have inflicted severe damage on Jessie. Her hips, by then, were audibly scraping bone.

What else would my poor dog have to suffer through?

The EMTs pulled up the boy's trouser leg, and I went over to look. Jessie had not broken the skin. Even in agony, even cruelly awakened to what had to be incredibly confusing for her, she had restrained herself. Teeth that crushed three thick raw chicken legs in seconds every morning hadn't cut into his flesh. The sole evidence of what she'd done to him were two sets of semicircular indentations.

Protection training had instilled in her a respect for biting so absolute, even in shock and excruciating pain, she didn't forget that she wasn't supposed to bite except to protect me. The two nips she inflicted were out of her mouth, so to speak, before she was fully conscious.

Even so, the parents, the EMTs, and the police blamed Jessie.

But eight customers at the café came over to give me a card or a slip of paper on which their names and phone numbers appeared.

"Saw the whole thing," each of them said. "If you need a witness, call."

The thought that Toronto Animal Control might want to euthanize Jessie made me nearly hysterical. Two days later an official called me to demand she be quarantined for a month. I squawked like an angry parrot.

"I can't keep her in for that long. She's got arthritis. She has to exercise, or it's going to get much worse."

"Sorry. But she bit someone, and now she must be quarantined."

"Look. I have her rabies certificate. Why doesn't that mean there's no problem?"

"It's the law."

"Well, screw the law," I said. "She didn't do anything wrong, and I won't punish her for the stupidity that put a little kid on a busy public street to learn how to ride a bike."

"If your dog is seen off your property, she'll be taken in."

I slammed the phone down. After a while, when my temperature had fallen a few hundred degrees, it came to me that there was no way Jessie could be "seen" off our property. What? Would they have her photograph posted in every police station? A "Ten Most Wanted Dogs" poster? Toronto is a city of nearly three million people, about half of whom own a dog or two. Some of those dogs had to look like Jessie.

The man who insisted I quarantine her couldn't have had any confidence in my compliance with the law, nor, I suspect, did he much care. He'd simply followed established bureaucratic procedures, the source of so much misery in life.

As Jessie approached the age of thirteen, our relationship changed. Cataracts turned her beautiful eyes milky. Her intense enthusiasm for everything waned. She began to feel vulnerable, which hit me hard when she barked at a passing dog that hadn't even glanced at her.

Old age, it's said, is when a person accesses 90 percent of the medical care she needs in her lifetime. The same happens with dogs. I was keeping the Pill Pocket people in business, administering dozens of nutraceuticals that promised to ease Jessie's joint pain and keep her mobile. She still chased a ball—although I made my throws shorter and cut off our sessions quicker—because I felt sure her life without a ball to chase wasn't worth living. Once, in the alleyway behind our house, she spotted a neighbor's dog playing fetch. Jessie, leashed, let out a cry that tore me apart. The neighbor insisted my girl wanted to hurt her dog. In vain, I said no, she just wanted that ball.

Around that time, we investigated stem cell implants that might renew the cartilage in her joints. The procedure was still experimental, but if it would give her some freedom from a body that steadily dragged her down, we were ready to try it. Unfortunately, the X-rays showed her hip dysplasia was so severe that there was no path to insert the needle.

The biggest blow came shortly after this. She was diagnosed with degenerative myelopathy of the spine. Slowly and inexorably, the myelopathy would take away her control over her back legs. Neither cure nor treatment was available. As of this writing, there is still no cure. The disease is painless but deadly. German shepherds, among other large breeds, are prone to it. Ethical breeders now DNA test their dogs to avoid breeding carrier dogs.

I was determined to give Jessie (and us) as many more months as I could, and to make those months sweet for her as well as for Charles and me. I made weekly appointments for water therapy, in which she stood on a treadmill in a tank of water. This increased or at least maintained some muscle tone while minimizing pain caused by dysplasia. Jessie disliked the exercises. I suppose they bored her. She tried to figure out a way around the treadmill's insistence that she walk forward aimlessly, and she did figure it out. She discovered that, by placing her feet to either side of the treadmill to rest on the thin edges, she could stop walking. The tech had to rig up ropes that kept Jessie in place. As she rigged them, the tech was laughing. "I've never had a dog figure that out."

I also found a source of infrared treatments and acupuncture. Probably a waste of time and money, given the nature of her affliction, but I felt I had to fight for her. I had to give her every chance to live more comfortably.

Once or twice a week, I took her to a doggy swimming pool. I'd throw in a rubber toy, and she'd swim after it. Whenever Jessie got the toy, she would swim back to her base, and hover at the shallow end, gnawing on the rubber. Unless I could think of a way to keep her from getting hold of the toy, she wouldn't get the exercise I wanted her to have. My solution was to tie a long piece of string around the rubber duck's neck; whenever Jessie got close to it, I yanked it out. The rules of the pool mandated she wear a life jacket, which the staff provided. One Velcro strap on her life jacket had lost its adhesive surface and hung limp on her chest. My poor baby got so frustrated she clamped her teeth down on the hanging strap. She would have some oral satisfaction from all that swimming.

I thought of Henry's end, and I knew this wasn't Jessie's situation. She had a life worth living, one she took pleasure in every day. Knowing that kept me from feeling unconscionably selfish about all I was putting her through.

Losing Jessie

We left Toronto to move to Evanston, Illinois, where Charles had been offered a part-time position at Northwestern. The trip was traumatic. By then, Jessie's back legs were only minimally functional. We used a sling under her to hold her up to potty. I had to lift her from the car at rest stops, and I too was thirteen years older. We waddled across the grass with me urging her to "do a hurry up," our code for "squat and do your business." But she wouldn't. Probably it was her pride refusing the indignity of the sling.

The house we rented in Evanston had three stories and steps up to the first floor. Jessie had to be carried down to the street and up to the ground floor. The sling wasn't getting us anywhere, so we decided to buy a wheelchair for her.

The instructions that came with the chair warned that the dog would push backward at first. No way. As soon as we got her hitched into it, she took off. We were far more challenged by it than she was. In the beginning, it took us about forty minutes to get her into the contraption and get all the straps in the correct configuration. Then we had to jointly carry her and the chair down to ground level where we could walk. Those walks were among the sweetest we ever took with her, so conscious were we that her time with us was drawing to a close.

In the morning, we'd go out together for a long stroll. Then, at noon, Charles would come home from the university to take another walk. In the evening, we'd take her to a nearby park, where we'd stockpiled sticks to throw for her. The first time we did this, she and the wheelchair toppled from a short ledge. She kicked and thrashed as we ran over to right her. After that, whenever she fell, she waited patiently for us to fix the problem.

On one occasion, she saw another dog chasing a ball she wanted to snag. She took off, with me panting after her. I caught her just as she was about to snatch his ball. Bringing her back, I said to Charles, "What does it mean when I can't catch a dog in a wheelchair?"

He smiled. "It means she still has more gas in her engine than you do."

In the house, Jessie pulled herself along the floor with her muscular front legs. The landlord's youngest daughter, a darling six-year-old, showed up almost every afternoon to ask, "Can I come in and touch Jessie?" Jessie, having already heard the little girl, was pulling herself toward the door to be "touched."

We'd been in Evanston for three months when Thanksgiving arrived. Several members of Charles's family joined us that year. Our landlords were going away and asked us to keep their little dog, Coco. That wasn't a problem. Coco was an adorable moppet. He'd been purchased from a pet store, something no one would risk if they'd investigated the source of pet store dogs. The bulk of those dogs come from canine factory farms, otherwise known as puppy mills, run by breeders who couldn't care less about the miserable quality of life suffered by their dogs. Puppies provided by them often end up costing loving owners thousands of dollars in medical bills for congenital disorders.

Coco was a clear exception. Not only was he smart, but he was also agile in the extreme, acrobatically kicking his back legs up and over his head every time he peed. He was friendly too, rarely barked, and never nipped. Nevertheless, stable as he was at home and familiar as he was with me, nine strangers, none of whom were his owners, made him tremble and pace and whine. He needed help to settle.

Recalling a TV dog trainer in Toronto who advocated a practice he called "umbilical," I leashed Coco to my belt. From there, I gave my attention to cooking. Coco had to keep his eyes on me to avoid being jerked back and forth as I prepared our dinner. Focusing on me distracted him from his fears. As soon as I hooked him up, he ceased whining. After an hour tied to me, he was calm, so I let him go. He ran off to wow the crowd and get some caresses in before dinner. From then on, he was a delightful house guest.

Meanwhile, Jessie's condition had worsened.

After Charles's family went home two days after Thanksgiving, we contacted Dr. Reinhardt, a mobile vet. The morning of the day he was coming, we strapped Jessie into her wheelchair for the last time.

As we took her for that final walk, a neighbor, walking her dog, called out, "How's she doing?" Choking back tears, I told her this was Jessie's last day. She said something I barely heard. But I knew she understood our pain.

At home I took six pounds of hamburger out and fed them to Jessie. Then I started giving her all the treats in the house. She kept eating, which was sweet and bittersweet. If she could eat and walk in her wheelchair, couldn't she go on living? But she couldn't. The paralysis had advanced and the vet urged us to let her go.

Dr. Reinhardt came too soon. Coming at all was too soon for me. We ushered him in and led him to our girl, who lay unmoving on a plastic sheet. He stooped to say a gentle hello to her, and to run his fingers through her coat before administering the first shot. As with Henry, Jessie's strong heart kept beating. I leaned down to kiss her face while he slipped a second dose into her leg.

As she died, something brushed my cheek, and I knew that was her indomitable spirit, leaving me.

Vela

Pictured on a website for a kennel in the mountains of New Mexico, Vela was a long-haired, red-and-black pup, nine months old. Her face didn't look like Jessie's face, and her body looked somewhat rangy, but she was a beautiful dog. I fell in love with her photograph, largely because she had lovely eyes and her coat reminded me of Jessie's.

The warning signs—surprise, surprise—were clear to anyone bright enough to heed them. The breeder didn't know if Vela was house-trained. She advised me not to feed Vela on Sundays because fast growth in a German shepherd creates joint problems. Having imported the dog from Germany, she knew little about her. All this should've given me pause, especially the part about her having been imported.

In my defense, I hadn't been totally imprudent. The breeder had excellent reviews all over the web. I could find no bad reviews, and so decided she must be okay. Any philosophy major would've told me what was wrong with that logic.

Sometime after I got Vela, I read that the breeder had been sued by a woman whose German shepherd bitch ate her puppies, a story the aggrieved buyer posted on the internet. The breeder countersued for defamation and won. The absence of critical reviews alone should've given me pause—under the rubric that if everybody likes someone, there has to be something wrong with her. Nobody pleases everybody. This is especially true for those dealing with the public.

At the time, Charles and I were living in Evanston, and driving to New Mexico for the puppy would've involved massive complications and delays. Instead, I agreed that the breeder could crate her and ship her to O'Hare.

It took us a while to find Vela at the airport. When we did, her crate was standing in a warehouse doorway, no one within a hundred feet of her. Had it been a hot day, she would've died. That couldn't be charged against the breeder, but I wondered who would've rescued her had we been in a car accident on our way to the airport?

When I opened the crate, I saw a cringing emaciated dog. Gently, I coaxed her out, growing increasingly indignant as her poor condition became more and more apparent.

"It wasn't only on Sunday she starved this dog," I told Charles. Vela looked like a furry xylophone.

I felt sure she hadn't been beaten because she wasn't hand shy. But I was more than certain she'd suffered neglect and deprivation. I knew the breeder's rationale for starving Vela, although I don't know if that was her only motive. It's true enough that German shepherd puppies should not be overfed. Too much weight on soft bones can lead to joint problems later on. But under-nourishing a puppy causes its own damage. I hope the pennies the breeder saved on Vela's kibble paid for better overall conditions at her kennel.

We wedged the crate into the backseat of our Maxima, leaving approximately eight inches for me to cram in next to her. I'd brought treats. Every time she stopped whimpering, I fed her one. By the time we were halfway home, she was quiet. I kept feeding her.

When we got her in the house, we discovered she was infested with scores of ticks. In the mountains of New Mexico, ticks abound, and apparently so do jerks who think letting ticks feed on a dog is preferable to using a chemical to get rid of them. If she didn't like to use pesticides, the breeder—whom I was close to hating at that point—should've at least pulled the bloodsuckers out. It took us hours, working together, to get them all.

At home I filled Vela's bowl with fresh hamburger. She hung over it, swaying a bit, looking queasy. Then she turned away. *Reasonable*, I thought. She'd had a rough day. Her appetite probably vanished from the trauma of the flight—although she'd gobbled treats by the handful. What didn't occur to me was that Vela did not like raw meat.

Unfortunately, I had a meeting to go to on her first evening with us. I was gone two hours and came home to a frantic Charles. Vela leapt at me as if she were drowning and I was a lifeguard.

"She started screaming the second you left—literally screaming. The only way I could get her to stop was to walk her outside the whole time."

"That was smart."

"Why didn't you answer your phone?"

"I had to turn it off, honey. It's rude to have your cell ring in a meeting."

"Well, for once, I wish you'd been rude."

Vela's behavior was intolerable on walks. She exploded when she caught sight of another dog. Moreover, nearly everything in our house spooked her: the stairs, the kitchen, the noises from next door. Strangely, after the trauma she'd just experienced flying in her crate, she felt more comfortable there. When I wanted respite from feeling sorry for her and angry at the breeder, I'd kennel her for an hour. Finally, feeding her wasn't going well. She wouldn't eat most of what I gave her. If the breeder hadn't suggested fasting her every Sunday, I'd have revised my opinion of the source of Vela's scrawniness. What little she did eat led to diarrhea or pudding-like stools.

The vet looked her over and said, "I wouldn't mind coming home to this dog every night." Her low weight concerned him, but he declared her otherwise healthy.

What most depressed me was the unlikelihood of my living long enough to adopt another German shepherd after Vela. But I sure didn't want this dog to be my last. The comparison between Jessie and Vela devastated me, a trip from the sublime to the subprime. I obsessed over whether her environment had caused Vela's weaknesses, or whether those were inherent in her breeding, and, therefore, potentially unfixable.

What I acknowledged to myself was my part in this mess. Once again, I'd leapt without looking. Swept away warning signs. Taken onto myself thoroughly misplaced confidence. I could fix anything, couldn't I? Oh, for a smidgen of shrewdness in lieu of this abundance of impulsivity! What on earth was holding up delivery of my share of venerable wisdom?

Superficial similarities between Vela and Jessie had lured me into assuming—without admitting, even to myself, that I had assumed as much—that poor Vela could be my next Jessie. All the two shepherds had in common was a long red and black coat.

Vela looked like what she was, a German reject whose long legs ended in paws slewed like duck feet, and a veritable pothole at the base of her spine.

Of the three of us—Vela, the breeder, and me—only Vela was innocent, and only Vela had been victimized.

After wallowing in self-pity for two weeks, I pulled myself together. Whatever I could do to make Vela's life work for both of us, I was determined to do.

While she was a sweetheart in some ways, Vela was also pig-headed. Before she got to Chicago, we put down gravel in a corner of the yard where we wanted her to relieve herself. Each time I took her over, she wouldn't squat. I crated her and waited an hour. Took her out again, but no dice. Another hour. Took her there once more. Nada. Another hour, again. Again nothing. And again, throughout that day.

She never did use the gravel. Vela was the first and the only dog I had that rejected *dry* pea gravel. All my dogs have hated gravel when it rains. In Toronto we had installed a run in a narrow patch between the house and the fence. Since there were no windows and the space had no use other than for a dog run, we figured it would work perfectly. Mostly, it did. However, let the rocks get the slightest bit wet, and we had to keep an eye on Jessie after sending her out, or she'd squat on the herringbone brick patio. Some dog quirks are as hard to crack as safes.

Vela's stubbornness included food. Whenever I placed a bowl of fresh meat in front of her, she turned away. She would've preferred Welsh rarebit, I suppose. But I kept offering raw meat: chicken, pork, beef, meaty bones, liver, even ground bison. Cats may starve if they don't get what they want, but I felt confident (with no data supporting that confidence, mind you) that when she got hungry enough she'd eat. She skipped meal after meal. When at last she did accept something on offer, she ate as if it were full of thorns, and she stayed skinny.

I gave in, filled her bowl with kibble, and those accordion ribs eventually sank below a sleek layer of fat.

Vela

What became crucial to address was her dog aggression. Another dog—across the street, down the street, on a balcony—transformed Vela from mild-mannered Dr. Jekyll into fiendish Mr. Hyde. Several times she nearly pulled me to the sidewalk.

Of course I had a theory. For months she'd lived in the mountains with a pack of adult German shepherds. Knowing dogs can be bullies, especially in a pack, I figured those shepherds had tormented puppy Vela. The breeder, who overlooked a glut of ticks and a skeletal body, who didn't even know if the dog she was selling was house-trained—that woman would not have noticed a pup needing help.

But I had no clue how to rehabilitate this quaking dog.

Google proved unhelpful. The ubiquitous suggestion was—duh—*find a trainer.* Other advice ranged from turn her around, walk in a circle, distract her with treats, never offer treats because they would reinforce bad behavior, and put her through a playbook of obedience commands. The dumbest idea was to anticipate her reactivity before it took over. Spotting a dog before Vela spotted it wasn't going to happen, at least not consistently. She had her nose. I had my cataracts.

And the only time Vela rejected a treat was when she was fully submerged in her boiling hatred of dogs. Our denial of our inability to fix her problem on our own crashed into reality when Charles and I decided to attend a community fair downtown. We'd made it all the way to the booths without encountering another dog. As we sauntered down the walkway between pottery displays, bad paintings, and overpriced earrings, Vela caught sight of a tiny dog.

And went berserk.

I felt every pair of eyes turning toward us, every person condemning us. We fled, wrestling a wild animal. Ten million dogs populated formerly canine-devoid streets. Vela had it in for every one of them.

I couldn't live this way, and neither could she.

As with Henry, I found it easy to find classes in sit and stay, not so easy to find classes in "please don't get hysterical whenever you see another dog." I didn't see the point of attending a class in what Vela had already mastered, so I searched for trainers who claimed to handle aggression. Most of the approaches seemed wrong for Vela. At last, I found a website for a doggy bootcamp run by a man who rehabilitated pit bulls that had been thrown into fighting rings. He also took in troubled dogs of all breeds and cross-breeds. I figured a fighting–pit bull reformer would find our shy Vela a piece of cake.

His training facility was miles away, but he held weekly obedience classes at a nearby neighborhood house. We decided to take Vela to a sit-and-stay session, so we could see what we thought of this guy. It was risky, given her vitriol, but what did we have to lose? If she pitched a fit, we'd see how the trainer reacted to her bad behavior.

Nevertheless, we braced ourselves for a humiliating experience. With our teeth clenched, we leashed her up and inched forward into the building where a dozen dogs were tolerating one another quite nicely. As we entered the lobby, anticipating Vela's meltdown, she began to issue low growls at the dogs swarming around us. Even so, she didn't, as we expected, hurl herself at them in a frenzy. The offending dogs ignored her.

All the while we were waiting for the time bomb we'd brought to this obedience class to go off. I prayed we'd get started soon so I could get a sense of Jeff, the trainer, before Vela upended the evening. But of all the horrible scenarios we dreaded, what she actually did astonished us.

Vela was the class's star pupil.

So much for the axiom that human tension invariably spreads to the dog.

As Jeff issued commands and directives on how to get the dogs to comply with those commands, Vela sat, stood, lay down, and heeled exactly as I asked her to. A Mensa scholar explaining quantum mechanics while playing Chopin on the piano had nothing on our dog that night.

Jeff came over and said the obvious. "Looks like she already knows every-thing I'm going to cover. May I?" He held out his hand for her leash.

As he walked her into the center of the room, Vela gave those novice dogs a demonstration of elegant conduct. Jeff heeled her past every dog there, close enough for an exchange of wafting fur. Vela didn't so much as lift a lip.

I didn't know whether to rejoice or be furious. If she could remain calm in a room full of dogs, why couldn't she do the same thing on a walk? Would Jeff even believe this stellar dog could act as we were going to tell him she did?

When the time came, we explained that the compliant Dr. Jekyll who attended his class, the one who had practically led the other dogs in a round of "Kumbaya," became Mr. Hyde at the sight of another dog. As we chatted, Vela tired of all that good behavior. She didn't go into full metal jacket, but she was amping up. We got out of there before her disguise crumbled.

The following week, I drove to Vernon Hills to Jeff's impressive dog reformatory.

"I've got some dogs in the exercise yard." He took Vela's leash. "Let's see how she does. You stay here."

I knew what that meant. He thought I was the problem, and no wonder, given Vela's performance in class. Which almost made me hope Vela would show him how horrid she could be. Half an hour later, he brought her out.

"Take a look."

He showed me a video. Vela at first stood close to him, her tail tucked. He told her to sit and she sat. A large white pit bull lumbered over and sat down next to her. He didn't look at her, and she didn't look at him. After a few minutes, Jeff unhooked Vela's leash, and she dashed out to play, just as if she'd spent her life frolicking with strange dogs.

Vela stayed with Jeff for a month. Once a week, I drove up and trained with her. At playtime, I'd go back to the recreation yard and watch her merrily join the other dogs. In my view, Jeff was a miracle worker.

I watched him rehabilitate a pit bull that hated bicycles the way Vela hated dogs. The two women who owned him weren't strong, so he'd broken away from the leash more than once when he saw a bike. The women didn't know whether they were more frightened about the possibility he'd be run over or the possibility he would catch up to a cyclist and maul them.

Jeff took the pit bull and walked him while rolling a bike. After three minutes of that, he climbed on the bike and pedaled forward. The dog loped along next to him.

Length of time to improved pit bull behavior: five minutes.

Length of time to improve Vela's tolerance of dogs: five minutes.

I am not naïve enough to believe that pit's owners could take him home and all would be well. Watching Jeff, I thought of Avery driving my Acura while Henry watched her in the mirror, disinclined to launch into one of his operettas. Projecting authority works. That was Jeff's magic as well as Avery's. Jeff knew the pit bull would do what he asked of him.

When I collected Vela after the month ended, Jeff urged me to be protective of her, to put myself between her and any dog that was getting pushy or any dog she seemed wary of. He stressed that she needed her confidence built up.

Adhering to Jeff's advice caused friction with Charles. He's a laissez-faire nurturer. Whenever I intervened as some dog sought to bully Vela or whenever she looked tense, Charles gave me a look.

And I would tell him where he could put his disapproval. No way was I going to throw away the progress Jeff had made with her.

Before we left boot camp for the last time, Jeff had invited me to watch Schutzhund training in the play yard. In Schutzhund, a dog earns points for executing a variety of maneuvers, not least of which is trapping a "bad guy" in a teepee. When the dog successfully attacks, he's given the padded sleeve as a reward. Which I thought a bad idea for developing a protective instinct. I imagined Jessie tearing off the sleeve of an attacker's shirt and prancing away with it.

But Schutzhund isn't about protection. It's a competition.

Vela wasn't invited to observe with me. Having parked in deep shade, I opened the sunroof and lowered all the windows a quarter of the way down. I figured she'd be cool enough for the fifteen minutes I would be away from her.

Three minutes later, one of Jeff's assistants came running to the back. "Your dog's wandering around the parking lot. I think she's looking for you."

As I led Vela back to the Maxima, a woman asked me, "How on earth did she get out of the car?"

I said, "She probably climbed out through the sunroof."

"She did!" her little boy burst out. His eyes like saucers, he added, "I saw her!"

When the Schutzhund class ended, Jeff told me to bring Vela to the play yard where the class had been held. He thought she had more moxie in her than we'd suspected. I was dubious, but I brought her out. The Schutzhund trainer slapped the ground next to her with a long piece of leather. Vela barely noticed. She focused on the large number of people sitting around the yard watching her. I could see they made her anxious. And I could see he wasn't going to get anything out of her. Finally, he gave her back to me with a look of disdain.

Years later, Vela reenacted her feat from that day. Charles and I were attending an outdoor dinner at a winery near our cabin. We'd brought her along but left her in the car with the sunroof and windows cracked. The evening was warm, but far from hot.

As I sipped a buttery chardonnay, my eye fell on a dog that looked a lot like Vela. Dogs in attendance at winery events were not uncommon. The owners were dog lovers and, in fact, had their own German shepherd.

But the look-alike wasn't a look-alike. It *was* Vela. Charles took her back to the car, adjusting the sunroof just enough to ensure a decent flow of air, but not enough, he thought, for another escape. A few seconds after we sat down to eat, I felt a dog nose my leg.

"Impossible!" Charles insisted. "She couldn't have gotten out. I only opened the sunroof a few inches."

I smiled and reached down to pet her. "And yet," I said, "here she is."

When we lived in Evanston and Vela was still a puppy, I often walked her down to the dog beach at Lake Michigan. She loved to wade and, even more, to plop herself down to cool off while peacefully looking around. From time to time, she'd rise up and leap into the air, water exploding from her fur. In the sun, those droplets glittered like diamonds.

These outings were somewhat of a sacrifice for me since her fur collected acres of sand. The dog beach officials provided a hose at the gate, excellent for removing sand from a short-haired dog, but ineffectual on Vela's long, thick coat. At home, it took me the better part of forty-five minutes, awkwardly bending over her, to cull the beach out of the dog.

Nevertheless, I couldn't have sacrificed the joy we both got from those beach romps. I have photos of her at Lake Michigan, trailing a pack of galloping dogs. When she ran, I'd watch in fascination. Her form was classier than that of any of the dogs she trailed. But she always trailed. Loping along, Vela looked as elegant as a thoroughbred, but she was one of the slowest dogs I've ever seen. She didn't care.

She also didn't care that other dogs ignored her. At every dog park I took her to over the years, she developed a passionate unrequited crush. At the Oakland dog park, she worshipped a Formosan mountain dog named Ginzu. From his point of view, Vela's adoration was nothing but a nuisance. He got cranky whenever she distracted him from his romps with the dogs he liked. At the dog park in Evanston, she fixated on Sarabel, a poodle, who for years had been in a monogamous relationship with Kodiak, a husky. Every time Vela spotted Sarabel at the gate, she raced toward her. When Sarabel and Kodiak began to chase each other, Vela pursued them, barking incessantly. Neither of them ever noticed her, and she never quit chasing them until they left or we did.

Unless she sighted a squirrel. For that, Vela would desert an idol. She was a patient hunter, sitting at the base of a tree for the entire hour I sat on a bench, hoping she'd get some aerobic exercise. If the squirrel didn't move, neither did she.

Too bad squirrels can't be trained to run on demand.

Vela never did figure out how to play with other dogs. While Henry thought humping would lead to satisfactory interaction, Vela relied on barking. She was never going to be the belle of the park. Whenever she expressed love for a dog that spurned her, I thought of the woman "in the helping professions" at Ohlone Park. Like her, I found it difficult not to see rejections from my own childhood in those Vela experienced. To my credit, I never did scream at an aloof dog, "You can't talk to my girl that way, you bitch!"

After her rehabilitation, Vela just avoided any dog she didn't like. If she couldn't, I was her backup. On one occasion that cost me years of a sore thumb, a rottweiler pursued her, and to get away from him, she hid behind me. That didn't work. I was seated on a log, which he circumnavigated. I turned around awkwardly to yank him off her. When I did, I hyperextended my thumb. It took years before it stopped aching.

In Evanston, a volunteer for the SPCA frequently brought a huge German shepherd named Morgan to the park. No one spoke to her about it, as we should've, because that shepherd, weighing over a hundred pounds, was aggressive. On more than one occasion, he looked for trouble, although he hadn't bitten another dog—yet. One day Vela rose to the top of his target list. At seventy pounds, she was no match for him. Without warning, Morgan hurled himself at her, crashing into her with such force, she shrieked. I rushed over and put myself between him and Vela, yelling, "Get away!" I was terrified that Jeff's work had been demolished. Drawing Vela close, I stroked her until she stopped shaking, at which point I was about to take her home.

Vela had other ideas, trotting back out into the roiling pack to find a likeable dog to bark at.

When I had Jessie, I had longed to involve her in activities beyond protection workouts. In particular, I wished she could herd sheep and participate in agility classes. Neither were readily available when she was young enough to benefit from them. Now I looked for an agility class for Vela, believing the more exposure she had to new places, people, and dogs, the better.

After Jeff, Vela liked almost all friendly dogs, but she took an intense dislike to malamutes. I couldn't figure it out. It couldn't have been the size of the dog because she showed no concern over other massive breeds. And it couldn't have been the face mask because she had no such reaction to

Kodiak's face. At the agility class, Vela spotted Poppy, a malamute, and flew into a rage. Poppy, bless her, ignored her, but we couldn't redirect Vela. As we made the rounds of the equipment, every time she caught sight of Poppy, Vela barked and lunged.

At the dog beach a few weeks later, Vela spotted another malamute. He was in the water, his owners supporting him on either side. I thought it a touching scene, that mammoth dog held aloft by two people who loved him and wanted him to experience the pleasure of swimming.

Vela didn't see it that way, and she waded out to tell him so. We went home.

After completing the group agility lessons, I enrolled her in private tutoring. She liked private sessions better because she monopolized all the attention and ate all the treats. She did okay but would never be a competitor—not that I had any interest in taking her around the state or investing time in strenuous daily bouts of training. We were just having fun.

Whenever she navigated the weave poles, Vela tried to skip a pole or two. I'd watched in amazement the blur of various border collies threading weave poles at dizzying speeds. It was unlikely anyone would ever admire Vela's weaving expertise. Like her running, she moved slowly, moseying after me as I held a treat in front of her nose.

In the group lessons, the equipment had been minimal. The private trainer, Sarah, had everything. She was a serious agility competitor with a couple of well-trained dogs she occasionally brought in for demonstration.

She began Vela's instruction on the teeter-totter by kneeling at one end while feeding Vela treats as she lowered the board until it produced a soft thud. More treats. We'd be lucky to finish these sessions before Vela weighed ninety pounds. Very slowly, Sarah increased the intensity of the plank slapping the floor, finally producing the explosive racket a big dog makes on the descent. After that, Sarah encouraged Vela to put her paw on the board and press down. In no time, Vela was happily banging that board against the floor all on her own. Like a rambunctious kid, she seemed to delight in the commotion.

With a treat, Sarah lured her, bit by bit, up the ramp. In no time, Vela ascended and descended jubilantly. Sarah's job now was to slow her down so she didn't hit the end with enough force to potentially injure her hips. But that wasn't happening. Each time Vela mounted the board, she moved with more speed than she'd ever shown.

Vela

A mattress, probably eight feet tall, stood against the wall near the tee-ter-totter. Something must've jarred it, and it fell, landing right in front of Vela, who jumped back, and then immediately trotted forward to sniff at it.

Sarah nodded approval. "That shows her excellent breeding."

My question answered, perhaps. Vela's awful experience at the hands of the New Mexico breeder could've provoked her shyness, her fear of dogs, the overall instability we witnessed in our first months with her. She'd been shipped here from Germany, presumably because her conformation defects prevented her being a registered shepherd. Selling her in the EU would've been difficult. The Verein für Deutsche Schäferhunde (SV) is the Society for German Shepherd Dogs founded by Max von Stephanitz, and his colleague, Arthur Meyer, in 1899. The SV registers puppies from licensed parents. To get an SV license to breed, each German shepherd must meet breed standards, which exclude, together with malformation, dogs that bite and/or are skittish or timid. A German breeder may crank out impaired dogs, but he can't register them, so they won't be worth much in Germany. These excluded dogs are often shipped to the US to be sold by breeders with less interest in improving the American German shepherd.

In the US, German shepherds with health or temperament defects are registered without question and sold for whatever the clientele is willing to pay. Anyone, whether knowledgeable and ethical or simply greedy, can register any litter, as long as the sire and dam have AKC papers, which are as easy to get as sand from a beach. Even worse, whenever a gullible customer gets scammed by an unethical breeder—with consequences far worse than I have suffered—the AKC isn't on the consumer's side. Breeders, not buyers, pay the AKC's bills. The organization, shamefully, has even lobbied Congress against bills outlawing puppy mills!

In the US, money makes the dog world go round.

Given her physical flaws, it seemed entirely possible that Vela had come from stable parents, in which case she might develop into the solid German shepherd she was meant to be.

Except for the damned barking.

That was the worst of Vela's misdemeanors. Her stubbornness was annoying, but also amusing. Her compulsive licking—well, that was just annoying. No human nor canine within reach easily escaped Vela's tongue. She wielded it with the fanaticism of a stalker, convinced every complaint harbored an intense desire to be licked some more.

Her barking, however, drove me mad. She barked in the car for however long I was away from it. (Admittedly, I regarded this as an improvement—albeit still plenty irritating—on Henry barking only when I was *in* the car.) She barked nonstop whenever I abandoned her (as she regarded it) at home. She barked the entire time we were at the dog park, unless she'd volunteered for squirrel-ogling duty. At the beach, she barked. At home, if anything breathed on the street, she barked.

In the first two years of having her, while we were still living in Evanston, whenever I left her at home, Vela raided the winter basket I kept near the door to the garage. She'd take out all my wool scarves, every mitten, and each of my knitted beanies. Making a nest, she'd settle down in it and watch the door. Barking.

For a time, I took her to doggy day care once a week, hoping to strengthen her self-confidence by spending time with dogs away from me. Each time, she seemed eager to go. But, one day, when I picked her up, I noticed a deep indentation around her muzzle.

"What's this?"

The attendant glanced up and smiled. "Oh, that," she said, waving her hand dismissively. "We put a rubber band around her mouth to keep her from barking."

"You what?"

"It's an old trick."

"It's not an old trick. It's abuse. You should've picked up the phone. Congratulations. She won't be back."

I tried the trick of "teaching her to bark" so I could teach her not to bark, but Vela quickly put paid to that strategy. No matter what I did, she wouldn't bark. It was easy to feel like a fool trying to ramp her up. When I was leaping around, making weird noises, she sat there, like Henry before her, regarding me with mute disdain. I leashed her to a post, and, just out of her reach, I waggled the fuzzy toy dangling from her flirt pole. She loved that game, but not when I wanted her to love it. I might've been trying to engage her in a game of fetch, in which she had no more interest than had Henry before her.

The doorbell, an instant goad to bark in the normal course of things, prompted nothing. Within less than twenty minutes, I'd run out of ideas. She'd mastered me once more.

The funniest example of Vela's refusal to do something just because I wanted her to do it involved a bell I'd placed on the door handle. Supposedly, she would ring it to signal a need to go out to relieve herself. I showed her how to use it by ringing it repeatedly, each time opening the door. She didn't yawn, but she might've, if she'd thought of it.

Her self-approved method was to stare hard at me. I'd say, "Ring the bell, Vela." She wouldn't move, would just keep staring, as if she had no idea what I was talking about. I'd repeat, trying to introduce some zing in the words, "Vela! Go ring the bell!" No dice. Around then, I'd lead her to the door, saying, "Ring the bell." When she'd had enough of this nonsense, and had grown desperate to get outside, she'd ease her nose up to the bell so cautiously, only the faintest tinkle emerged.

She reminded me of Jessie when I'd urge her to take a drink of water before a walk. "Have some water," I'd say, and then repeat. She'd stare at me as if I were babbling in tongues. If I kept insisting, she'd finally lower her muzzle to the water, dip it fleetingly, and then look at me as if to say "There. Satisfied?"

Vela and I did the bell polka every day, and every day she'd wind up treating the bell as if it were radioactive. Did I learn? Nope. I persevered. But she persevered harder.

Except. In the evening, if Charles and I went upstairs to change, she knew we were about to go out. She'd run to the back door and swing that bell until it nearly came off its hook. Our neighbors, had they been in on the purpose of the bell, would've come over and let her out.

I signed Vela up for swimming lessons. Although she loved to wade, she never ventured far enough in to swim. During the first swim session, her crazed thrashing flooded the concrete deck. She wanted nothing more than to get out of that pool. Given time, I thought she might've drained it. Nevertheless, I kept bringing her, and eventually she easily swam the length of the pool and back. After several weeks of her swimming, I accepted that it was never going to be her favorite activity. What mattered to me was knowing that, if she ever got caught in deep water, she'd be able to handle herself. And she had conquered her fear. Another plus for her confidence.

We had moved back to Oakland when Charles told me he wanted to get Vela trained for protection. He knew I'd felt insecure ever since Jessie had died.

He said, "I tried calling Avery but got that *no longer in service* bleep. Went by anyway, just in case. The place's for sale. Doesn't look like there's gonna be a bidding war. You can't see the fence for all the crumbling flyers."

"Give it up," I said. "You won't find anybody. I looked. People around here—that kind of training goes against their religion."

"There have to be a few atheists who train dogs."

"You're a mathematician, Charles. No clients equals no trainers."

"I don't get it. Why should this area be different from everywhere else?"

I shrugged. "It's the Bay Area. No gluten and no 'attack' dogs."

A few days later, as I poured my coffee and considered whether I'd have eggs or cereal, Charles said, "I found somebody."

"For what, honey?"

"To train Vela."

"Huh. That's a surprise." I took half-and-half from the fridge. "But maybe we shouldn't do this. Don't forget. Jeff tested her back in Illinois. She didn't have what it takes. She's a soft dog."

"She was a puppy when Jeff tried her."

"She was over a year old, Charles. Jessie had been training for a couple of months at that age."

Charles shrugged. "It can't hurt to have this guy take a look at Vela."

One week later, Charles was screwing a bolt into the fence in our side yard.

"What's that for?" I asked.

"This guy, Ethan. The trainer. He wants her tied up."

"Jeff didn't tie her up. He doesn't have to worry. I won't let go of her."

"He's not worried. He wants to ramp up her frustration."

Ethan turned out to be a tall, muscular Black man with the vocabulary of a public school–trained Englishman—public school in the UK meaning hoity-toity to the hoi polloi.

He was in our living room, but he took over. Right away I could see him working a dog. Unlike me, he didn't fidget. He projected alert serenity. If only it were contagious.

I'd locked Vela in the bedroom. If she came out, she'd lick him to death. Well, no. Clearly, Ethan could handle a dog with far more gumption than our Vela. But I would've paid to see what he'd do if she applied herself to obsessively washing him.

After we'd talked for a while about his approach, which didn't sound different from Avery's, he said, "Let's take this girl out for a test drive."

Holding a leather strap, Ethan jumped at Vela, the leather slapping the ground. To my astonishment, she lunged at him, straining against the tether, barking frenetically. Her barking at the slightest provocation I knew all too well. But my placid dog looked astonishingly aggressive.

After several repetitions of this, Ethan, huffing, nodded at us. "She'll do."

I was too stunned to rejoice.

Back in the house, he took out a contract and explained the terms. Charles asked for the bottom line. "Ten thousand dollars," Ethan said, without blushing.

Charles's eyes flew open. "Well," he said.

For a moment, I couldn't say anything. Finally, I said, "I got my first German shepherd plus lifetime protection training for five."

Spreading his hands in a helpless gesture, Ethan said, "Inflation. It's a bitch."

"What do we get for our ten thousand? I mean, since we already own the dog."

"I'll work with her until you're satisfied."

"Satisfied or disappointed?"

"You won't be disappointed. Vela will make an excellent protector. She's got the nerve and the drive."

I wasn't sure how he knew she had the nerve and the drive. Jeff hadn't thought so. Even though she was a far more stable dog than the one we'd collected from O'Hare, she didn't strike me as a dog ready to be my defender.

I said, "What makes you so sure it's not just prey drive you're seeing? She lunges like that at the flirt pole. Let one squirrel show up, and she gets manic."

"Vela showed fight as well as prey drive. Anyway, it's a game to the dog. They're playing. She wants to get in on the party."

Jessie never saw it as a game; I was her responsibility. She was the Secret Service, and I was the president. Close to the end of her life, when her back legs were all but gone, she saw me climb the stairs with a man who was going to supply me with new drapes for the bedroom. As I waited for him to finish measuring the windows, I heard the crash of my beloved girl tumbling down the stairs. Using only her front legs, Jessie had pulled herself just short of the top, where her strength had given out. Protection was her mission in life, from her very first day with me.

"That's the thing," I said now to Ethan. "Vela never played. Not really. She doesn't know how."

"Play can be taught. Drives can't."

"Look, I'm not questioning your expertise. But this dog has no passion. She's—I don't know—phlegmatic. A trainer in Illinois tested her for protection. He got nothing."

Ethan seemed not a bit perturbed by my questioning his judgment. "I can't account for what happened in Illinois. But the dog I saw today has the drives she needs. You told me about all the work you've done to build up her confidence. It took."

Charles and I looked at each other, but I couldn't read him, and probably he couldn't read me. Hell, I couldn't read myself. After a moment, Ethan stood. "Up to you folks. You have my opinion."

Charles held out his hand. "We'll let you know."

We watched as Ethan drove away. "What do you think?"

"Like Ethan said, honey: up to you. Vela's your dog."

"No, she isn't."

"You've done all the work with her. Like he said, it took."

"Maybe. But that's way too much money for it to be up to me."

"Do we have a choice?"

"We do. We can leave her as she is. If he's right, she'd protect me anyway. If he's wrong, we don't want to throw away ten grand."

Charles shook his head. "This is less about what Vela might do than it is about how you feel. I want you to feel as safe as you did when Jessie was alive."

"I'd like that too."

"We can afford it," he said at last. "And since we can't find anyone else in this chardonnay-sipping, tofu-addicted town, let's go for it."

No problem with getting Vela to stare at the "bad guy." No problem with getting her to bark when I said to. Her mastering that command dismantled the theory that training a dog to bark on cue was the best way to train them to stop barking.

But when she took her first bite on a sleeve, she was happy to stop barking. Like Jessie, she thought biting was the dessert. With a bite coming, barking was spinach.

With Avery, Jessie had trained almost exclusively in the yard. With Ethan at the helm, we traveled. I took Vela to Laney College and Merritt College, where I was "attacked" by men I'd never seen, men from Ethan's seemingly bottomless supply of personnel. At Merritt, men from two directions loudly cursed at me. They sounded serious. When one moved toward me, Vela pivoted and bit him. When he withdrew as the other advanced, she whirled and bit him. In a bank parking lot, I lowered the car window and went to the ATM, pretending to withdraw money. Another "attacker" came at me, waving some kind of fake weapon. Vela clambered out the window and went for him.

There was, however, a serious problem with how she was being trained, and it had to do with the way dogs understand the world. Dogs connect events to objects or conditions. Because I hate shoes, whenever I put them on, my dogs know I'm going out—hopefully with the dog.

Ethan's "bad guy" assistants were Black men, whose color became a trigger for Vela's learned aggression. Soon, whenever we drove past a Black guy, she barked. I'd begged Ethan to find at least one white guy to attack me. When I told him about an incident at the dog park, he finally found somebody.

People of color aren't frequent visitors to that park. It's located in the Oakland Hills, where the population tends to be decidedly pale. We had just entered the park when Vela saw a Black man chatting with friends. Before I could stop her, she ran at him, barking. The man, accustomed to dogs, glanced at her without concern, and without animosity. I felt a rush of gratitude as he shrugged off my apology. I didn't want to think about reasons he might not be surprised by a white woman's dog charging him.

A movie called *White Dog* explores the phenomenon of training a dog to behave as a racist. But, such training, sadly, doesn't even have to be intentional. White dog owners can instill negative reactions to dark skin, merely by tightening their hold on the leash whenever a person of color appears. If the owner feels fear, the dog can sense it.

We are always training our dogs, whether we want to or not.

Ethan made countless appointments but kept them randomly. Nevertheless, his training worked. On a hot day in Alameda, Vela proved it.

The parking lot at the Alameda dog park is tiny and, naturally, frequently full. As if that wasn't irritating enough, only one parking space was available on our side of the street, and it was far from roomy for the Maxima.

The four-lane street fronting the park serves as a main thoroughfare, which meant every time I abandoned an abortive attempt to squeeze in close to the curb, I had to wait for a break in traffic before moving out to make another pass. Whenever I drove forward and began to back up, I was holding up other drivers. After ten minutes of this frustration, I shook so hard, I had to give up.

When I was younger, I could park a semi in a walnut. In my twenties, on Mission Street, one of San Francisco's busiest, with a bus right behind me, I whipped my Chevy Impala into a pocket-sized parking space so fast, the bus driver gave me two thumbs up. Had he been behind me in Alameda that day, his thumbs would've taken a different direction.

Across the street, a huge space gaped at me. I executed a zippy U-turn across four lanes of traffic to slip into it. But I had cut off a motorcycle. The rider was livid, and I couldn't blame him.

I got out of the Maxima, my legs like water, both from the strain of trying to park and from wondering if this guy was going to hit me. He looked to be the stereotypical motorcycle rider: burly, with tattoos coiling from his neck to his wrists. He wore leathers and had at least a foot over my height and easily a hundred pounds over my weight. He shouted I'd have to pay if I'd done something to his "hog." I had no idea what I could've done. He used the word "stripping," I think. If he'd had to damage his bike to avoid hitting me, I knew I was responsible. He couldn't hear my apologies over his own yelling, but I wasn't in a position to order him to pipe down.

Something moved next to me. I looked down, and there was Vela. She'd jumped from the car window, just as she'd been trained to do, and she stood ready for me to tell her what should happen next. My heart soared, even as I—thoroughly rattled—led her back to the car. She'd made it clear I wasn't defenseless.

Mr. Tattoos demanded to see my license, once again warning me about my obligation to repair his bike. He cursed me again as I handed it to him. I wondered if I was too submissive, a lure for his inner bully. But I was at fault, and I thought of my own anger when a driver made a boneheaded move in front of me.

He glanced at my license, and then looked harder at it. Then he looked at me. "You're seventy?"

"Now you know why I couldn't park my car."

He shook his head, flung the license at me, and roared away. Maybe I reminded him of his grandma.

Shortly after that, Ethan disappeared for good. His job done, his outrageous fee for his erratic performance perhaps now piloting him through Europe.

Bob used to say that when the money's gone, it's gone, and it's pointless to dwell on how it went. It seemed wise to adopt his philosophy.

Vela began to show more than a little stiffness in her hind legs. And I'd never found out what that depression at the base of her spine meant. The UC Davis veterinary college runs a clinic, presumably for veterinary interns to learn the ropes, so I made an appointment. The examination must've been thorough; it lasted more than three hours. All I saw of it, because I was excluded from being present, was the vets walking Vela up and down stairs. When they presented their finding, they told me they had videotaped her walking. What else they did, I have no idea. Most of the news turned out to be positive—meaning the tests were negative.

They saw no evidence of hip dysplasia. They did a DNA test for degenerative myelopathy of the spine, and I got the result weeks later: she didn't have the gene. I was overjoyed. What she had, they told me, was a malformation of her pelvis. It could be corrected with surgery, but they didn't recommend it. She was functioning well for her age. If she grew worse, surgery could always be an option. In short, she was a healthy dog.

Vela and Pilar

Vela disliked going to the cabin. Because there were no other dogs, there was nothing for her to do—no trips to the dog park, no unresponsive love objects to chase, no chances to sit in the car and bark. Charles didn't care whether she had fun or lay around all day, dreaming of—what? What would paradise be for a dog like Vela? Canine autocracy? Having me enslaved? A cot at the dog beach to rest on in between soaks and chases?

His attitude was, "She's a dog," meaning, we make the decisions, and the dog lives with them. I coveted his ability to shut out distractions such as an unhappy Vela. He loved her, maybe even a bit more than I did, but he didn't fret over any need to cram her days with pleasurable moments. He felt she could reasonably expect some "down time," having given her what he believed was fair. In my conscience, I couldn't locate a yardstick for "fair."

A second German shepherd would solve my problem and Vela's. She'd have her playmate, and my conscience would take a sabbatical. Charles wasn't in favor. Even if he didn't realize that doubling the number of dogs quadruples, at best, the number of problems, he did know there would be more barking, more hair garnishing every surface, more kibble to buy, and, since what goes in must come out, more poop to clean up.

If my happiness hadn't meant the world to him, he would've continued to hold out. But it did—why do you think I married him?—so he agreed.

This time, I told myself, I'd get a problem-free dog.

Avery had once recommended a kennel to the north. To me, it looked like a canine Walmart. We weren't invited in to take a look. The excuse was the breeder needed to avoid potential disease. Apparently, however, it was fine for us to pick up any pup and rub his sweet little nose against our big, contaminated ones, just as long as we weren't inside the facility. Fresh air cures all ills, I guess.

In less than five minutes of the breeder vanishing, at least a dozen German shepherd puppies romped out into the grass. Fat little bodies tumbled around like water-logged balloons.

I wanted them all.

This time, I told myself, I'd get a short-haired shepherd. Long-haired shepherds are especially beautiful, but those coats demand hours of combing every week. Moreover, the prodigious skill of any shepherd to blanket a house in dog fur finds its apotheosis in the long-haired version. Hundreds of furry tumbleweeds skidded over our floors, landing under anything with an underside, and on anything with an overside. My black jeans hadn't visited my legs in years. I wouldn't become Yeti for the sake of twenty seconds of being chic.

Novice German shepherd owners whine about the relentless shedding: "What can I do?" There's only one answer: "Live with it." Some comedians, having spent decades trashing one wrecked vacuum cleaner after another, will now and then offer a tip, such as "Add it to stir fry." Pointless advice. The fur's undoubtedly already in the stir fry.

When I'd chosen a darling little puppy, I found Charles squatting by the gate, watching a long-haired pup "attack" Vela, occasionally whipping around to taste the cuffs of his pants.

"How about this girl?"

He barely glanced at the pup I held. "That's the one," he said, pointing to the puppy tormenting Vela. "She's got moxie."

As I paid and the breeder filled out the papers, I asked about genetic testing for hip dysplasia and degenerative myelopathy of the spine. "Don't believe in it," she snapped, slipping our check into a drawer. Okay. I should've asked the question before she got her grubby little hands on our money. As I watched the drawer slam shut, a dark feeling came over me. *What have I done?*

The breeder walked us out to our car, probably to make sure we didn't hang around and invade that off-limits building. But she cried out in alarm as we plopped Pilar into the backseat next to Vela. "You're sure your dog won't hurt her?"

Far as I knew, there were two dogs on the backseat and both of them were ours.

All during the long drive home, Pilar sat back there, alert, interested. She'd not been the least bit concerned about her home disappearing in the back window. At the halfway point, I took her out in a vacant lot. She squatted and peed, nosed around a bit. When I put her back, she moved closer to Vela.

Pilar liked everybody, and everybody liked her—everybody except those incomprehensible people who hate dogs. She had an endearing expression, made more charming by the folded pancake ears pasted to the top of her noggin. German shepherd ears come up whenever they feel like it, generally before six months. With Pilar, when her ears peeled off her head, the left one decided on a halfway measure, sticking out like an airplane wing. The other shot straight up and stayed there. Nearly everyone who saw her rhapsodized about that indecisive ear. Up, I told it. Up!

Like many fans of the breed, I was passionate about the alert look of German shepherd ears. Often, on the Bayview trail, long before I had Pilar, I'd encounter a woman walking a large elderly shepherd with floppy ears. Each and every time we came abreast of one another, she'd say mournfully, "They never came up." I thought it sad that a dog she undoubtedly loved should cause her shame whenever someone walking a perky eared shepherd came along.

The techs at the vet clinic where I took Pilar loved that low-flying ear.

"Oh, that ear!" they'd croon. "That adorable ear."

But they were Pilar fans, once greeting her with, "Oh, Pilar! We saw your name on the appointment sheet, and we've been waiting all day to see you!"

They meant it. I know that because they never greeted any other dog of mine with that much enthusiasm, even though they seemed to like them all and said nice things about them. One vet told me she wished her German shepherd were as well behaved as my two.

Google advised me that if Pilar's ear hadn't levitated by six months, it never would. Some people insisted gluing would cure an uncooperative ear. Others said baloney. So, I glued poor Pilar's ear, only to experience humiliation at the dog park when someone, peering down at her, exclaimed in amazement, "You glued it!"

Sometimes the ear would pop up for no apparent reason, a few minutes later lowering back into semaphore position. It never drooped, just kept signaling "turn left," as if patiently awaiting compliance. Every time I looked at it, I felt dismayed, and simultaneously chagrined. What was wrong with me? Did everything have to be perfect? My short answer was *yes*, and my longer answer was *yes indeed*.

In time, I made my sluggish way to acceptance of Pilar's Flying Nun ear. That right-angle projection, I told myself, played a vital role in her goofy magnificence. I wouldn't just tolerate it. I would embrace it. And feel proud of my open mind. Sure.

And then something weird happened. When Pilar turned three, as if to celebrate her birthday, her ear slid up into the AKC-authorized position. And stayed there. Out of curiosity, I searched for a precedent online. Combing through hundreds of posts in dozens of sites where German shepherd ears were discussed—and yes, the ears of a German shepherd are a major interest of their owners—I couldn't find a single instance of an ear that waited three years to launch.

But, once it was gone, I missed that semaphore.

The Maxima had seen better days. For an eight-year-old car, even so, it looked pretty good. The trouble didn't begin until Pilar turned one year old. After that, our car was her oyster. To shuck. She zeroed in on the inside of the doors, functioning as if she'd majored in rapid demolition at a canine vocational school. Thankfully, she never chewed on the leather seats. However, in short order, the upholstery on the doors looked as if Leatherface had used power tools on them. Whenever I opened one, scraps fluttered in the breeze.

Having taken my son Seth's dog with my two shepherds to a dog park, I didn't have time to ferry them home before visiting a terminally ill friend. I'd been at her bedside about twenty minutes when hospital security buzzed my cell phone.

"We've got three dogs here."

"No, no, not possible. I left them in the car."

"Your number's on the tags of two of 'em."

"I can't believe it," I muttered. "I'll be right there."

How on earth had those dogs escaped? It made no sense. When I got to the garage's security office, there they were, my shepherds and my son's big mutt. Despite my annoyance, I was relieved that they'd stuck together. But they didn't have the decency to look ashamed of themselves. Instead, they raced up to me, exhibiting completely inappropriate joie de vivre. I thanked the guard and told the dogs to stay with me as I navigated through traffic to where I'd parked.

My brain fired questions into empty space. Did someone open the door so three huge dogs could jump them? Vela would've been barking hysterically. Maybe all three would've barked as someone jimmied the lock. But why would anyone jimmy the lock? The Maxima was old, so no prize, parked amid dozens of classier vehicles. And why, seeing these barking animals, didn't a presumptive car thief experience trepidation?

And that was it, wasn't it? The car had been locked. I was sure of it, recalling that sweet little beep-beep that says, "You can go now; I've got this covered."

Did I even have a car anymore? If I didn't, how was I going to keep control of three dogs while I worked out how to get home with them? I couldn't imagine a cab stopping to pick up the four of us.

The car stood where I'd left it, one back door fully open. Okay. Someone had let my dogs out. They must've.

As I rounded the car, reality cleared away my brain fog. The upholstery covering the lock had been gnawed to pieces that now festooned the seat and the floor.

Pilar had mastered the art of picking a lock.

I was determined that Pilar would have the benefit of a diet rich in raw meat and organs. She had a healthy appetite, and her palate, unlike Vela's, wasn't finicky. For much of the first year, I chopped up her meat and offal or served it ground. After that, I dumped chicken drumsticks into her dish, the same chicken drumsticks I'd fed Jessie for years.

It's commonly known among raw feeders that cooked chicken bones splinter. Uncooked, everything's copacetic.

When she was about nine months old, Pilar, in the dog run, let out a horrible screech. At first, I couldn't figure out what was wrong. But turning her around—to my horror—I spotted a chicken bone protruding from her anus. Seth scooped her up and held her still as I drove as fast as possible to the emergency clinic. They rushed her into the back, and twenty minutes later came out to report no damage, except to our bank account.

Okay. A raw chicken leg splintered. Well . . . but . . . still . . . we must avoid feeding her a chicken leg that's been cooked. That could perforate her intestines.

Months later, a six-pound roasted chicken rested on our kitchen counter while Charles and I sipped wine in the living room. Pilar was a skilled and sneaky counter surfer, so we should've known better than to leave aromatic meat within her reach.

Ready to feast, we went to the kitchen. All that was left of six pounds of chicken was a small splotch of grease on the tile floor. Pilar had licked up most of that.

Having distanced herself from the scene of her crime, she slept the sleep of the just fed. And, astonishingly, there were no ill effects. Which proves even an ironclad rule can splinter.

Vela and Pilar had chronically loose stools. Having given up on raw feeding altogether following the chicken bone catastrophe, I'd tried one brand of kibble after another, and had finally settled on one that didn't seem to irritate their guts. But I wasn't satisfied because it looked to me as if more came out of them than went into them.

I'd bought the hype about grain-free food because it fit with my conviction that raw meat, bones, and organs were all a dog needed. Grain-free boutique kibble isn't cheap, but like all dog lovers who can afford it, I bought what I thought would give my dogs the nourishment they required. After a lot of research, I started feeding them one of the more expensive kibbles.

Choosing that one might've been one of the worst decisions I ever made for any of my dogs.

Frequently, people asked me if my shepherds were Belgians. At that time, long-haired German shepherds were not common in the States. Some people were openly astonished when I said they were Germans. One man shook his head in disgust over my dishonesty. At Lake Merritt, a tipsy woman insisted they were Malinois. I thought I might set her straight.

"Malinois," I pointed out, trying not to sound like the teacher I'd been, "are short-haired dogs."

"I was a vet tech for years," she spat at me. "I know what a Malinois looks like." She paused briefly, perhaps to give me an opportunity to make an even greater fool of myself. I passed. "Malinois," she said by way of having the final word, "have long hair!"

At the time, I thought only that liquor had addled her brain. Eventually, I suspected what had led to our pointless quibbling. Three varieties of shepherds were under discussion: German shepherds. Belgian shepherds. And Belgian Malinois, sometimes also referred to as Belgian shepherds—no doubt the source of my debater's confusion.

One night, in my dreams, someone came to me and said confidently, "Your dogs really are Belgians, you know."

The day after the dream, while I was walking them on a leash-free trail, a man stopped me to ask me . . . if they were Belgians.

He was nice, so I didn't tell him what I wanted to say the next time I was asked that question, or any other about their provenance.

"Djibouti shepherds," I would say, if I could get my tongue around it. Let them mull that one over.

At the cabin, Pilar was Vela's number one fan. All day the two of them roamed free, shoulder to shoulder. As I'd hoped, Vela's aversion to the cabin was gone. Now she loved it as much as Jessie had. One of their favorite cabin games was to stand up on their hind legs and bat at each other. They lay nose to nose on the floor to carry on 'tooth wars,' banging their fangs together while emitting weird sounds. Vela thrived on Pilar's adulation and responded by lapping at her partner's face until even patient Pilar tired of it. They dozed next to each other, sometimes with the front leg of one stretched across the body of the other.

They loved to explore, and the cabin gave them acres for that. For a long time, they restricted their romps to our property. But there came an evening when we left them in the car close to our neighbors' yurt, where we were having dinner. Big mistake.

A day later, a polite but chilly voice informed us that our dogs had come down the road for a visit. We apologized and hopped in the car to fetch them. The following day, those ne'er-do-wells hightailed it right back to our neighbors' yurt. We were distraught. And so were the neighbors, especially because they had a cat.

Charles started saying we'd have to give up the cabin. We'd have to sell it. This was the end. We'd never be able to relax there again. No, we couldn't tie the dogs up. What kind of life would that be for them? It was over. Nothing could fix this.

Did I mention that he inclined toward the apocalyptic?

Naturally, I decided something would fix this. Ironically, he's the usual fixer, and I'm the usual make-a-mess-of-it-er. Trusty old Google didn't offer many options, but, following my usual inclination, I settled on an expensive one. Desperate, Charles—most of the time more reluctant than I am to spend a lot of money—agreed.

And that's how we came to invest in overpriced equipment that promised to tell us where our dogs were at all times, and—most important of all—to alert us whenever they wandered off the property. We accepted the difficulty of parsing the indecipherable directions that supposedly explained how to access the countless functions of the antenna-sprouting collars. Whenever they wore them, our dogs looked like Martians, just off the mother ship.

Predictably, the collars were a failure, and not just because we never did figure out most of the directions. The canopy of trees shading our property ensured that we received a steady stream of inaccurate data from each collar.

Back to Google. (How on earth did we cope before the internet?) We could, some experts assured me, establish boundaries the dogs would respect by teaching them the location of those boundaries. This struck me as a ludicrous proposition. My dogs knew the boundaries of our property already, didn't they? Or did they?

At least it wasn't an expensive experiment. Charles and I resigned ourselves to the drudgery of repeatedly walking the perimeter first with one dog, then with the other, several times a day. Neither of us held out much hope for advice that looked like the ambulatory version of snake oil, but we kept at it anyway.

After a week of this exercise, our dogs stayed on the property. We were flabbergasted.

At Safeway in Oakland, I ran into one of Avery's other clients, whose name I couldn't recall, although I did remember her dog's name was Lucy. She too remembered only my dog's name.

"Long time no see," she said. "How's Jessie?"

"Gone a while ago."

She rolled her eyes. "Stupid me. Lucy passed years ago, so I should've figured. Hell, I lose track of time. Have you got a dog now?" I nodded. "Me too. She's in training with Avery."

"Really? I thought Avery went out of business."

"Nah. She's up in Sacramento. Got a bigger place. Doing well. It's a slog to drive up there every week, but what can you do? She's the best."

I could've saved us ten thousand dollars, although I might've spent half that on gas for a weekly three-hour roundtrip. (That would be in good traffic, which that freeway rarely hosts.) Okay, I had to give myself some consolation for all that money spent on a flake of a dog trainer—who nevertheless did a great job with Vela.

Because Pilar was four and a half years younger than Vela, I hoped she could be prepared to move into the role of my protector when she became my only shepherd. Avery was happy to take her on as a client. Things looked up, at the start.

Pilar bit with enthusiasm. Frank said her grip was intense. And she loved the sessions. But as I watched her, Ethan's theory about dogs seeing protection as a game came back to me. With Jessie, and even with Vela, I didn't believe he was right. They were dead serious about protecting me. With Pilar, however, it did seem to be a game. I suspected that everything she learned in Sacramento would stay in Sacramento. I wondered if her attachment to Vela, stronger, I believed, than her attachment to us, was the cause.

In talking about her with Avery, I mentioned that my son's shepherd, Zephyr, intimidated Pilar. Every time he showed up, she hid behind me. It didn't help that Zephyr was something of a bully and obsessed with her. For him, Vela, trying to horn in on the fun, was background noise. Pilar, quivering behind me, was the target. At such moments, I pitied Vela, recalling the times my grandmother practically elbowed me out of the way as she rushed to embrace my brother. But Vela's reaction was healthier than mine. She viewed being ignored as an accident persistence would remedy.

Pilar's fear of Zephyr came when he got bigger. When he'd been a puppy, she'd tried to shelter him. Seth made a video of the three dogs together during that time. In the video, Vela is intently gnawing a bone, Pilar by her side, with puppy Zephyr facing the two of them. He keeps his eyes on Vela's bone while Pilar observes him fixedly. She looks concerned. After several minutes, she moves, dropping down between Zephyr and Vela, blocking his view of Vela's bone.

In time, however, Zephyr's visits became a misery for Pilar.

"She won't defend herself," I told Avery.

"Okay," she said. "Let's see where she stands."

I thought maybe the time to "see where she stands" would've been months ago, before we began training. But what did I know?

She took Pilar's leash and moved to the fence, some distance from me and from Frank. He came right at me with a "bat." As I screamed, "Help!" he pretended to pummel my head. Pilar didn't move. She didn't even look over at us.

Avery ordered her to go for Frank, but Pilar looked confused. Gone was the pattern she understood—the one with her by my side, facing Frank, the "bad guy." Our unfamiliar positions left her in the dark as to what she should do.

I thought of the guy in Pinole, the one who had assured me Jessie lacked the drive to make a solid protection dog. I remembered him saying he was going to get rid of his little Muley because that tiny dog didn't like to bite. She bit whenever he told her to, but she lacked passion for it. I had almost laughed in his face. Muley's teeth were the size of baby peas and equally lethal. She weighed less than twenty pounds. Good thing she didn't like to bite. Even with the soft shoes I normally wear, I could've kicked her halfway across the state. Imagine what a man's boot would've done to her.

But her sweetness, her perfect obedience, and her devotion meant nothing to him. Maybe he had gotten her in the first place simply to show her off as comic relief at Schutzhund trials, warming up the crowd before the main event. Imagine the guffaws as that tiny dog bared her teeth and lunged at a 250-pound decoy.

I kissed the top of Pilar's head and held the car door open for her. We drove back to Oakland from protection training for the last time.

When Vela was seven, I enrolled her and Pilar in herding lessons. Charles and I had attended a few sheep herding contests at the fairgrounds near the cabin. They were fun to watch. The dogs were border collies of all colors. Border collies have the energy and intelligence to work a herd for hours. We watched as each dog maneuvered three sheep through narrow obstacles into a pen. The sheep varied in response to all this. One cluster pressed themselves against the fence, slithering toward the exit gate. As they huddled there, the emcee asked, unnecessarily, whether the contestant wanted a different herd.

As another lamb trio was pressed toward the opening in a low fence, one plucky ewe whirled around and stamped her foot right in front of the dog. The border collie skittered back, but only momentarily. I liked that ewe. I always root for the underdog, although in this case, I was hoping the under-sheep could gain the upper foot.

Vela loved herding so much, I regretted not getting her into it years before, when her body wasn't starting to show signs of breaking down. Heidi, a squat woman with a whip, ran the operation. Every time Vela came close to nipping one of the sheep, Heidi cracked that whip. She had to crack it a lot because Vela kept trying to nip those sheep. Each time the leather tip landed near her, Vela would pause but then, without a glance at Heidi or the whip, plunge back toward those delectable sheep. She was having a ball.

As she aged, Vela increasingly showed me the level of self-assurance I associated with the best German shepherds. Her indifference to that whip coming down near her confirmed my theory that the breeding in Germany that produced her flawed body had nonetheless produced a solid dog, one with courage and character.

Pilar was different. She hated herding. At first the sheep excited her, but when Heidi snapped the whip, Pilar raced over to me, trembling, her tail tucked. I put her back in the truck.

Had she not weighed seventy pounds, Pilar would've made a good lap dog. I was in love with her, but she would've appalled Max Emil Friedrich von Stephanitz, the man who bred the original lionhearted German shepherds. He would've been horrified to see how many American German shepherds lack the courage and excellent structure he carefully bred into his dogs over a century ago.

I hadn't considered how hard herding would be on Vela's body. The question that eventually faced me was one we all face, not only with our pets but with ourselves and others close to us. Should we deny pleasure in pursuit of a longer life?

I wanted a long life for Vela, but I also wanted her to enjoy her life. After she'd had half a dozen lessons, I had to decide. She hadn't jumped into the car in years. Her difficulty in rising from the floor clawed at my heart. In herding, the dog swivels rapidly, leaning into the hip. I didn't need a veterinary degree to picture the damage these movements might be inflicting on Vela's joints. Maybe it was selfish, but I decided, if there were ways to avoid it, I wouldn't subject her and me to the steady, long-term destruction of her mobility. While I hated to deprive her of so much pleasure, I decided to withdraw Vela from herding.

Dogs handle pain well, but I don't.

In the category of don't believe everything you think, my son's German shepherd, Zephyr, is another fine example of the breed. He's beautiful, with solid joints and a straight back. At seven years old, he's been healthy all his life. He's courageous, stable, friendly, devoted to my son, and smart. He doesn't even bark that much. (Hear that, Vela?)

Zephyr watches television. He looks at videos on an iPhone. I don't mean he glances at them; he studies them until they end. Even more astonishing, he has a favorite movie, *Alpha*, about a prehistoric boy and wolf who befriend each other during the boy's quest to be reunited with his tribe. My son plays it often. When Zephyr hears it start up, he runs in from the yard, perches himself on the bed, and watches the entire film, whimpering over the sad parts.

I bought Zephyr for Seth from a backyard breeder. As was true with raw and cooked chicken bones, a rule of thumb isn't absolute. Unscrupulous backyard breeders should be avoided. But those who don't put together defective dogs may be turning out sturdier animals than breeders who fixate on and try to replicate one characteristic—a large head, a back sloped just right, etc.

German shepherds used to be jacks-of-all-trades. They might not have been the best at herding, personal protection, guiding the blind, emotional support, or tracking, but a well-bred German shepherd can do any one of those jobs satisfactorily. Nowadays police departments spurn shepherds in favor of the Malinois, a breed not yet popular enough to have been watered down or riddled with health problems. To be fair, Malinois are smaller and more agile, have energy to spare, and a smart one—which most are—can accomplish astonishing feats. I've seen videos of a Malinois climbing straight up a wall. Increasing shyness and/or structural defects among too many shepherds make them a poor choice for a career requiring sustained vigor and courage. The diamonds among them are getting harder to find among all the dross.

Here, and in Europe originally, German shepherds were the breed trained as guide dogs for the blind, almost without exception. Nowadays Labradors all but exclusively fill that role. Many factors fed into turning away from the shepherd as a mainstay among guide dogs, but, again, significant health and temperament problems of overbred German shepherds number among them.

You might say German shepherds are becoming increasingly unemployable.

Vela, Pilar, and Liam

I first encountered the Havanese breed at a dog show. Like long-haired German shepherds, Havanese in North America were then rare. The more I saw, the more I felt drawn to the little dogs despite being, for many years, a devotee of big dogs.

"I want a bed dog," was the way I put it to Charles.

"Hmm," he said, and rolled over to go back to sleep.

A year after I started lobbying for my bed dog, my daughter called to ask me for advice about a dog for her son. Right away, I suggested a Havanese and offered to find one for him. But litters were not to be found. With all unborn puppies destined for identified homes, I didn't stand a chance. I began to despair.

When I'd all but given up, a cream and butterscotch puppy became available. I snatched him up, although only figuratively. Charles and I had to drive down to Long Beach to collect him, a trip that turned out to be more of an adventure than we'd expected.

We checked into a seedy Motel 6. (Shades of Reno.) As we unlocked the door to our room, a brawny tattooed man in the room next to ours glowered at us. I ducked inside, feeling shaky. Charles too was unnerved. The scene reminded me of a noir movie. Was that man a hired killer, or had we woken him from a nap? Who knew? In our tiny room, with no way out except right past him, we were trapped. Maybe we'd be murdered.

Obviously, we'd been watching way too many crime shows on TV.

Once settled, I called to let the breeder know we'd arrived. She said she had a sick child she had to take to the ER. Assuming that went okay, she'd be over with the puppy afterward. We waited uneasily.

211

At last, a knock came at the door. When I opened it, a blowsy drunk woman holding the leash of a filthy dog said, "Hi." The dog's fur was stiff with grime, and he was missing an eye. He looked nothing like a Havanese. But all of a sudden I couldn't remember what a Havanese looked like. Was it possible? "Is this the puppy?" I asked.

She roared contemptuously. "Don't you even know a Pekingese when you see one? He looks nothing like a Havanese." She proceeded to tell us the history of her pitiful dog. He'd been a champion in the show ring, she claimed. Won medal after medal. That was difficult to imagine, but then I suppose at that time he'd been clean and combed. And he'd had two eyes.

She said a cat clawed out the dog's eye and his show ring career ended. Apparently, so did his access to grooming. It seemed reasonable to ask this woman why she was in our room, but we hate confrontation, so neither of us challenged her. We sat in silence, listening to this gabby inebriate for more than an hour.

Finally, she provided the information we wanted. The breeder had said to come by, presumably to assure us she existed and so did the puppy. The woman said the breeder was her best friend. Someone who hung out with this sorry human being and her neglected dog—I didn't know what to think about that. I knew I wanted nothing to do with her, and I wondered how an ethical breeder could be chummy with someone oblivious to her dog's filthy, matted coat.

As they used to say in gangster movies, I smelled a rat. Had we traveled all that way to be scammed? We were carrying the price of the puppy in cash. The breeder couldn't accept a check from strangers, after all. Perhaps our glowering neighbor in the next room knew about the money. Maybe he was part of the scam.

At last, the drunk tired of our dull company and left. Another hour passed. Then the breeder showed up with apologies for our long wait. She came in with a darling puppy. To my relief, they both looked clean. She carried a folder and went through the conditions of the purchase, including our commitment to return the pup to her if at any point he wasn't wanted. While not definitive, this is one sign of an ethical breeder. I liked the sweetness with which she treated the puppy. After chatting with her for quite a while, we gave her the money. She seemed reluctant to leave the pup. I think she'd gotten quite attached to him. One glance at him and I knew why. He was a doll.

He whimpered a bit after she left but soon settled down, and we all went to sleep, the pup snuggled between us. The next morning, we drove up to Los Angeles to deliver him to my grandson. I put the pup on the floor, and he toddled over to a full-length mirror. Riley said, "I'm naming him Narcissus."

Riley was a well-read twelve-year-old.

Now it was my turn. I'd had a regular stream of emails offering me Havanese mixes. I'd wanted the "real thing" for Riley so had dumped those offers in the trash. But some months after we took Narcissus to Riley, the animal shelter in San Jose wrote about Liam, an eight-month-old Havanese.

At the time, Charles was in Chicago for a conference. I had boarded the shepherds so Liam and I would have time to get acquainted without their noses poking in between us.

No one advised me against Liam. No one said he was a biter. No one said anything about him. He'd been found a week before, unneutered, wandering the rainy streets, without a collar or a microchip. Someone hadn't wanted him.

In a huge room lined with folding chairs, I sat away from the door as the volunteer went to collect Liam.

She brought in a small black dog with a white beard. He promptly lifted his leg and peed. After that, he squatted and pooped. Good signs. He hadn't soiled his kennel. With his tail high and a cocky tilt to his head, he began making the rounds of the empty chairs. His nonchalance astonished me. First, lost in the streets, then placed in a locked kennel in a strange place, then neutered, and now plopped down in a room practically the size of a gymnasium, with a strange woman (me) staring at him. He came right over to me, and I scooped him up, signed the papers, paid, and took him out to the car. Times had changed. He cost me considerably more than five dollars.

An intense rain lashed the car as I eased out of the parking lot. Visibility was all but absent when I swung onto the freeway. Dog claws were digging into my shoulder. For the hour and a half it took to reach Oakland, Liam did a convincing impersonation of a fox-head stole.

The first task, as I saw it, was to crate train him. I knew I couldn't leave him free in the house with the shepherds whenever I had to go out. I got down on the floor, placed a treat inside the crate, and watched Liam reach in and take it. I followed with a series of treats, each further into the crate. Liam repeatedly trotted inside, picked up the morsel, and trotted out again. We played this game for a few hours with no sign of progress. The shepherds were coming home the following day. I needed to make this happen.

I figured I had nothing to lose by acting decisively. I picked Liam up, set him in the crate, and shut the gate. He curled up and went to sleep. He's been happy to go in his crate ever since.

Unlike Vela, Liam holds out only so long, although, admittedly, there have been a few instances where he showed just as much determination as she ever had and more than I have.

He didn't look particularly cute: he'd been clipped close to the skin. I assumed his fur had been matted. Naturally, I concocted a theory about how he'd wound up on the street, a theory bolstered to some degree by the fact that no one had tried to find him and he had no identification on him. And he hadn't been neutered. Liam has a clubfoot. Only a thin layer of skin protects the bone on his rear left foot from contact with the ground. He walks fine, although now and then he lifts that paw, but it doesn't appear to bother him much.

I speculated that, given the relative rarity of the Havanese breed, someone had seen a possible fortune in him as a stud—until they spotted his club foot. Speculative, true, but I couldn't imagine how else someone could ignore the loss of such a wonderful dog. He rapidly learned everything I had to teach him.

But I started worrying about the shepherds. Seventy pounds times two against thirteen-pound Liam: What had I been thinking? Yeah, duh. While I knew they wouldn't intentionally hurt him—they were good-natured dogs— nevertheless, they could easily hurt him unintentionally just by stepping on him. This, I told myself, had been another one of my ill-thought-out moves.

If he couldn't be safe with me, I promised myself I'd find him a good home. But the idea tore me apart. I was already in love with him.

When the shepherds came home with Charles, I held my breath.

Vela and Pilar came in and sniffed Liam's parts thoroughly. I almost heard their assessment.

Interesting, eh?

Yep.

They lay down and took a snooze.

Only when Liam got the zoomies would they go into high alert. He'd imitate an acrobat on a flying trapeze, arcing from sofa to sofa to ottoman and back to sofa. I kept an eye on all of them, ordering the shepherds to leave the circus tent whenever they got too excited.

Somebody left a door open when I'd had Liam for less than a month. He shot through it before we noticed that he could. I was frantic. He'd be hit by a car. He'd never be found. He'd starve on the street, or a coyote would get him. Charles isn't the only apocalyptic member of our pack. We roamed the neighborhood in different directions, shouting for him. One of our neighbors was weeding his front yard when Charles asked if he'd seen a small black dog.

"You mean like that one?" the guy asked, pointing to a bush nearby, under which Liam was cheerfully feasting on grass.

About two months after Liam joined the family, Vela, Pilar, and my brash Havanese took a group walk on the leash-free trail. By then, I trusted him. He came when called, lay down when told to, sat nicely, and had learned to wait at doors. A family walk was just the thing, I thought. Yep.

This was his first outing, and he was having a grand time, diligently inspecting every whiff of canine urine. My attention was primarily on the shepherds as, unleashed, they liked to engage in a game of "intimidate the strange dog," which, understandably, enraged that dog's owner. I always managed to call them off before they launched full bore into what to them was a good joke.

I didn't immediately see the large pit bull puppy charging toward Liam. When I did, it was too late for me to sprint over and grab my Havanese. Although clearly the pup wasn't intent on hurting Liam, nevertheless, given his hefty size, his playful stunt could've caused a significant injury to my petite Havanese. The pit looked like a diminutive charging bull, his paws kicking up dirt as he rocketed forward. But just before he would've slammed into his target, Vela stepped in front of Liam and turned sideways, creating a wall behind which Liam, oblivious, continued exploring. The pup thought better of jousting with a seventy-pound German shepherd and veered off.

If Vela had craved raw meat, I would've given her a steak that night. As it was, I contented myself by heaping an extra scoop of kibble into her bowl. She seemed satisfied.

Liam lacked concern for the danger he'd been in because he hadn't noticed it. But he had enough moxie for ten dogs. He got in the faces of the shepherds whenever they annoyed him, and they'd back off. He was Magellan sailing into the new world. Nothing scared him, and everything intrigued him.

He's the perfect combination of dog and cat. At times, he purrs. (Years later, he snores as loudly as Charles. During bouts of insomnia, I enjoy stereophonic snoring.) In line with his cat-like behavior, one of Liam's favorite games is to respond to my calling him by stretching out, low to the ground, and stalking very slowly toward me, looking as if he's about to pounce on an unsuspecting mouse. However, his favorite sleeping posture is decidedly un-cattish. He lies on his back with his rear legs spread, airing it all out, like a manspreader taking up three seats on the subway.

If he's relaxed about how he sleeps, he's OCD when it comes to having everything in its place. He's worse than I am, and I've always been regarded as a neat freak by friends and family. Bob once told friends that, if he got up to pee in the middle of the night, when he got back, I'd made up his side of the bed. And, with that, you now know a bit more about why that marriage crumbled.

I'd hung dry cleaning from the ledge above the closet door, intending to remove the plastic later. I heard Liam growling and went to the bedroom to see what was going on. He stood, staring up at the disruptive dry cleaning. When I put it in the closet, he trotted away, mollified. But I learned not to set my purse down in places he didn't approve. He barked at it if I set it on the kitchen counter instead of hanging it up on its proper hook.

He stands ready to alert us to the danger of any incorrectly repositioned object. While his appropriating the map of our household items is rather charming, his other area of assertiveness isn't. I'd never had a dog that wouldn't accept my moving his food dish. Even Henry didn't mind that.

I don't make a habit of seizing food from my dogs, but there are occasions when I need a feasting dog to get out of my way. My kitchen is small and poorly adapted to accommodating more than one activity at a time. Marital advice, for instance, extols the pleasures of cooking dinner as a team. In our kitchen, romance gives way to crabby exchanges and elbow poking, if not outright shoving of an unmindful sink hog. Fixing dinner is a one-person operation. And sometimes a dog food bowl needs to be relocated.

That doesn't work for my Havanese, whom we've dubbed "Napoliam" for his dictatorial bent. If anyone approaches his dish while he's eating, he turns into Wolfman on a bad night. I tried all the conventional tricks, such as offering him something more delicious as an exchange. Nope. Tried feeding him by hand. Nothing worked. Oddly, Liam, like Jessie before him, can take a tiny bit of kibble from between my fingers without grazing my skin with his teeth. But I know better than to reach into his mouth to reclaim that kibble.

If there's ever a reason to move his dish, I use my foot.

In one other way, Liam engages in vigorous resource guarding. Whenever Charles approaches me for a kiss or a hug, Liam zips over to plant himself between us, grumbling. In the beginning, he tried to bite Charles, but that didn't fly. He wound up on the floor. Eventually, he contented himself with raising a verbal stink over it and, when the kissing ceased, sluicing my face to get rid of that other scent marking. We thought it hilarious, but occasionally, I had a vision of Liam at one hundred pounds, taking possession of the house and its contents, including me. While he was never going to get close to a hundred pounds, he had grown beyond the original thirteen—to twenty. We began to think of him as our Giant Havanese.

In line with regarding our house as his fiefdom, he found Zephyr intolerable from day one. Perhaps because Zephyr is an intact male, Liam feels threatened by him. When Seth regularly brought his boy for a visit, Liam started peeing in the kitchen. All the deodorizing cleaner in the world didn't stop him. I recalled a time I had a cat that peed in a different corner of the kitchen. To discourage this, I put furniture over that spot. She climbed through it. It became a jousting match between us, with me piling on more furniture and her wending her way through to deposit some urine.

We barred Zephyr. It took six vigilant months, a scat mat keeping Liam out of the kitchen, and quarts of enzymatic cleaner to curb the nasty habit of his. But—fingers crossed—I think we've finally convinced him he doesn't need to water the house to keep his primacy in it.

When Liam was four years old, we set off with him and only him on a long trip to the East Coast, planning to visit family in New York, New Jersey, Massachusetts, and New Hampshire. From there, we intended to go up to Toronto to see old friends, and then back down to Evanston, Illinois, to see other old friends. No way could we cart three dogs around the country. Even Motel 6 balks at three. We boarded Pilar and Vela.

Perched on the console between the two front seats, Liam was the ideal traveling companion. He'd place his head on Charles's lap now and then, often pressing his paw down on the car's "snow" button. It might've been intentional, but probably not, since he had no more idea than we did about that button. The car manual declined to elucidate. Presumably, every motorist automatically knows the purpose of a snow button, even in the Bay Area. But if he didn't intend to activate the snow button, he did intentionally open car windows. With him in the car, the windows had to be locked. I had to request window privileges from Charles before I could get some air.

At night, we'd get a room with two queen-sized beds, and Liam—released from bondage—would sail back and forth between them, getting his exercise for the day. His flights made us giggle. Charles would take him outside around nine for a last pee, and then Liam would settle down in his crate and sleep through the night.

I think he felt he'd struck gold.

We were late getting into Evanston, our last stop to see friends before returning to California, but the hosts for the BnB had stayed up to greet us. They fixed us a quick meal, served on their patio under the stars. Together, we drank good wine and got acquainted. The next morning, I had a date with a friend for breakfast, and the next evening we were to join a colleague of Charles's for dinner in Chicago.

All those plans crashed.

For some time, our shepherds had attended a fabulous doggy day care in Oakland once a week. The center had room for a huge play area for small dogs, as well as a number of big-dog spaces. And they had a sliding roof for rainy days. Vela loved their wading pools.

They also did overnight boarding, and our three dogs had spent several nights together in a comfortable spacious kennel. Liam, in his crate, stayed with his pack. We had no qualms about leaving the shepherds there, knowing they'd be playing all day and would be together at night.

When my phone rang, I assumed my friend was calling to confirm our plans. But it wasn't my friend. It was the kennel.

Pilar had woken in distress. She hadn't gotten up from her bed. They'd rushed her to the emergency vet clinic, where they were doing everything they could for her. But she was seriously ill. I burst into tears but calmed down enough to telephone the clinic and speak to the vet, who told me, "She has a condition called dilated cardiomyopathy. So far, I'm sorry to say, she hasn't responded to treatment."

According to the day care staff, she'd seemed fine the day before, playing and eating well. Her decline had been abrupt. Yet I began thinking of possible signs of heart problems I'd ignored, such as how, whenever Charles took both shepherds for a walk, Pilar came back a bit more tired out than Vela. The difference was subtle. Whenever I threw a ball for her, Pilar chased it only a couple of times before losing interest. I thought that, like Vela and Henry, she had little interest in retrieving. But maybe it had been more than that.

In many ways, she had always shown plenty of energy. One of our favorite photographs from the day care people was a picture of a joyous Pilar in midair, body stretched out, every hair quivering with elation. That picture was taken less than two months before she was rushed to the emergency vet hospital.

When I said I should've investigated her flopping on the floor right after a walk, the vet told me, "Even if you had, it's unlikely this condition would have been discovered. It's a silent disease, and often people have no idea their dog is sick until they go down."

I was halfway across the country, and Pilar needed me. No, the attending vet said, she's unconscious. She wouldn't know you were here.

But she would've felt my presence, wouldn't she? Wouldn't she have felt my love and fought harder to stay alive? Instead, the last time she saw me, I was abandoning her. I couldn't bear it.

We packed up and said a hurried and tearful goodbye to our hosts. Charles, unknown to me, planned to try to make it back to Oakland in one shot. That would've taken us more than thirty hours, and I knew we were too old to endure that kind of stress. Meanwhile, we were a mess. I wept nonstop.

Around midnight, we finally stopped at a motel. Exhausted, Charles dropped off to sleep. I called the clinic and was told there hadn't been any improvement in Pilar's condition. I lay on the bed, staring up at the ceiling, unable to close my eyes. I knew what was coming.

At two, my phone rang. Before I tapped the button, which I so did not want to do, I tried to stop sobbing. Pilar was in pain, and I needed to make a decision. My voice strangled; I choked out permission to end my girl's pain. For the rest of that night, tears steadily slid down my face onto my pillow. Even now, remembering, I'm weeping.

My beautiful dog was only four years old.

Two or three months after Pilar died, the FDA issued a bulletin about a notable uptick in the diagnosis of dilated cardiomyopathy in dogs from breeds not normally prone to it. The bulletin cited a possible connection between the condition and grain-free premium dog food. In its initial report, the FDA speculated that legumes in general, and peas in particular, interfered with the absorption of taurine, a vital amino acid for heart health.

They listed ten brands reported as having been fed to dogs that came down with the condition. One identified dog food was precisely the one I fed my dogs, right down to the type of meat.

I rushed to the kitchen and pulled out the bag. For the first time, I read the entire list of ingredients. As I did, I cursed myself and the diabolical manufacturer. The first ingredient listed was lamb, but in the next four were peas, pea fiber, rice, and pea meal. Since ingredients must be listed in the order of their concentration, the deviousness of breaking peas into three categories hid the fact that lamb was a secondary ingredient. I'd been feeding my dogs exorbitantly priced peas for two and a half years. For Pilar, still growing, that could've been the source of her failure to develop a strong heart.

Breaking an ingredient into deceptively named parts is a common commercial ruse, seen in prepared human food as well. Government agencies charged with ensuring the safety of food, as well as the accuracy of its representation, have nothing to say about this contemptible subterfuge. Bad enough that human beings, who can exercise choice, are victimized by this practice. Since dogs and most of their owners haven't got the wherewithal or the cash to lobby our esteemed politicians, the practice will persist, certainly with regard to kibble.

Admittedly, neither the FDA nor I can say with certainty that pricey low-quality dog food killed Pilar. But I carry the guilt for her death, knowing that, if only I'd read that list instead of trusting a profit-making corporation, I wouldn't have kept feeding her that inadequate kibble.

If I'd jettisoned the kibble, Pilar might be alive and thriving today.

If her death upset Vela, she gave no sign of it. Jessie's leg-lifting tribute to Henry wasn't anything Vela would've initiated. I thought how different things would've been if she had gone first. The loss of Pilar's best friend would've been traumatic for her.

Tildy

To take my mind off losing Pilar and the state of Vela's rickety bones, I volunteered to foster a dog. Tildy, a German shepherd mix, was shy and skittish. She'd been homed with the head of the adoption group for about three months, and I could see why. When adoption day at Petfood Express came around, Tildy didn't stack up well against the other shepherds, most being full shepherd, larger, and more confident. She wasn't homely, but her demeanor emphasized her rangy, undersized body.

Tildy wanted to stay in her crate. For the first day, I let her do that. But on the second day, ready to take Vela and Liam for a walk, I decided it was time to bring her out. After loading the car with my dogs, I went upstairs, fastened a leash to Tildy's collar, and placed gentle pressure on the lead. She held fast, but I kept the pressure on her, and gradually eased her out of the crate, across the floor, down the stairs, and over to the car.

She balked. So, I climbed into the car and got her to climb in after me. On the walk, she was fine. But when we got back, she went to her crate and settled in.

The next day, I again used steady, gentle force to encourage her out of the crate. This time she came quicker—not at all quick, but not nearly as slowly as the day before. We walked the lake, she returned to her crate, and we had our evening.

On the third day, as I turned around after putting Vela and Liam in the car, ready to go back upstairs and fetch Tildy, I saw her standing in the open doorway. She jumped into the car on her own.

A week later the group held an adoption event, and I brought Tildy. The president gaped when she saw Tildy.

"My God," she said. "She's a whole other dog."

After that, Tildy found her forever home.

Cancer

At eight, Vela developed more than stiff joints. One morning, although she ate well, she began vomiting. This was unusual, but what was more unusual and horrific was that her vomit contained putrid chunks of something unrecognizable. I telephoned the vet, and they took her in right away.

They examined her for what seemed hours. Surely it couldn't be serious, I kept telling myself. Dogs throw up. Something she ate, probably. Except Vela had been nowhere she could've gotten hold of anything toxic enough to keep her puking. I was chewing my cuticles bloody when the vet came to get me.

In the examining room, I put my face into Vela's ruff as the vet gave me the bad news. She had intestinal cancer and needed surgery immediately. After that, assuming the surgery didn't find any metastases, she'd need chemotherapy. They scheduled surgery for the next day. Stunned, I couldn't say anything through the lump in my throat. I paid the bill and walked Vela out the door. Outside, the world had retreated, and I saw nothing but a blur.

Vela's surgery took longer than expected. Apparently, the ultrasound had been misleading. The cancer wasn't located in a readily accessible part of her intestines. For hours, Charles and I sat mute, waiting. We couldn't lose another dog; we just couldn't.

At last, the call came to pick up Vela.

"Doing fine," the vet told me. "Vitals stable throughout."

The good news was the surgeons had seen no evidence that the cancer had spread. They thought they'd gotten it all.

"You should know, however," the vet warned me. "This cancer will certainly recur. We estimate that Vela has at most two more years."

While this was horrible news, we tried to focus on the good parts, that the cancer hadn't spread, and they'd gotten it all out.

When we got to the clinic, we saw Vela walking with great difficulty, held up by two techs. I was horrified. She was an hour out of surgery, groggy, and in pain. Why hadn't they put her on a stretcher?

With great difficulty, we got her into the back of our SUV. I climbed in with her and tried to stroke her gently. She growled at me, making it clear she wanted to be left alone. That showed me the ferocity of her suffering since Vela thrived on around-the-clock petting. Our vet clinic, where the surgery had been performed, didn't have overnight staff, so we were ferrying her to the ER hospital where she could be monitored around the clock. At the ER clinic, techs brought out a gurney, and I heaved a sigh of relief to see her treated so tenderly.

The next morning, she was alert and doing that normal dog thing of ignoring her pain. From there, her recovery was swift. In almost no time, she was back to nudging our hands as we tried to read the newspaper.

For months, every Thursday, I drove to Berkeley, where she was given chemotherapy. She hated it, especially because she had to remain there for hours, without me. But dogs, like children, tolerate chemotherapy better than adult humans. Vela didn't vomit. She didn't go bald, although there were floor-strewn-with-fur moments when I might've welcomed that. She ate as much as I was willing to give her and would've happily downed twice that. We were back in business.

Another Dog (Surprise)

With Pilar gone, I had only Liam and Vela, who was nine. I wanted another shepherd before I got too old to outlive her. Many would argue I was already too old, approaching my mid-seventies. I paid no attention to them.

This time I was determined to find a confident dog, one that wouldn't drain us of thousands of dollars for canine rehabilitation. After researching breeders on the internet, I found a kennel in southern California that had rave reviews and no complaints. Does this sound like déjà vu all over again?

This breeder sold working line dogs, mostly sables. My three shepherds were all show line. Working line shepherds receive consistent high marks for stability, courage, and loyalty. Those were the traits I sought in my next shepherd.

The kennel was located on a dirt road, far from any neighbors, on a large ranch. Jane came out and greeted us without noticeable warmth. I began to think of breeders as the original pioneers, stubborn, rugged, and individualistic. Opinionated loners with a penchant for dominating people as well as dogs. Probably that's an inaccurate characterization, since I have a very small field to draw on. But it does describe the few breeders I've encountered.

"Sit there," she said, pointing at two metal chairs she'd placed in the dirt. "Don't look at them and don't talk to them. And don't try to touch them."

I assumed she wasn't referring to the chairs.

At that, she went into the house, presumably to get the pups, although we were left to wonder.

She brought out three. One black-and-white girl that was going to be plush, if not long-haired. That dog was stunning. And confident. Immediately, Jane told us she would have to go to a working home. She had intense

227

drives and way too much self-assurance for a lightweight like me. "Whenever I washed down the run, from the time she was four weeks old, she challenged the hose." Probably would've jumped a vacuum cleaner and wrestled it to the floor, I thought. But if Jane had no intention of selling us that pup, why had she brought her out?

I reluctantly agreed we weren't the right people for the gorgeous pup. Without Avery at the helm, that dog would probably line us up every morning to hear the day's marching orders. I didn't have what it would take to shape her into a wonderful, obedient pet. Whoever bought her, I hoped they had it all. It was lovely to imagine that beautiful dog blossoming into another Jessie.

I dragged my eyes away from her.

The runt was an intersex, hospitalized immediately following her birth for an unspecified ailment. Jane urged us to take her. Because we were old, perhaps she assumed we were in our dotage, soft in the head to the point of pity-purchasing a dog that would never achieve the size of a German shepherd and would likely suffer lifelong health problems. Talk about preexisting conditions!

I didn't look directly at any of the pups. I didn't try to touch them. And I certainly didn't speak to them. I knew better. Ignoring a strange dog almost always brings that dog straight to you.

Which it did. One by one, each of the three puppies came up to me and put their paws on my legs. The healthy sable had a sweet face, a lovely expression, and she seemed friendly.

Even so, there were those damnable red flags that should've warned me that training and living with this dog might not be a piece of cake. The kennel appeared deserted except for Jane, who told us about a friend with cancer. She explained she hadn't had much time to spend with the puppies because her friend was hospitalized. Her friend also bred dogs, and her place was at a considerable distance from Jane's. As a result, she'd spent much of every day driving back and forth, tending to her friend's dogs, and giving her puppies the leftovers. None of which spoke well for the puppies' socialization.

"Socialization?" Jane spat out the word. "Ridiculous. People ruin dogs by trying to socialize them. A dog from my last litter came back because the owners said he was vicious. They'd done it themselves, trying to socialize him. I know someone who socialized her dog by having him climb steps in a stadium. That worked. We don't flood them with fear by forcing them into dealing with people."

Dealing with people? "Well, Jane," I began recklessly, "we don't all live miles from our neighbors. Most of us have people in from time to time. I hope that's not what you call 'flooding' a dog."

For a moment, I thought she might throw us off her property. The set of her jaw told me exactly what she thought of my opinion. I said, "We'll take the sable."

When I was pregnant for the first time, I read an article about "quick attachers" and "slow attachers." The article claimed some mothers took a day or two, or even longer, to feel motherly with their newborns, while others felt intensely protective and loving in the delivery room, or even sooner, from the moment they found out they were pregnant. As I lay on the birthing table being sewn up, I watched my daughter in the isolette, kicking at her blanket. Her feet lifted it over her face, where it settled.

"Get it off!" I shouted. "She'll smother!"

No question about the length of time it took me to attach, although there well might be questions about my judgment. But never mind. If I'm going to like someone, I like them pretty much immediately. I adored this sable even before we made it off Jane's property.

We named her Sparkle.

I'd planned for Sparkle to travel home in Liam's crate. She had other plans, and so did Charles. Within less than a mile, he'd stopped the car, I'd uncrated Sparkle, and she lay in my lap for the six-hour trip home.

She quickly mastered house training, and all the sit and stay stuff. What she hadn't come close to mastering was being outdoors and around people. In the beginning, I'd leash her up and take her out. She'd climb up my back. We moved down the driveway less than a foot a day.

At the vet, she was fine with being examined, oddly enough. Closed spaces seemed to comfort her. But a month passed before she and I reached the end of the driveway, and a month after that to get her to walk to the end and back of our very quiet block. Eventually, I thought she was ready for a walk at Lake Merritt. She didn't think so. She climbed my back.

With Jane growling in my ear about "flooding" the poor dog, I walked a tightrope between honoring Sparkle's fears and moving her forward. The question of letting people interact with her was touchy as well. Sometimes she seemed fine with it. At others, she seemed wary. I played it by ear, denying access when she seemed uneasy and keeping treats in my pocket to encourage her to focus on something other than her fear.

Trouble was, Sparkle wouldn't accept treats if she wasn't entirely comfortable. Even if I walked her around Merritt College, on a vacant path, she was too nervous to accept food.

When visitors came to the house, she'd bark. I put her in her crate until they'd been in the house for a while and then I would bring her out. She'd make the rounds, receive lots of petting, and that was that.

When she turned two, that wasn't that anymore.

Although we had little available floor space in our house, with Vela's sore joints, I felt a need to keep a second soft bed outside the bedroom for her. Amazon offered something called a donut bed. Reviews overwhelmingly described their dogs loving it. Dubious, but willing to take a chance, given Amazon's return policy, I ordered a large one in black. Black it had to be since, if successful, in seconds it would be coated in black dog fur. When the bed arrived, I set it up at one end of the dining room, a position that allowed Vela to keep track of us in the living room but didn't add to the general furniture overload down there. I needn't have worried about Vela not liking that bed. She spent most of her day lying in it. I bought a second for the cabin, where the floor can be icy in winter.

The funny thing was that Liam loved it too, but in an odd way. At least once a day, I still spot him, stretched out on his belly with his chin resting on the raised donut edge, his body on the floor. Praying, nursing, or meditating, one of those. Whenever Vela left the donut bed for the cool floor, Liam did muscle-building exercises by tugging it across the floor and back. Sometimes he tried with her in it.

Another Dog (Surprise)

Sparkle too loved the bed and waited for Vela to abandon it. Once, at the cabin, she had been snoozing in the donut for some time when Vela tired of lying on the cold hard floor. I'd never seen Vela fight for anything. Sure, she'd snarl at Pilar in the early days, teaching her what was and wasn't acceptable behavior—from Vela's point of view. However, she was primarily a licker and a lover, conflict averse. This time she surprised me. Without ado, she marched over to the occupied donut, and plopped herself down, nearly crushing Sparkle, who skittered out from under her and found somewhere else to lie. The sight of Vela asserting herself gladdened my heart.

Unlike Vela before Pilar, Sparkle instantly took to the cabin. She and Liam did circuits around it while Vela, reduced to standing by, lurched one way and then the other, only to watch her rocketing packmates zip by her. When Seth's shepherd, Zephyr, visited, he and Sparkle made those rounds, Liam bringing up the rear. In vain, Vela lurked nearby. Barking, of course.

Losing Vela

Vela didn't suffer a long downhill slide. She walked reasonably well until the week she died. After recovering from cancer, she never had a serious illness. Her two veterinary-prescribed years expired, but the cancer didn't return. When she turned twelve, however, she approached the finish line for the average German shepherd.

Her last days were spent at our cabin. Almost to the end, she engaged with life in ways that told me it wasn't time, despite how her joints ached and her back legs now and then gave out from under her.

But then she collapsed and didn't get back up. It was time, Charles and I told each other.

I wanted her euthanized at home, or rather at the cabin. But the closest towns were Boonville and Philo, neither of which had a vet. The one we used when we were at the cabin was an hour away. Trouble was, neither of us could lift her and she couldn't climb in our SUV. We were stuck.

Ever resourceful and never fazed by a challenge, Charles located a veterinarian in Fort Bragg who did "house calls."

"She'd never come all this way," I said.

"Probably not. But I'll send her an email and see."

Within less than a day, Karen responded that we were in luck. On the coming Friday, she'd planned to drive to Santa Rosa to catch a flight. She could leave a bit earlier and make a stop at our cabin.

As soon as the date had been confirmed, Vela got up. Her back legs wobbled, but she was going outside, eating as usual, drinking plenty of water, and seemed a quaky version of herself. My heart sank. If we canceled the appointment and Vela went down permanently a week later, we'd be out of luck. She'd have to endure the misery of dying slowly. But if we kept the appointment, we might be depriving her of time she deserved. I waffled without saying anything to Charles. He was confident the time had come.

Three days before the vet was to show up, Vela went down for good on our concrete porch. She stopped eating and only sipped a bit of water. I had to wash her several times a day to keep her skin from becoming inflamed by her increasingly concentrated urine.

Charles slept next to her on a chaise lounge, but she seemed less and less conscious of our presence. Even stroking her didn't get the usual nudging of my hand with her snout, urging me not to stop.

All my doubts vanished. She was ready to go. I wished we didn't have to wait until Friday because I knew she was suffering. Her eyes seemed trained inward, as if on the misery that gripped her. Every hour dragged by in seconds. What if the vet forgot us? What if she woke up late and had to skip us to catch her plane? What if she couldn't find the cabin? We were far back from the highway, deep in the hills.

The day finally came, and, thank heavens, so did the vet. Karen was gentle, first giving Vela a sedative to put her to sleep. Then the final shot. Vela's heart quit instantly. Karen said quietly, "She was ready."

Charles had spent the week before the end digging Vela's grave in hardpan soil on a plateau above the cabin. After the vet left, we lowered Vela's body into it. Charles covered her, placing heavy rocks over the dirt to keep animals from disturbing her grave.

I felt comforted to have her on our property. My other dogs had all been whisked away, one way or another. My mother's body had been cremated, and one day it hit me that she was nowhere on this earth. I had no marker of her existence. And that had been true of every one of my lost dogs.

Except now. Now there was Vela.

My Sweet, Awful Sparkle

Sparkle's barking whenever someone approached the door increased as she matured. When she settled down, I'd bring her out of her crate, and she'd make the rounds, accepting cuddles. My friends thought of her as friendly. So did I. But one night I saw her growl at a guest, a man who suffers from serious ailments. Before I could get to her, she turned away and paid no more attention to him. I breathed a sigh of relief and found the excuse. Sickness emits odors, which, to a dog, can signal trouble. I chose to believe she was instinctively trying to eject an impaired individual from the pack. Right.

One afternoon our petite downhill neighbor stopped to offer us a handful of loquats when Charles, Sparkle, and I were out for a walk. Neither of us like loquats, but we took a few to be polite. The tiny woman, no doubt assuming we weren't taking as many as we wanted out of courtesy, moved toward Charles, urging him to accept more. He stepped backward and raised his hand, saying, "No, no." Without growling, without barking, Sparkle lunged. Only the leash prevented disaster.

I told myself that she misunderstood what was happening. Charles putting up his hand as the woman kept advancing signaled danger to her. Considering the woman's size, her demeanor, and the lack of anxiety in Charles's voice, Sparkle had behaved stupidly. But I gave her a pass for trying to protect us. Ha ha. How often had I been annoyed by someone saying their Fido was protective when he tried to attack anyone coming near them? Now it was my dog, and I was pedaling furiously away from the truth.

Most dogs wouldn't have sensed danger when a petite woman offered fruit to an owner who declined to take it. The dogs that did imagine something amiss would've growled or barked as a warning. Not our Sparkle.

Weeks later, I was expecting people for a meeting. My door was unlocked, and the first attendee entered the house while I was in the back. Sparkle, having never seen the man before, bit him on the rump, bruising him and tearing his pants. When he exited the house, she didn't follow him, and that I took for a positive sign. She'd been protecting the property. It didn't occur to me that my friend must've been sprinting out the door when she attacked because, otherwise, she couldn't have bitten his butt. Having successfully ejected him, a dog protecting territory ought to rest on their laurels. But I clung to the position that she was merely defending our house.

There it was: my ugly lineup of excuses. Sparkle saw illness as a threat to the pack. Charles needed protection from a woman who weighed almost less than Sparkle did. My guard dog stopped a stranger who could've been a burglar. Everything was going along just as it should, and I was happily at work socializing her.

At the cabin, Charles waited for a delivery of propane one morning. He stood on the porch with Sparkle as the big truck rumbled up our driveway. We weren't oblivious enough to take her out unleashed, but Charles focused on the driver when he should've focused on Sparkle. When the man exited the cab of the truck, she turned into Attila the Hun. Bolting to the end of the leash, she bruised his leg and ripped his pants.

Okay, I thought. Territorial. But she hadn't broken the skin. If we were reasonably cautious, she'd be okay.

Everything was going to be fine.

Because Charles and I had the comorbidity of age, we moved into the cabin to sit out the first year and a half of the Covid-19 pandemic. It did occur to me that it was far less than ideal for Sparkle's socialization. Increasing isolation wasn't a cure for what ailed her. Yet neither of us were willing to risk contracting Covid, not after seeing images of comatose people with tubes down their throats, and not after reading the daily infection and death statistics. At that time, a vaccine was still in development, so our primary protection came from staying away from people.

Against what I thought was common sense, however, Charles had begun to spend part of his day helping a neighbor with work on his truck. Neither of them wore a mask, and this man traveled back and forth from Santa Rosa, where he lived with an employed girlfriend. In other words, plenty of opportunities to pick up the virus. I resented the risk of being exposed to Covid. But isolation is boring, and helping a neighbor was in my husband's genes, so I tried to be gracious and let it go.

Until he brought Steve to the cabin. I don't know whether Sparkle picked up on my anger as the two men entered, or whether Steve's proximity to Charles (he looked as if he were glued to my husband's back) triggered her, but before either of us could stop her, she sank her teeth deep into the flesh just above Steve's ankle.

I pushed her out the door and slammed it. On my way to the bathroom to collect a bandage and disinfectant, I glanced outside and was shocked to see her gamboling around as if she's just opened a package from Omaha Steaks. She looked positively giddy. Again, there'd been no warning, no growling, no barking, no baring of teeth.

Was it possible that the act of biting released some happiness hormone into her system? If she'd been tense before she bit, I didn't pick up on it. She hadn't had time to get tense. Okay. She certainly heard them coming before I did. But really, she'd looked relaxed one minute, a fiend from hell the next.

Steve's ankle was deeply gashed. I cleaned the wound and bandaged it, but he had to go to the hospital for stitches and an antibiotic. The bite took a couple of months to heal. Although the doctor who treated him asked for the name of the dog that attacked him, Steve said it was a stray. I was grateful for that.

But I finally accepted that Sparkle was a dangerous dog, one that didn't give warning of her aggression before acting on it. We had to do something.

I dialed Avery's number in Sacramento, but I didn't recognize the voice on the phone.

She said, "You're the first in a long time."

"Excuse me?"

"When I got this number, I'd get all kinds of calls for her. Dog trainer, right? Sorry, I don't know diddly-squat about dogs."

"Do you know anything about where Avery is?"

"Sorry, no."

My trainer must've finally retired.

How could I find a replacement? I needed a strong recommendation from someone I could trust, preferably someone who'd had such a dog and found a trainer to fix it. But I didn't know anyone who'd had a dog like Sparkle. Hell, I wasn't sure there was another dog like her.

I cruised Google and found Vera Donaldson. She kept dogs in her home for training and listed treating aggression among her skills. I emailed her a description of the issues with Sparkle, spending more than an hour writing and editing to make my dog's problems crystal clear, and to make sure she understood this wasn't the usual case of an aggressive dog.

Within a day Vera responded. She wouldn't come to my house, which, although it annoyed me, I somewhat understood. The pandemic was still raging. If I gave her $200, she would meet me in Lafayette at a public park, where she would conduct an evaluation. Okay. I figured I had nothing but $200 to lose.

I parked next to her van. She stood, arms crossed, next to it, and said she'd like to talk for a minute before I brought Sparkle out. As she questioned me, I realized she either didn't remember or hadn't read my email.

As usual with Sparkle in a strange environment, as soon as I took her out of the car, she shrank back. Vera dangled a toy in front of her. Predictably, Sparkle ignored it. Vera asked me to walk her around and then issue some commands, which I did. Sparkle obediently sat, lay down, stood, heeled, and stayed as I walked away from her. Vera took the leash. Sparkle trotted next to her, tail tucked.

"I thought she'd be more forward," Vera said. *Forward*? Everything I'd written and everything I'd subsequently told her amounted to a fearful dog that withdrew except on her own property.

Vera, scarcely looking at my dog, repeated a few times that she'd expected her to be more forward, and the "evaluation" was over.

While I felt uneasy—Vera had established no rapport with Sparkle—I felt I had no other option. Just because she was neither a careful reader nor a focused listener didn't mean she couldn't work well with a dog. Maybe she was autistic, or maybe she had social anxiety disorder.

Within days, Vera offered me a date for Sparkle to begin boarding with her. A week later, she telephoned to say she had to go up to Oregon, but she could take Sparkle with her. My uneasiness spiked. A week after that, she called to say she'd booked another client and Sparkle would have to wait two months for training.

"You didn't book," she said.

"What are you talking about? You gave me a date."

"I'm sorry, but I never make a commitment until the booking fee has been paid. You didn't pay, so no booking."

"That's crap and you know it. You never asked me for a booking fee. What's going on is you know you can't change my dog's behavior. Fine. Send me back my deposit, and let's forget we ever met."

"You paid two hundred for an evaluation. I gave you an evaluation."

I was astounded. "Saying you thought she'd be more 'forward' is your idea of an evaluation? Give me back my deposit or you can expect to see this sorry story spread across the internet."

She returned my deposit.

Avery called. "Just checking in to see how the pups are doing."

This was weird. She'd never checked in with me before. "They're fine. No. They're not fine. Vela's dead."

"I heard. I'm so sorry."

"How did you hear?"

"Karen told me."

"Karen?"

"The vet. The one that put Vela down. From Fort Bragg?"

"Oh. But how did she—?"

"Said you was looking for me."

I couldn't recall saying anything about Avery, but I'd had other things on my mind.

The good news was I had her on the phone. Avery, who could train the bugs out of the trees. "Are you still training? Because I've got a dog that needs training more than any dog I've ever owned, including Henry."

"Nah. So what's the problem?"

I explained.

"Yup." I heard her clicking her tongue and knew she was shaking her head, probably recalling how stupid I could be. "Better get somebody for the punk quick. I don't gotta tell you she's heading for your bank account, big time."

"Do you know anyone?" I told her about Vera, and she clicked her tongue again, then blew some air into the phone, presumably considering a possible reference to give me.

"Got it. And she ain't far from you—in Alameda. Name's Laura something—can't remember, but she's the real deal."

I took down Laura's phone number and called her immediately. She didn't pick up. Reluctant to leave a message after the screw-up with Vera, I tried several more times and finally reached her.

Laura said she'd take a look and see if she could help, and she gave me an appointment to bring Sparkle to her training academy.

"Unclip the leash. I wanna see what she does."

Sparkle nosed around her office and then sat at my feet.

"No socialization, eh?" Laura said when I told her about Jane's comment. "Dumbass."

She came over, sat next to me, and stroked Sparkle's head.

"I'll take her on. She needs to stay here for a month. The cost is twenty-five hundred."

"When can she start?"

"How about now?"

Driving home, I felt ambivalent. On one hand, I was relieved to have Sparkle in the hands of someone with confidence she could reform her. On the other, I already missed her. Charles would miss her even more.

Laura called me after five days. "Just wanted to let you know, we're doing fine."

"Is she okay? Anxious?"

"Oh yeah. But she'll get over it."

For the next ten days, I heard nothing. When Laura called again, she sounded optimistic. "She's a great dog. Watch out. I'm getting to love her. Might not give her back."

I laughed. "How's your security system? I've got a cat burglar outfit I've been wanting to try out."

"It's hard to tell how much she's improving since she's only aggressive on your property. But so far, so good. I'll be in touch next week about when you start coming in to train with her."

That week had feet of concrete. Meanwhile, Liam was relishing the extra attention of being our lone dog. He was funny and sweet, but we sorely missed Sparkle. Finally, the time to join the training came. I showed up half an hour early.

"She did really well," Laura said. "At first, she was freaked out, but that's natural. Every time I went down to see her, I gave her a treat. After a bit, she decided seeing me meant yum!" Laura reached into her desk and handed me a sheet of paper. "Those are instructions for when you get her home. Look them over, and if you have questions, we can talk about them tomorrow. Now I'm going to bring her in. Brace yourself. Don't let her walk all over you."

Sparkle came in, wild, keening, trying to climb into my lap. Laura wasn't pleased with my slow reaction to her out-of-control behavior.

"Tell her 'down!'" she snapped. "Now, if she moves, give a little pop on her leash, say 'no,' and make sure she settles. We're going to talk a bit, and then we'll walk across the floor, testing her. If she gets up, you go back, pick up her leash, take her back to where she was, and tell her, 'down.'"

"Got it."

"Seen any good movies lately?"

I laughed. "No. Have you?"

"Never go. Let's walk to the door." We did, and Sparkle stayed put. I was proud of her. "Okay. Let's go sit down. Read any good books lately?"

"A few. But I can't remember the titles. How about you?"

"Never read," she said. "Not unless it says 'dog' on the cover." She smiled. "Now tell her what a good girl she is. Like she saved your kid from drowning."

When we brought Sparkle home, I believed our troubles were over. The regimen Laura prescribed, however, was demanding. Sparkle had to stay on her mat except for when we took her out for exercise or she was crated. All day she wore a leash. She wasn't to do anything unless we said so. She looked unhappy, and that made me unhappy. But if our unhappiness would end in a well-behaved—meaning never biting—dog, I'd bear it.

After a month, we loosened the reins, and she became a house pet once more. We reminded ourselves, almost as a daily ritual, that Laura had warned me she could never be trusted, but she could be controlled.

Uh huh.

I'd been looking for someone to clean my house. While I could do most of the work myself, giving it the kind of thorough cleaning I like exceeds my energy level. When an applicant came, Sparkle was in the dog run. I took Lily through the house, showing her what needed to be done. She seemed to half-listen. We went into the bedroom, where Sparkle stood watching us through the sliding-glass door.

We chatted, in full view of Sparkle. I was about to tell Lily I'd call her because I knew I wasn't going to hire her and never calling seemed the best way out of telling her she hadn't made a good impression. Before we said goodbye, however, I wanted to expose Sparkle to a moment of social inter-action. I was always looking for opportunities to have her meet strangers. Lily and I had been chatting in full view for about ten minutes when I said, "I'd like you to meet my dog." Lily shrugged with the same energy she'd discussed cleaning my house.

I opened the glass door. Before I could grab her, Sparkle leapt at Lily, nipped her thigh, and whirled around, apparently ready to go at her again. I flew across the room and shocked myself by slapping my dog's face. Opening the bathroom door, I threw her inside.

Lily's eyes had a "gotcha" expression. Would she sue? I doubted it, but the possibility alarmed me. Sparkle hadn't torn her pants, so that was good. There was nothing for it but to hire her to do an "in-depth" cleaning, some-thing she accomplished while talking on her phone through the three hours she gave my house a slapdash once-over. Her fee was unreasonable, but I paid it.

We were both delighted to say goodbye for the last time.

Back at my old enemy, square one. That month of keeping Sparkle under strict control, useless misery for all of us. Her attack on Lily was a romp. I couldn't understand it. Dogs bite out of fear or maybe pain or just plain viciousness. Sometimes they defend someone from an actual threat. But I never heard of a dog biting people to amuse herself.

Yes, she's from the Czech working line, and yes, that lineage is reputedly prone to aggression, particularly when, as a puppy, the dog gets no socialization. But this wasn't the type of aggression typically seen in an unstable dog. When she bit, she wasn't showing anger or hostility or fear. She was having a blast.

"She didn't growl or bark," I told Charles. "Her hackles weren't even up. It was like she thought we'd all have a laugh over it."

He sighed. "I guess we can't let her loose in the house when people come over."

"I'm supposed to keep her crated for hours? How's that work? If somebody shows up, she has to go in the crate. If I shut her up in our bedroom so she can move around, I'll be anxious whenever somebody gets up to go to the bathroom. What if they open the wrong door? I don't want to live like that. I want her to behave herself, damnit! We paid for her to behave better, didn't we?"

I almost took to my bed. We'd put Sparkle and ourselves through the stress of following Laura's agenda for a lousy month. Maybe I should've known. Laura had told me about a client who kept returning his aggressive German shepherd, over and over. She said it was his fault because he didn't follow her instructions whenever he took the dog home. Well, we had followed her instructions. And look where *we* were.

During sleepless nights, I imagined Sparkle in the gas chamber and us in the poor house.

Over the next eight months, I played musical habitats with Sparkle, ferrying her back and forth, from room to crate to outside to crate outside, then back inside behind a closed door. When I finally found a satisfactory housekeeper, I had to kennel Sparkle outside. The housekeeper needed to clean the glass doors, inside and out. She worked six long hours. I hated to confine my dog for six hours. Once I took her to the garage and put her in the car for a couple of hours.

The situation was intolerable.

Online, I saw an ad for a company that boards the dogs in their trainers' homes. Shades of Vera. They, too, listed aggression among the behaviors they could cure. I called and asked if they'd ever successfully cured a dog of biting people. They said they had and then asked me penetrating questions about her.

"Our trainers take the dog into their home. They get inside the dog's head. But they accept a dog only if they feel they can connect with it. I can send Jordan to see you if you like."

Jordan came over. She seemed mellow, and I could tell she not only liked dogs, but she also liked Sparkle, who liked her in return.

Charles was skeptical. I wasn't surprised.

"Another trainer? How many are we going to try?"

"Just this one. If it doesn't work, I'm through. I'll just have to live with her problem and be unhappy for the rest of her life."

Jordan took Sparkle home later that month, promising to send me a video twice a week so I could see how things were going.

I told Charles, "Maybe she can get back to the way she was before she turned two. Remember? She was friendly to everybody then."

"Not quite. There was the woman with the loquats."

"But that was a hell of a lot more understandable than biting Lily for fun."

The videos started out with discouraging footage of Sparkle, tail tucked, refusing a treat. By the next week, she was accepting the treat. By four weeks, she was lying in an aisle at Home Depot's garden center—most certainly, early in the morning—waiting calmly while Jordan walked away. When Jordan released her, Sparkle raced forward and gobbled up her treat. Even so, given the extreme level her of instability, Jordan and I both thought she could benefit from two more weeks.

Video from week six showed Jordan and Sparkle with four other trainers and four other dogs in San Francisco's downtown. Buses rolling past, traffic loud, buzzing conversations as people passed by. The dogs were placed in a circle. The trainers stood five or six feet away from them.

The only dog that looked relaxed was Sparkle. My heart soared.

It's been more than two years since Sparkle last turned my life into musical doors. Now, whenever we have company, she lies on her cot until I feel confident she's accepted them. Even then, I exercise caution, transitioning her for a bit to her donut bed, which occupies a space near the end of the dining room table. There, she can inhale the human scents and (hopefully) accept these visitors as benign. When I release her, she wanders around, scarfing up affectionate tousling.

The first serious test of her rehabilitation came when some of Charles's family visited from the East Coast weeks after she'd come home from Jordan's training. She'd never seen these people. Chatting, they stood around in the living room, inches from her cot. I'd asked them not to look at her and not to touch her. To my astonishment, she dozed on her bed all the while. Eventually, each of the dog lovers got to pet her.

Despite her troubling history, Sparkle is a sweet girl, eager to please. We know we will always need to remain vigilant, but her territorialism no longer distorts the way we live.

Afterword

Sparkle never walks down stairs; she flings herself at them, oblivious to potentially injurious collisions with the steps. Liam never clambers from the sofa to retrieve his chew toy; he hurls himself at the floor. Dogs are 150 percent into anything they are into at all. As someone who has always entered a pool toe first, fully wet a good ten or fifteen minutes later, I live vicariously through their enthusiasm.

This morning, as I brushed Sparkle—who, despite daily brushing, persists in generously sharing her bountiful coat with the floor—I stroked her, and she turned to kiss me. Pleasure ricocheted between us. Whenever I return to the car after mailing a letter or buying a few groceries, Liam sluices my face as if I'd been gone a year. A normally fastidious person, I nevertheless feel honored while I clean myself up.

Each dog in this book enriched my life. Each has revealed to me some aspect of myself—sometimes not one I wanted to see, so I'll skip those.

Henry made me realize how determined (or, as some regard it, how pig-headed) I am. I take a bit of pride in my ability to see—when he was far from wonderful—how wonderful he could be.

Jessie gave me unconditional devotion from the first day. Because of her, I got to experience the sense of security taken from me when I was a child.

Vela showed me how much a dog could grow from a sorry beginning, and Pilar taught me how much I can love a dog, even when disappointed by them.

For most of my life, I thought only big dogs were real dogs. Liam has demolished that notion. Who knew how much life and intelligence a "giant" (eighteen-pound) Havanese can contain? Okay, I get it. A lot of people knew.

Afterword

Finally, every day Sparkle reminds me that dogs are a mystery, one I will never solve.

I can live with that.